Designing Public Policies

This textbook provides a concise and accessible introduction to the principles and elements of policy design in contemporary governance. Howlett seeks to examine in detail the range of substantive and procedural policy instruments that together comprise the toolbox from which governments select specific tools expected to resolve policy problems.

Guiding students through the study of the instruments used by governments in carrying out their tasks, adapting to, and altering their environments, this book:

- Discusses several current trends in instrument use often linked to factors such as globalization and the increasingly networked nature of modern society.
- Considers the principles behind the selection and use of specific types of instruments in contemporary government.
- Evaluates in detail the merits, demerits and rationales for the use of specific organization, regulatory, financial and information-based tools and the trends visible in their use
- Addresses the issues of instrument mixes and their (re)design in a discussion of the future research agenda of policy design.

Providing a comprehensive overview of this essential component of modern governance and featuring helpful definitions of key concepts and further reading, this book is essential reading for all students of public policy, administration and management.

Michael Howlett is Burnaby Mountain Chair in the Department of Political Science at Simon Fraser University and Visiting Professor at the Lee Kuan Yew School of Public Policy at the National University of Singapore, specializing in public policy analysis, political economy, and resource and environmental policy.

Routledge Textbooks in Policy Studies

This series provides high-quality textbooks and teaching materials for upper-level courses on all aspects of public policy as well as policy analysis, design, practice and evaluation. Each text is authored or edited by a leading scholar in the field and aims both to survey established areas and present the latest thinking on emerging topics.

The Public Policy Primer
Managing the policy process
Xun Wu, M. Ramesh, Michael Howlett and Scott Fritzen

Designing Public Policies
Principles and instruments
Michael Howlett

Designing Public Policies

Principles and instruments

Michael Howlett

Routledge
Taylor & Francis Group

LONDON AND NEW YORK

First published 2011
by Routledge
2 Park Square, Milton Park, Abingdon, Oxon, OX14 4RN

Simultaneously published in the USA and Canada by
Routledge 270 Madison Avenue, New York, NY 10016

Routledge is an imprint of the Taylor & Francis Group, an informa business

© 2011 Michael Howlett

The right of Michael Howlett to be identified as author of this work
has been asserted by him in accordance with the Copyright, Designs
and Patent Act 1988.

Typeset in Sabon by
Keystroke, Tettenhall, Wolverhampton
Printed and bound in Great Britain by
CPI Antony Rowe, Chippenham, Wiltshire

British Library Cataloguing in Publication Data
A catalogue record for this book is available from the British Library

Library of Congress Cataloging in Publication Data
Howlett, Michael, 1955–
    Designing public policies: principles and instruments / Michael Howlett.
        p. cm.—(Routledge textbooks in policy studies)
    Includes bibliographical references and index.
    1. Policy sciences. 2. Political planning. I. Title.
    JF1525.P6H69 2010
    320.6–dc22
    2010021029

ISBN: 978–0–415–78132–9 (hbk)
ISBN: 978–0–415–78133–6 (pbk)
ISBN: 978–0–203–83863–1 (ebk)

Oh, philosophers may sing
Of the troubles of a King;
Yet the duties are delightful, and the privileges great;
But the privilege and pleasure
That we treasure beyond measure
Is to run on little errands for the Ministers of State.
(*The Gondoliers or The King of Barataria*.
Libretto by William S. Gilbert;
music by Arthur S. Sullivan)

Contents

CONTENTS

CONTENTS

Figures and tables

Preface

This book introduces students to the principles and elements of policy design in contemporary governance. It does so through the study of the implementation instruments used by governments in carrying out their tasks and adapting to, and altering, their environments. These form the basic foundations or structures upon which policies and programmes rest. An essential component of modern governance, the range of substantive and procedural policy instruments together comprise the toolbox from which governments select specific tools expected to resolve policy problems. The book begins with the discussion of several aspects of instrument use in contemporary government often linked to factors such as globalization and the increasingly networked nature of modern society. It then moves on to consider the principles behind the selection and use of specific types of instruments in the process of policy formulation. The merits, demerits and rationales for the use of specific organization, regulatory, financial and information-based tools and the trends visible in their use are set out in separate sections of the book. Finally, by way of conclusion, the issues of instrument mixes and their origins are addressed in a discussion of the future research agenda of policy (re)design.

Acknowledgements

The book could not have been written without the pioneering work of the many, many scholars who individually and collectively have spent a great deal of time and effort developing the empirical cases and carefully building the many frameworks and models used throughout the text. Many colleagues have also more directly helped contribute to the ideas, models and concepts found in the book. They include M. Ramesh, Richard Simeon, Laurent Dobuzinskis, G. Bruce Doern, Vince Wilson, Ken Woodside, Keith Brownsey, Luc Bernier, Jeremy Rayner, Chris Tollefson, Ben Cashore, Adam Wellstead, Colin Bennett, Hans de Bruijn, Ernst ten Heuvelhof, Peter May, David Weimer, Leslie Pal, George Hoberg, David Laycock, Pearl Eliadis, Rejean Landry, Margaret Hill, Evert Lindquist, Iris Geva-May, Michael Mintrom, Christine Rothmayr, Allan McConnell, Adam Wellstead, Evert Vedung, B. Guy Peters, Giliberto Capano, Frederic Varone, Dietmar Braun, Anthony Perl, Eva Heidbreder, Wu Xun, Aidan Vining, Scott Fritzen, and the participants in a variety of workshops and students in many classes held in North America, Europe, Asia and Australia over the years where papers on aspects of policy design and instrument choice were delivered and critiqued. A special debt is owed to Rebecca Raglon for her support and encouragement. Thank you all for your ideas and inspiration.

Part I

INTRODUCTION

Policy design and the modern state

Chapter 1

Understanding contemporary policy mixes

Policy design is a complex subject with many nuances and variations to consider. In Davis Bobrow's (2006) apt phrase, policy design is 'ubiquitous, necessary and difficult' but surprisingly little studied and understood. Over the past three decades it has received some treatment in the existing policy literature, but not as much, or in as much detail, as is necessary (May 1981, 1991 and 2003; Weimer 1992; Bobrow 2006). Within the policy sciences it has been linked to studies of policy implementation and policy instruments (May 2003) and to those of policy ideas and policy formulation (Linder and Peters 1990; James and Jorgensen 2009), but without systematic attention being paid to such basic elements as the definition of key terms and concepts. In addition, it has been a large, if typically implicit, part of a more recent trend towards the study of governance, and even 'meta-governance', but again, without the benefit of clear and systematic analysis (Meuleman 2009; 2010). This book surveys the existing literature, clarifies key terms and concepts, and brings clarity to the study of this important aspect of public policy-making.

In this regard it is important to note that despite the vagueness and uncertainties currently associated with its principles and elements, the purpose and expectations of policy design have always been clear. That is, it is an activity conducted by a number of policy actors in the hope of improving policy-making and policy outcomes through the accurate anticipation of the consequences of government actions (Tinbergen 1958; 1967; Schon 1992). It thus is situated firmly in the 'rational' tradition of policy studies, one aimed at improving policy outcomes through the application of policy-relevant and policy-specific knowledge to policy-making processes, specifically in the crafting of alternative possible courses of action intended to address social, political, economic and other kinds of policy problems (Cahill and Overman 1990; Bobrow 2006).

3

While somewhat similar in this regard to activities such as planning and strategic management, policy design is much less technocratic in nature than these other efforts at 'scientific' government and administration (Forester 1989; Voss et al. 2009). However, it too is oriented towards avoiding many of the inefficiencies and inadequacies apparent in other, less knowledge-informed ways of formulating policy, such as pure political bargaining, ad hocism, or trial and error (Bobrow 2006). In general, it is less specific than planning in developing alternatives rather than detailed 'plans', fully acknowledges the uncertainty of the future and the contingent nature of policy outcomes (Voss et al. 2009) and is more open than strategic management to the idea that there are alternative sources of knowledge and design criteria than those residing in, or proposed by, experts (Fischer and Forester 1987; May 1991).

As May (2003: 226) has argued, rather than treating design as simply a technical activity of finding the best design, it should be seen to involve channelling the energies of disparate actors towards agreement in working towards similar goals. In this sense, policy design contains both a substantive component – a set of alternative arrangements potentially capable of resolving or addressing some aspect of a policy problem, one or more of which is ultimately put into practice – as well as a procedural component – a set of activities related to securing some level of agreement among those charged with formulating, deciding upon, and administering that alternative. It thus overlaps and straddles both policy formulation and policy implementation and involves actors, ideas and interests present at both these stages of the policy process (Howlett, Ramesh and Perl 2009).

The contextual orientation of policy design

Conceived of as both a process and outcome, policy design is very much situated in the 'contextual' orientation which is characteristic of modern policy science (Torgerson 1985; May 2003). That is, it is an activity or set of activities which takes place within a specific historical and institutional context that largely determines its content (Clemens and Cook 1999). Which alternatives can be imagined, and prove feasible or acceptable at any given point in time, change as conditions evolve and different sets of actors and ideas alter their calculations of both the consequences and appropriateness of particular policy options or implemented designs (March and Olsen 2004; Goldmann 2005).

This contextual orientation has led many observers of policy outcomes and policy deliberations to focus on the policy environment as a key factor affecting policy designs (May 1991) and upon changes in that environment as a key determinant of any trends or patterns existing in design choices. There is a broad agreement among many popular commentators on globalization, for example, that this phenomenon has fundamentally altered many aspects of contemporary governance and policy designs.[1] As a result of golobalization, it is often alleged, states' governance practices have been greatly constrained; not only in what states do but also in how they do it (Cerny 1996; Reinicke

1998). That is, as globalization has proceeded apace, states' options in terms of the policy instruments available to them in order to realize their ends have been argued to have changed in response to their growing inability to manage public policy-making processes and outcomes as they had in past eras. This process has therefore altered the nature of the kinds of policy options which are feasible in the new global circumstances, affecting the kinds of designs which emerge from policy formulation processes and can be successfully implemented.

Similarly, many commentators have also argued, either separately or in conjunction with the globalization thesis, that state practices have also been changing as societies are being transformed by improved information and communication technologies to become ever more complex networks of inter-organizational actors (Mayntz 1993; Castells, 1996). This increased 'network-ization' of society, it is argued, has meant that many functions and activities traditionally undertaken exclusively by governments increasingly involve ever-larger varieties of non-governmental actors, themselves involved in increasingly complex relationships with other societal, and state, actors (Foster and Plowden 1996). This second movement towards the development of networked societies, it is often argued, has further complicated the situation and accentuated the constraints globalization has imposed upon the capabilities of domestic states, further reducing their capacity for independent action and limiting their design choices and alternatives (Dobuzinskis 1987; Lehmbruch 1991).

The result of these dual processes, many commentators have suggested, is that implementation practices have become more participatory and consultative over the last several decades (Alshuwaikhat and Nkwenti 2002; Arellano-Gault and Vera-Cortes 2005) as networkization has increased, while over this same time period and longer many public enterprises have also been privatized and previously government-provided services contracted-out to non-governmental organizations (NGOs) as globalization has advanced. In addition, it has also been argued that in some sectors regulatory activities have shifted from 'enforcement' to 'compliance' regimes; tax incentives have increasingly substituted for earlier systems of subsidies and grants; and many countries now place an increasing emphasis on public information and other similar types of campaigns, replacing or supplementing more coercive forms of government activity (Woodside 1983; Hawkins and Thomas 1989; Hood 1991; Howlett and Ramesh 1993; Weiss and Tschirhart 1994; Doern and Wilks 1998).

However, while the evidence of some changes in how governments func-tion in the contemporary era is undeniable and will be discussed in depth in Chapters 5–9 below, the scope, significance and causes of these changes remain contentious. Especially contentious is the belief that the changes in formulation and implementation practices which have occurred have been triggered solely by the changes in the domestic and international spheres encapsulated in the dual movements of globalization and 'networkization' cited above. And even more contentious is the closely related idea that governments have no choice in their policy designs but to continue these transformations and continue to work towards the reduction of the state presence in the economy and society as these dual processes continue to unfold and intensify (Levi-Faur 2009; O'Toole and Meier 2010).

Assessing the effects of internationalization on policy design: the globalization hypothesis

In order to assess the actual effects and impact of environmental changes on state behaviour, it is necessary to acknowledge that serious gaps exist in our understanding of the workings and characteristics of globalization and its policy consequences (Hay 2006). Contrary to what is commonly believed and often advocated, in our global era the domestic state remains far from overwhelmed and lacking autonomous decision-making capacity (Weiss 2003; Braithwaite 2008) and the source of many of the changes in the patterns of policy-making and instrument choice found in contemporary society very often lies in the domestic rather than the international arena (Scott et al. 2004; Levi-Faur 2009). Domestic states, be they national or sub-national, do not just react to changes in their international environments but also are very much still involved in the design and implementation of policies expected to achieve their ends (Lynn 1980; Vogel 2001). And, to the extent that global factors have had an impact on domestic policy designs and governance practices, it is often through what can be termed more 'indirect' and 'opportunity' effects spilling over from trade and other activities, rather than from the 'direct' effects that advocates of design alterations typically cite in arguing that state behaviour must change (Howlett and Ramesh 2006).[2]

That is, there is little doubt that economic, diplomatic, military and aid-related relations among nations help shape many choices of policies and policy tools. It is well known, for example, that many countries are aggressive in pressuring other countries to weaken regulations or preferential tax or subsidy treatments that restrict international firms' business activities and global and regional multilateral agreements are the most direct ways by which extra-territorial factors shape the choice of policy instruments. But these exist only in very few sectors, and often have large areas of exclusion even when they are present. Trade and investment agreements such as the World Trade Organization (WTO) agreements and the North American Free Trade Agreement (NAFTA), for instance, often specify in great detail the measures that governments can or cannot adopt vis-à-vis domestic and international producers. But, powerful as these treaties are, they only prohibit the use of a small number of very specific instruments such as tariffs and quotas to assist domestic producers, and even then they often contain exceptions to those bans. The use of subsidies of various kinds specifically intended to assist domestic producers, for example, is restricted by countervailing duty clauses and other similar measures, but activities in the cultural and agricultural realms are usually excluded from these measures.

Similarly, more general political agreements, whether formal or informal, can also have a constraining direct effect on the choice of policies and policy tools. The European Union is an extreme case of the formal transfer of decision-making authority to a supra-national centre, for example, which often severely limits what national governments can do and the instruments they can employ to effect their decisions (Kassim and Le Galès 2010). However even here the restrictions on national governments' abilities to employ regulatory and fiscal tools on their own are often less significant than often assumed (Halpern 2010). And, even when they are, national governments are often able to craft their own specific solutions to ongoing policy problems with little regard to EU policy through mechanisms such as 'subsidiarity' or the 'Open Method of Co-ordination' which allow local states to determine and design their own policy responses to EU-level initiatives (Meuleman 2010; Heidbreder 2010; Lierse 2010; Tholoniat 2010).

Thus, while there is no doubt that the evolution of these kinds of international treaties and arrangements is an important development, in many sectors and areas of government activity they impose only very minimal or no constraints on the choice of policy tools utilized by governments; nowhere near those alleged by both proponents and opponents of globalization-led pro-market reforms (see especially Palan and Abbott 1996; Clark 1998; Weiss 1999; Bernhagen 2003). There are few international agreements that specifically require governments to privatize or deregulate, for example, and the sectors which have experienced the deepest deregulation and privatization in recent decades – financial, telecommunications and air transportation services – predate the General Agreement on Trade in Services (GATS) negotiated under the WTO umbrella.

Hence, to date, the actual impact of globalization on domestic state policy designs is much less than often alleged, outside of several well-known sectors and events. The direct international constraints on policy designs typically cited by proponents of the globalization thesis have largely been confined to cross-border economic exchanges and do not cover much of what governments do and how they do it. Traditional command and control instruments of governance, such as regulation by government or independent regulatory commissions, state-owned enterprises and direct taxation and subsidization, are far from antithetical to globalization as is evident in their continued, and at times even increasing, use in policy designs in a variety of national and sectoral settings (Jayasuriya 2001, 2004; Vogel and Kagan 2002; Jordana and Levi-Faur 2004; Ramesh and Howlett 2006).

Assessing network effects: the 'government to governance' hypothesis

Similarly, the need to shift toward the greater use of network management tools and activities put forward by adherents of the argument that states have moved 'from government to governance' as a result of changes in society and the way in which government interacts with it, is also lacking a great deal of empirical evidence (Howlett, Rayner and Tollefson 2009; Schout, Jordan and

Twena 2010). While it is clear that the development of modern information and communications technologies have had a serious impact on the way in which individuals and organizations interact and organize themselves in contemporary societies, it is not clear that these developments have had an equally direct effect in altering traditional governance practices or policy designs (Hood 2006; Hood and Margetts 2007b).

Governing involves the establishment of a basic set of relationships between governments and their citizens which can vary from highly structured and controlled to arrangements that are monitored only loosely and informally, if at all. In its broadest sense, 'governance' is a term used to describe the *mode* of coordination exercised by state actors in their interactions with societal actors and organizations (de Bruijn and ten Heuvelhof 1995; Kooiman 1993 and 2000; Rhodes 1996; Klijn and Koppenjan 2000). 'Governance' is thus about establishing, promoting and supporting a specific type of relationship between governmental and non-governmental actors in the governing process.

Changes in governance modes entail both alterations in the abilities of various state and non-state actors to prevail in policy formulation disputes and decisions, as well as shifts in the choices of policy instruments used to implement public policy (Scharpf 1991; Weaver and Rockman 1993; March and Olson 1996; Offe 2006). But much is unclear about the application of the concept of governance to considerations of policy design.

Typical management activities related to network modes of governance are those which affect network creation, recognition, capacity-building, and content creation or alteration. Robert Agranoff (Agranoff and McGuire 1999), for example, has observed that in a typical 'network management' situation 'the primary activities of . . . [a] manager involve selecting appropriate actors and resources, shaping the operating context of the network and developing ways to cope with strategic and operational complexity' (21). Such definitions of network management activities, however, are very vague and their design implications unclear.

Many early proponents of the idea of increased 'networkization' simply expected governance arrangements to shift evenly away from sets of formal institutions, coercive power relations and substantive regulatory tools found in hierarchical systems towards more informal institutions, non-coercive relationships of power and a marked preference for procedural instruments and soft law in more plurilateral systems (Dunsire 1993; Kooiman 1993). However the possible variations in governance types and outcomes are a good deal more complicated once the possibility of sectoral variations is taken into account (van Kersbergen and van Waarden, 2004; Meuleman 2009).

Mark Considine and his colleagues, for example, have investigated these arrangements and linkages and identified four common governance arrangements found in modern liberal-democratic states which they relate to specific policy foci, forms of state-society interactions and overall governance aims (see Table 1.1).

Table 1.1 Modes of governance (empirical content)

Mode of governance	Central focus of governance activity	Form of state control of relationships	Overall governance aim	Prime service delivery mechanism	Key procedural tool for policy implementation
Legal governance	Legality – promotion of law and order in social relationships	Legislation, law and administration	Legitimacy – voluntary compliance	Rights – property, civil, human	Courts and litigation
Corporate governance	Management – of major organized social actors	Plans	Controlled and balanced rates of socio-economic development	Targets – operational objectives, subsidies and grants	Specialized and privileged advisory committees
Market governance	Competition – promotion of small- and medium-sized enterprises	Contracts and regulations	Resource/cost efficiency and control	Regulatory boards, prices – controlling for externalities, supply and demand	Tribunals and commissions
Network governance	Relationships – promotion of inter-actor organizational activity	Collaboration	Co-optation of dissent and self-organization of social actors	Networks of governmental, and non-governmental organizations	Network brokerage activities

Source: Modified from Considine, M. 2001. *Enterprising States: The Public Management of Welfare-to-Work*. Cambridge, Cambridge University Press; and English, L. M. and M. Skellern. 2005. 'Public-Private Partnerships and Public Sector Management Reform; A Comparative Analysis'. *International Journal of Public Policy* 1, nos. 1/2: 1–21.

While a change in governance mode involving a shift from hierarchical, imperative state-led coordination to 'steering' through reflexive self-organization ('plurilateralism') is basic to the idea of a shift from 'governing' to 'governance', such a shift may be present in only some sectors and also represents only one axis along which different modes of governance can be located (Harrop 1992; Cerny 1993; Pontusson 1995; Daugbjerg 1998; Haas 2004; Zielonka 2007). As observers such as Knill and Lehmkuhl have noted, governance arrangements feature different relative strengths of the public and private actors involved (Knill and Lehmkuhl 2002; Jordan et al. 2005) and vary according to whether these relationships are expressed in formal or informal terms (Treib et al. 2007; Kritzinger and Pulzl 2008).[3]

These dual dimensions of governance arrangements cover the four modes of governance Considine identified (see Table 1.2) and suggest 'network governance' is only one such possible arrangement in any given governing circumstance (Heidbreder 2010).

The existence of several possible alternative types or 'modes' of governance existing simultaneously at the sectoral level suggests a more complex picture of governance arrangements, instrument choices and policy designs than the one-to-one national level, multi-sectoral shift towards the use of more participatory and less 'command and control' tools often proposed by adherents of the 'government to governance' thesis (Koppenjan and Klijn 2004; Barnett et al. 2009; Esmark 2009; Hysing 2009; Edelenbos et al. 2010; Hardiman and Scott 2010; Schout et al. 2010).

Table 1.2 Multiple modes of governance (logic)

		Nature of rules	
		Explicit	Implicit
Nature of state–societal interactions	Hierarchical	Type I governance mode – legal governance	Type II governance mode – corporatist governance
	Non-hierarchical	Type III governance mode – market governance	Type IV governance mode – network governance

Source: Adapted from Heidbreder, Eva. 2011. 'Structuring the European Administrative Space: Policy Instruments of Multi-Level Administration'. *Journal of European Public Policy*, June forthcoming.

Conclusion: moving beyond globalization and networks in the study of policy design

The recognition of the continued vitality of the state in a globalized environment along with the existence of multiple modern sectoral modes of governance suggests a more subtle and nuanced account of policy design trends and influences is required than is typically found in the discussions about instrument use and policy design which have flowed from many current studies of globalization and network governance. However, many existing debates about policy design often continue to fixate on the impact of these two processes and, as a result, much of the existing discussion of policy tools and policy design is characterized by misinformation, ideological predilection, and unnecessarily polarized position taking.

Fortunately, other scholarship on policy design and policy instrument choice has offered pathways to a better understanding of instrument selection and policy design by grounding it more carefully in empirical studies and in more nuanced and sophisticated analyses of policy-making practices and activities (Bressers and O'Toole 1998; de Bruijn and Hufen 1998; Van Nispen and Ringeling 1998). As the discussion in this book will show, embedding the discussion of policy design in the Procrustean bed of globalization and network theory is not a useful way to advance thinking on the subject. Understanding contemporary policy design requires an effort to develop a more nuanced understanding of the policy formulation and implementation activities of governments than is provided by adhering to either or both of the 'globalization' and 'government to governance' hypotheses. A more detailed and systematic understanding of the kinds of policy choice open to governments and of their ability to choose specific combinations of policy tools in their efforts to create and manage public policy-making is needed to advance our understanding of policy design (Ingraham 1987). This book is intended to help facilitate this understanding.

Readings

Bobrow, Davis. 2006. 'Policy Design: Ubiquitous, Necessary and Difficult'. In *Handbook of Public Policy*, ed. B. Guy Peters and Jon Pierre. Beverly Hills, CA: Sage, 75–96.

Cerny, Philip G. 2010. 'The Competition State Today: From Raison d'État to Raison du Monde'. *Policy Studies* 31, no. 1: 5–21.

Cerny, P. G. 1996. 'International Finance and the Erosion of State Policy Capacity'. In *Globalization and Public Policy*, ed. P. Gummett. Cheltenham: Edward Elgar, 83–104.

de Bruijn, J. A. and E. F. ten Heuvelhof. 1995. 'Policy Networks and Governance.' In *Institutional Design*, ed. D.L. weiner. Boston: Kluwer Academic Publishers, 161–79.

Hobson, J. and M. Ramesh. 2002. 'Globalisation Makes of States What States Make of It: Between Agency and Structure in the State/Globalisation Debate'. *New Political Economy* 7, no. 1: 5–22.

Howlett, M. and M. Ramesh. 2006. 'Globalization and the Choice of Governing Instruments: The Direct, Indirect and Opportunity Effects of Internationalization'. *International Public Management Journal* 9, no. 2: 175–94.

Ingraham, P. 1987. 'Toward More Systematic Considerations of Policy Design'. *Policy Studies Journal* 15, no. 4: 611–28.

Kooiman, J. 1993. 'Governance and Governability: Using Complexity, Dynamics and Diversity'. In *Modern Governance*. London: Sage, 35–50.

Kooiman, J. 2000. 'Societal Governance: Levels, Models, and Orders of Social-Political Interaction'. In *Debating Governance*, ed. J. Pierre. Oxford: Oxford University Press, 138–66.

May, Peter J. 2003. 'Policy Design and Implementation'. In *Handbook of Public Administration*, ed. B. Guy Peters and Jon Pierre. Beverly Hills, CA: Sage, 223–33.

Milward, H. B. and K. G. Provan. 2000. 'Governing the Hollow State'. *Journal of Public Administration Research and Theory* 10, no. 2: 359–80.

Milward, H. B., K. G. Provan, and B. A. Else 1993. 'What Does the "Hollow State" Look Like?' In *Public Management: The State of the Art*, ed. J. Bozeman. San Francisco, CA: Jossey-Bass, 309–23.

Rhodes, R. A. W. 1994. 'The Hollowing Out of the State: The Changing Nature of the Public Service in Britain'. *The Political Quarterly* 65, no. 2: 138–51.

—— 1996. 'The New Governance: Governing Without Government'. *Political Studies* 44: 652–67.

Treib, Olivier, Holger Bahr and Gerda Falkner. 2007. 'Modes of Governance: Towards a Conceptual Clarification'. *Journal of European Public Policy* 14, no. 1: 1–20.

Vans Kersbergen, K. and F. Van Waarden. 2004. '"Governance" as a Bridge Between Disciplines: Cross-Disciplinary Inspiration Regarding Shifts in Governance and Problems of Governability, Accountability and Legitimacy'. *European Journal of Political Research* 43: 143–71.

Weiss, L. 1998. *The Myth of the Powerless State: Governing the Economy in a Global Era*. Cambridge: Polity Press.

—— 2003. *States in the Global Economy: Bringing Domestic Institutions Back In*. Cambridge: Cambridge University Press.

—— 2005. 'The State-Augmenting Effects of Globalisation'. *New Political Economy* 10, no. 3: 345–53.

Part II

SYSTEMATICALLY STUDYING POLICY DESIGN

Chapter 2

Key definitions and concepts in the study of policy design

Providing a better, more nuanced understanding of policy design and the factors which influence it is the goal of this book. Before moving to a discussion of the evolution of current thinking in the field, however, it is helpful to go back a step and provide several definitions and key concepts commonly used in the study of policy design.

What is public policy?

The first term which requires definition is 'public policy'. The most concise formal definition of a public policy is probably that set out by Thomas Dye in his early and best-selling text on the subject where he defined policy simply as 'what government chooses to do or not to do' (Dye 1972). This is a useful definition in so far as it underscores the notions that policies are conscious choices and not accidents or accidental occurrences; that they result from government decisions and not those of other actors in society such as private companies or other non-governmental organizations; and that so-called 'negative decisions' – that is, decisions to consciously avoid changing the status quo – are just as much public policies as the more commonly understood 'positive decisions' which do in fact alter some aspect of current circumstances.

This definition, however, is not all that helpful from a design perspective because it does not reveal anything about the *processes* through which policies are made, nor the *substantive content* of government decisions and the different elements which go into making them up. In addressing these two issues, a second definition put forward almost two decades before Dye's by one of the earliest proponents of the modern policy sciences, the University of Chicago political scientist Harold Lasswell, is quite helpful. Lasswell, like Dye, also defined public policies as government decisions but noted that they were composed of two interrelated elements: *policy goals* and *policy means* operating at different levels of abstraction (Lasswell 1958). Policy goals in this sense are the basic aims and expectations governments have in deciding to pursue (or not) some course of action, while policy means are the techniques they use to attain those goals (Walsh 1994). Both these elements can be focused on a range of activities, from abstract principles associated with governance arrangements, to much more concrete administrative programme specifications.

In terms of *content*, this suggests that policies are composed of a number of analytically distinct elements, with some policies focused on attaining concrete outputs while others focus on less tangible normative and cognitive aspects of policy-making. However, the situation is much more complex than it might first appear. A typical substantive policy, for example, involves some very abstract general 'aims' or goals, such as, in the cases of criminal justice or education policy, attaining a just society or a prosperous one; along with a set of less abstract 'objectives' actually expected to achieve those aims such as, in the examples provided above, reducing crime or providing better educational opportunities to members of the public. Further, those objectives themselves must be concretized in a set of specific targets or measures which allow policy resources to be directed towards goal attainment, such as reducing specific types of crimes to specific levels within specified periods of time or increasing post-secondary educational attendance within some set temporal period (Cashore and Howlett 2007; Kooiman 2008; Stavins 2008; Howlett and Cashore 2009).

Similarly, the means or techniques for achieving these goals also exist on several levels. These run from highly abstract preferences for specific forms of policy implementation, such as a preference for the use of market, government or non-profit forms of organization to implement policy goals in areas such as health care, or crime prevention; to the more concrete level of the use of specific governing tools or mechanisms such as regulation, information campaigns, public enterprises or government subsidies to alter actor behaviour in order to promote or increase wellness or prevent crime; to the most specific level of deciding or determining exactly how those tools should be 'calibrated' in order to achieve policy targets. This latter activity, to continue the examples, might include providing a specific number of additional police on the streets within a specified period of time, or a specific level of subsidy to non-profit groups to provide additional hospital beds or other types of health service within the same set period of time (Howlett 2005; 2009; Stavins 2008).

Policies are thus complex entities composed of policy goals and means arranged in several layers, ranging from the most general level of a relatively abstract governance mode, to the level of a policy regime and finally to the level of specific programme settings (Cashore and Howlett 2006; 2007; Howlett and Cashore 2009). The principle 'components' of public policies involved in any policy design, following this logic, are set out in Table 2.1 below.

In terms of policy-making *processes*, Lasswell (1956) also discussed this subject in a useful way. He did so by using one of the historically most popular

Table 2.1 Components of public policies involved in policy design

	Policy level		
	Governance mode: high-level abstraction	*Policy regime: programme-level operationalization*	*Programme settings specific on-the-ground measures*
Policy goals	General abstract policy aims: The most general macro-level statement of government aims and ambitions in a specific policy area	Operationalizable policy objectives: The specific meso-level areas that policies are expected to address in order to achieve policy aims	Specific policy targets: The specific, on-the-ground, micro-requirements necessary to attain policy objectives
Policy component			
Policy means	General policy implementation preferences: The long-term preferences of government in terms of the types of organizational devices to be used in addressing policy aims	Policy tool choices: The specific types of governing instruments to be used to address programme-level objectives	Specific policy tool calibrations: The specific 'settings' of policy tools required to attain policy targets

Source: Howlett, Michael and Benjamin Cashore. 2009. 'The Dependent Variable Problem in the Study of Policy Change: Understanding Policy Change as a Methodological Problem'. *Journal of Comparative Policy Analysis: Research and Practice* 11, no.1: 33–46.

models for analyzing public policy-making, which has been to think of it as a process; that is, as a set of interrelated stages through which policy issues and deliberations flow in a more or less sequential fashion from 'inputs' (problems) to 'outputs' (policies). The resulting sequence of stages is often referred to as the 'policy cycle' (Jann and Wegrich 2007; Howlett, Ramesh and Perl 2009).

The idea of a policy cycle has received somewhat different treatment in the hands of different authors. In his own work, for example, Lasswell (1971) divided the policy process into seven stages, which, in his view, described not only how public policies were actually made but also how they should be made: (1) intelligence, (2) promotion, (3) prescription, (4) invocation, (5) application, (6) termination, (7) appraisal. In this construct, the policy process began with intelligence-gathering, that is, the collection, processing, and dissemination of information for those who participate in decision-making. It then moved to the promotion of particular options by those involved in making the decision. In the third stage the decision-makers prescribed a course of action. In the fourth stage the prescribed course of action was invoked alongside a set of sanctions to penalize those who fail to comply with these prescriptions. The policy was then applied by the courts and the bureaucracy and ran its course until it was terminated or cancelled. Finally, the results of the policy were appraised or evaluated against the original aims and goals.

In this view, policy-making is viewed not as primarily a random, ritualistic or symbolic form of state activity,[1] but as a conscious matter of attempting to match the means of policy implementation to formulated policy goals. That is, policy-making is viewed as an *instrumental* problem-solving activity, one in which various governing resources are marshalled into a set of techniques which could at least potentially or theoretically achieve the aims, objectives and goals of policy-makers.

Lasswell's original formulation provided the basis for many other later models of the policy process (Lyden et al. 1968; Simmons et al. 1974; Brewer 1974; Anderson 1983; Brewer and deLeon 1983; Jones 1984). Each contained slightly different interpretations of the names, number, and order of stages in the cycle but used the same logic to describe them; that of 'applied problem solving' (deLeon 1999; Hill and Hupe 2006). The stages in applied problem-solving and the corresponding stages in the policy process are depicted in Figure 2.1.

In this model, *agenda-setting* refers to the process by which problems come to the attention of governments; *policy formulation* refers to how policy options are formulated within government; *decision-making* is the process by which governments adopt a particular course of action or non-action; *policy implementation* relates to how governments put policies into effect; and *policy evaluation* refers to the processes by which the results of policies are monitored by both state and societal actors, the outcome of which may be reconceptualization of policy problems and solutions. As we have seen, policy design activity occurs at the policy formulation stage of the policy process but is not synonymous with that stage. Rather it represents the articulation of sets of ideas about policy-making and possible policy outcomes which may or may not be actually adopted, in whole or in part, in practice (Goggin 1987).

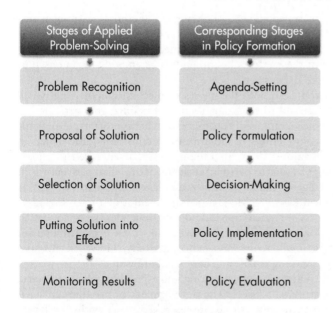

Figure 2.1 The five stages of the policy cycle and their relationship to applied problem-solving

The idea of a policy process or cycle has often been used to view policy-making in essentially pragmatic terms, as the embodiment of effort to improve the human condition through harnessing reason to guide human activities, in this case, in the process of governing (Hawkesworth 1992). In this view, policy means or instruments are often viewed mainly as *technical* mechanisms used to attain policy goals and as existing only in the stages of policy formulation – when policy means are proposed, and policy implementation – when they are put into effect. However, a process model can also be used to describe policy-making as a much more overtly social or political process in which actors compete with each other in order to attain their goals or collectively 'puzzle' through towards the solution to an issue (Howlett, Ramesh and Perl 2009; Wu et al. 2010). In this view, policy instruments are thought of as much less technical than political in nature and are typically viewed as extending to activities located in all stages of the policy process, including not just policy formulation and implementation, but also agenda-setting, decision-making and policy evaluation.

What is policy design?

This discussion raises several important issues related to the idea of 'policy design'. That is, public policies are the results of efforts made by governments to alter aspects of their own or social behaviour in order to carry out some end or purpose and, as discussed above, are comprised of complex arrangements of policy goals and policy means. These efforts can be more or less systematic and the ends and purposes attempted to be attained are multifarious and wide-ranging. Should all of these efforts be thought of as embodying a conscious 'design'? In most cases the answer is 'yes'.

Policy design extends to both the means or mechanisms through which goals are given effect, and to the goals themselves, since goal articulation inevitably involves considerations of feasibility, or what is practical or possible to achieve in given conjunctures or circumstances considering the means at hand (Huitt 1968; Majone 1975; Ingraham 1987). Even when the goals pursued are not laudable, such as personal enrichment or military adventurism, or when the knowledge or the means utilized is less than scientific, such as religious or ideologically inspired dogma or implementation preferences, and even when these efforts are much more ad hoc and much less systematic than might be desired, as long as a desire for effective resource use in goal attainment guides policy-making, it will involve some effort at design. However, this does not mean that all designs are equal or generate equal results.

As discussed in Chapter 1, policy-making and especially policy tool selection is a highly constrained process. The development of programme level-objectives and means choices, for example, takes place within a larger governance context in which sets of institutions, actors and practices are 'defined' which make up the 'environment' within which policy-making takes place. Some of the key elements which comprise a policy, notably, abstract policy aims and general implementation processes, are defined at this 'meta' level of policy-making. Hence, as we have seen, a legal mode of governance contains a preference for the use of laws while a market mode involves a preference for regulation; a corporatist mode – a preferences for plans and organization; and a network mode – a preference for the use of information tools. Thus choices of programme-level tools and targets are constrained by the existing governance mode, while a policy regime logic (Skodkin, Gulbergand Aakre 2010), that is, the choices of meso-level programme objectives and policy instruments, similarly constrains micro-level targeting and programme goals. The multi-level, nested, nature of policy tool choices, therefore, must be taken into account in any effort to design or plan policy outcomes. Better designs are more effective at doing this, generating policy processes and outcomes which are more consistent with their environments.

In this regard it is important for policy designers to incorporate into their thinking the knowledge that the exact processes by which policy decisions are taken vary greatly by jurisdiction and sector and reflect the great differences, and nuances, that exist between different forms of government – from military regimes to liberal democracies and within each type – as well as the particular configuration of issues, actors and problems various governments, of whatever type, face in particular areas or sectors of activity – such as health or education policy, industrial policy, transportation or energy policy, social policy and many others (Ingraham 1987; Howlett, Ramesh and Perl 2009). In some circumstances, policy decisions will be more highly contingent and 'irrational', that is, driven by situational logics and opportunism rather than careful deliberation and assessment, than others (Cohen et al. 1979; Dryzek 1983; Kingdon 1984; Eijlander 2005; Franchino and Hoyland 2009). This high level of contingency in decision-making has led some critics and observers of policy design efforts to suggest that policies cannot be 'designed' in the sense that a house or a piece of furniture can be (Dryzek and Ripley 1988). However, many other scholars disagree with this assessment.

In their many works on the subject in the late 1980s and early 1990s for example, Stephen H. Linder and B. Guy Peters argued that the actual process of public policy decision-making could, in an analytical sense, be divorced from the abstract concept of policy design, in the same way that an abstract architectural concept can be divorced from its engineering manifestation. Policy designs in this sense they argued, can be thought of as 'ideal types', that is, as ideal configurations of sets of policy elements which can reasonably be expected, if adopted as set out within a specific contextual setting, to deliver a specific outcome. Whether or not all of the aspects of such contextual configurations are actually adopted in practice, in their view, is more or less incidental to the design, except in so far as such variations suggest the expected outcome may be less stable or reliable than the original design assumptions would augur. As Linder and Peters (1988) argued:

> Design then, is not synonymous with instrumental reasoning but certainly relies greatly on that form of reasoning. Moreover, the invention or fashioning of policy options is not designing itself and may not even call on any design. While somewhat at odds with conventional (mis)usage, our treatment focuses attention on the conceptual underpinnings of policy rather than its content, on the antecedent intellectual scheme rather than the manifest arrangement of elements. As a result, the study of design is properly 'meta-oriented' and, therefore, one step removed from the study of policy and policy-making.
>
> (Linder and Peters 1988: 744)

However it is conducted, the idea of policy design is inextricably linked with the idea of improving government actions through the conscious consideration at the stage of policy formulation of the likely outcomes of policy implementation activities. This is a concern both for non-governmental actors concerned with bearing the costs of government failures and incompetence, as well as for governmental ones who may be tasked with carrying out impossible duties and meeting unrealistic expectations. Regardless of regime and issue type, and regardless of the specific weight given by governments to different substantive and procedural aims, all governments wish to have their goals effectively achieved and usually wish to do so in an efficient way, that is, with a minimum of effort and cost (Weimer 1993). Thus all governments, of whatever stripe, are interested in applying knowledge and experience about policy issues in such a way as to ensure the more or less efficient and effective realization of their aims (deLeon 1999; Potoski 2002).

This desire to husband resources involved in goal attainment involves governments of all types and persuasions in processes of more or less conscious and rational efforts at design (Dryzek 1983). It also allows us to define the term as *the effort to more or less systematically develop efficient and effective policies through the application of knowledge about policy means gained from experience, and reason, to the development and adoption of courses of action that are likely to succeed in attaining their desired goals or aims within specific policy contexts* (Bobrow and Dryzek 1987; Bobrow 2006; Montpetit 2008).

Again as Linder and Peters (1990) argued:

> A design orientation to analysis can illuminate the variety of means implicit in policy alternatives, questioning the choice of instruments and their aptness in particular contexts. The central role it assigns means in policy performance may also be a normative vantage point for appraising design implications of other analytical approaches. More important, such an orientation can be a counterweight to the design biases implicit in other approaches and potentially redefine the fashioning of policy proposals. (304)

What is a policy instrument?

The policy alternatives which policy designers create are composed of different sets or combinations of the policy elements described above. And, as Linder and Peters noted, policy instruments[2] are especially significant in this process as they are the techniques or means through which states attempt to attain their goals. They are the subject of deliberation and activity at all stages of the policy process and affect both the agenda-setting and policy formulation processes as well as being the subject of decision-making policy implementation, and evaluation (Howlett 2005; Howlett, Ramesh and Perl 2009).

These tools have a special place in the consideration and study of policy design because, taken together, they comprise the contents of the toolbox from which governments must choose in building or creating public policies. Policy design elevates the analysis and practice of policy instrument choice – specifically tools for policy implementation – to a central focus of study, making their understanding and analysis a key design concern (Salamon 1981; Linder and Peters 1990). Instrument choice, from this perspective, in a sense, *is* public policy-making, and understanding and analyzing potential instrument choices involved in implementation activity *is* policy design. One role of a textbook in policy design is thus assisting 'in constructing an inventory of potential public capabilities and resources that might be pertinent in any problem-solving situation' (Anderson 1975: 122).

It is important to repeat, however, that policy instruments exist at *all* stages of the policy process – with specific tools such as stakeholder consultations and government reviews intricately linked to agenda-setting activities, ones like legislative rules and norms linked to decision-making behaviour and outcomes, and others linked to policy evaluation, such as the use of ex-post, or after-the-fact, cost–benefit analyses (see Figure 2.2).

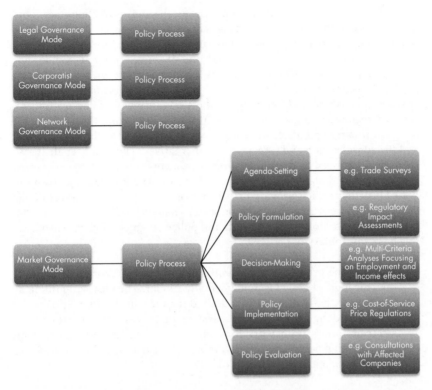

Figure 2.2 An example of the range of policy instruments by governance mode and stage of the policy cycle

Policy tools are thus in a sense 'multi-purpose', since, for example, regulation can appear in the implementation activities of several governance modes, while some tools, like impact assessments, can also appear within several stages of the cycle. However, a regulation appearing within the implementation phase of a network mode of governance which mandates information disclosure, for example, serves a different purpose than a regulation found in a market mode which limits a firm to ownership of only a specific percentage of an industry. Similarly, consultations which take place in the agenda-setting stage of the policy process have a different purpose and effect than those which take place after a decision has been made. While the general terminology may be similar, pains must be taken to distinguish these tools and activities in order to avoid confusion and errant efforts at instrument selection and policy design.

Although policy instruments appear in all stages of the policy process, however, those affecting the agenda-setting, decision-making and evaluation stages of the policy process, while very significant and important in public management (Wu et al. 2010), are less so with respect to policy design activities. This is because, as we've seen, policy design largely takes place at the formulation stage of the policy cycle and deals with plans for the implementation stage. Thus the key sets of policy instruments of concern to policy designers are those linked to policy implementation, in the first instance, and to policy formulation, in the second. In the first category we would find examples of many well-known governing tools such as public enterprises and regulatory agencies which are expected to alter or affect the delivery of goods and services to the public and government (Salamon 2002), while in the second we would find instruments such as regulatory impact or environmental impact appraisals which are designed to alter and affect some aspect of the nature of policy deliberations and the consideration and assessment of alternatives (Turnpenny et al. 2009).

The role played by implementation instruments in policy design, however, is key to policy design and is the central focus of many of the chapters of this book. It is they which provide the substance or content of whatever design deliberations occur at the formulation stage. Thus, as Linder and Peters (1984) noted, it is critical for policy scientists and policy designers alike to understand this basic vocabulary of design:

> Whether the problem is an architectural, mechanical or administrative one, the logic of design is fundamentally similar. The idea is to fashion an instrument that will work in a desired manner. In the context of policy problems, design involves both a systematic process for generating basic strategies and a framework for comparing them. Examining problems from a design perspective offers a more productive way of organizing our thinking and analytical efforts. (253)

What is an implementation tool?

Implementation tools are thus key to policy design. They are policy instruments which affect either the content or processes of policy implementation, that is, which alter the way goods and services are delivered to the public or the manner in which such implementation processes take place (Howlett 2000).

One common type of implementation instrument proposes to alter the actual *substance* of the kinds of day-to-day production, distribution and consumption activity carried out in society, while the other focuses upon altering political or policy behaviour in the *process* of the articulation of implementation goals and means. *Substantive* implementation instruments are those used to directly affect the production, distribution and consumption of goods and services in society while *procedural* implementation instruments accomplish the second purpose (Ostrom 1986; Howlett 2000; 2005).[3]

Substantive instruments are expected to alter some aspect of the production, distribution and delivery of goods and services in society: broadly conceived to include both mundane goods and services like school lunches to crude vices such as gambling or illicit drug use, to more common individual virtues such as charitable giving or volunteer work with the physically challenged, and include the attainment of sublime collective goals like peace and security, sustainability, happiness and well-being. We can thus define substantive policy instruments as those policy techniques or mechanisms designed to directly or indirectly affect the behaviour of those involved in the production, consumption and distribution of different kinds of goods and services in society (Schneider and Ingram 1990; 1993; 1994). This is a large field of action since it extends not only to goods and services provided or affected by markets, but also well beyond to state or public provision and regulation, as well as to those goods and services typically provided by the family, community, non-profit and voluntary means often with neither a firm market nor state basis (Salamon 1989; 2002).

Substantive implementation instruments can affect many aspects of production, distribution and consumption of goods and services regardless of their institutional basis. Production effects, for example, include determining or influencing:

1   Who produces it – for example, via licencing, bureaucracy/procurement, or subsidies for new start-ups.
2   The types of goods and services produced – for example, through bans or limits or encouragement.
3   The quantity of goods or services provided – for example, via subsidies or quotas.
4   The quality of goods or services produced – for example, via product standards, warranties.
5   Methods of production – for example, via environmental standards or subsidies for modernization.
6   Conditions of production – for example, via health and safety standards, employment standards acts, minimum wage laws, inspections.
7   The organization of production – for example, via unionization rules, anti-trust or anti-combines legislation, securities legislation, or tax laws.

Consumption and distribution effects are also manifold. Some examples of these are:

1   Prices of goods and services – such as regulated taxi fares or wartime rationing.
2   Actual distribution of produced goods and services – affecting the location and types of schools or hospitals, forest tenures or leases.
3   Level of consumer demand for specific goods – for example, through information release, nutritional and dangerous goods labelling (cigarettes), export and import taxes and bans and similar activities.
4   Level of consumer demand in general – via interest rate, monetary and fiscal policy.

Procedurally oriented implementation tools, on the other hand, affect production, consumption and distribution processes only indirectly, if at all. Rather they instead affect the behaviour of actors involved in policy implementation. Policy actors are arrayed in various kinds of policy communities, and just as they can alter or affect the actions of citizens in the productive realm, so too can they affect and alter aspects of policy-making behaviour (Knoke 1987; 1991; 1993). Procedural implementation tools are an important part of government activities aimed at altering policy interaction within policy sub-systems but, as Klijn et al. (1995) put it, they 'structure . . . the game without determining its outcome' (441). That is, these behavioural modifications affect the manner in which implementation unfolds but without predetermining the results of substantive implementation activities.

Some of the kinds of implementation-related activities that can be affected by the use of procedural tools (Klijn et al. 1995; Goldsmith and Eggers 2004; Klijn and Koppenjan (2006) include:

1 changing actor policy positions
2 setting down, defining or refining actor positions
3 adding actors to policy networks
4 changing access rules for actors to governments and networks
5 influencing network formation
6 promoting network self-regulation
7 modifying system-level policy parameters (e.g. levels of market reliance)
8 changing evaluative criteria for assessing policy outcomes, success and failure
9 influencing the pay-off structure for policy actors
10 influencing professional and other codes of conduct affecting policy actor behaviour
11 regulating inter-actor policy conflict
12 changing policy actors' interaction procedures
13 certifying or sanctioning certain types of policy-relevant behaviour
14 changing supervisory relations between actors.

Policy designs typically contain 'bundles' or 'mixes' of procedural and sub-stantive implementation tools (Howlett 2000; 2002). For reasons discussed in Chapter 4 below, procedural implementation tools and their effects are not as well studied or understood as are substantive instruments, although several procedural techniques, such as the use of specialized investigatory commissions and government reorganizations, are quite old and well-used and have been the objects of study in fields such as public administration, public management and organizational behaviour (Woodley 2008; Schneider and Sidney 2009). Nevertheless, just like their substantive counterparts, they are a key part of policy designs and policy design activity.

Conclusion: policy design and policy instrument choice

As Charles Anderson (1971) noted, policy design is virtually synonymous with 'statecraft' or the practice of government as 'the art of the possible'. It is always a matter of making choices from the possibilities offered by a given historical situation and cultural context. From this vantage point, the institutions and procedures of the state to shape the course of economy and society become the equipment provided by a society to its leaders for the solution of public problems. (121)

Policy designers use the tools of the trade of statecraft and, as Anderson (1971) also noted, 'the skillful policy maker, then, is [one] who can find appropriate possibilities in the institutional equipment of . . . society' to best obtain their goals.

The nature and type of the specific policy implementation instruments available to policy designers are dealt with in more detail in Chapters 4–8. Before moving on to this discussion, however, the next chapter examines the policy formulation process in more detail; setting out the basic characteristics of this stage of the policy process and reviewing the sets of actors who formulate policy options and the kinds of ideas which go into their preparation and appraisal of implementation alternatives.

Readings

Bobrow, D. B. and J. S. Dryzek. 1987. *Policy Analysis by Design*. Pittsburgh, PA: University of Pittsburgh Press.

Bressers, H. T. A. and L. J. O'Toole. 1998. 'The Selection of Policy Instruments: A Network-based Perspective'. *Journal of Public Policy* 18, no. 3: 213–39.

—— 2005. 'Instrument Selection and Implementation in a Networked Context'. In *Designing Government: From Instruments to Governance*, ed. P. Eliadis, M. Hill and M. Howlett. Montreal: McGill-Queen's University Press, 132–53.

Dryzek, John. 1983. 'Don't Toss Coins in Garbage Cans: A Prologue to Policy Design'. *Journal of Public Policy* 3, no. 4: 345–67.

Dryzek, J. S. and B. Ripley. 1988. 'The Ambitions of Policy Design'. *Policy Studies Review* 7, no. 4: 705–19.

Dye, T. R. 1972. *Understanding Public Policy*. Englewood Cliffs, NJ: Prentice-Hall.

Hill, M. and P. Hupe. 2002. *Implementing Public Policy: Governance in Theory and Practice*. London: Sage Publications.

—— 2003. 'The Multi-Layer Problem in Implementation Research'. *Public Management Review* 5, no. 4: 471–90.

—— 2006. 'Analysing Policy Processes as Multiple Governance: Accountability in Social Policy'. *Policy and Politics* 34, no. 3: 557–73.

Howlett, M. 2000. 'Managing the "Hollow State": Procedural Policy Instruments and Modern Governance'. *Canadian Public Administration* 43, no. 4: 412–31.

Howlett, Michael and Benjamin Cashore. 2009. 'The Dependent Variable Problem in the Study of Policy Change: Understanding Policy Change as a Methodological Problem'. *Journal of Comparative Policy Analysis: Research and Practice* 11, no. 1: 33–46.

Howlett, M. 2005. 'What is a Policy Instrument? Policy Tools, Policy Mixes and Policy Implementation Styles'. In *Designing Government: From Instruments to Governance*, ed. P. Eliadis, M. Hill and M. Howlett. Montreal: McGill-Queen's University Press, 31–50.

Lasswell, H. D. 1956. *The Decision Process: Seven Categories of Functional Analysis.* College Park, MD: University of Maryland Press.

—— 1958. *Politics: Who Gets What, When, How.* New York: Meridian.

Linder, S. H. and B. G. Peters. 1984. 'From Social Theory to Policy Design'. *Journal of Public Policy* 4, no. 3: 237–59.

—— 1988. 'The Analysis of Design or the Design of Analysis?' *Policy Studies Review* 7, no. 4: 738–50.

—— 1990a. 'Policy Formulation and the Challenge of Conscious Design'. *Evaluation and Program Planning* 13: 303–11.

—— 1990b. 'Research Perspectives on the Design of Public Policy: Implementation, Formulation, and Design'. In *Implementation and the Policy Process: Opening up the Black Box*, ed. D. J. Palumbo and D. J. Calista. New York: Greenwood Press, 51–66.

—— 1990c. 'The Design of Instruments for Public Policy'. In *Policy Theory and Policy Evaluation: Concepts, Knowledge, Causes, and Norms*, ed. S. S. Nagel, 103–19. New York: Greenwood Press.

—— 1991. 'The Logic of Public Policy Design: Linking Policy Actors and Plausible Instruments'. *Knowledge in Society* 4: 125–51.

—— 1992. 'A Metatheoretic Analysis of Policy Design'. In *Advances in Policy Studies Since 1950*, ed. W. N. Dunn and R. M. Kelly. New Brunswick, NJ: Transaction Publishers, 201–38.

Weimer, D. L. 1992. 'The Craft of Policy Design: Can It Be More Than Art?' *Policy Studies Review* 11, no. 3/4: 370–88.

—— 1993. 'The Current State of Design Craft: Borrowing, Tinkering, and Problem Solving'. *Public Administration Review* 53, no. 2 (April): 110–20.

Chapter 3

Policy design as policy formulation

As we have seen, policy instruments exist at all stages of public policy-making. There are specific instruments, like consultative mechanisms such as public hearings or investigatory commissions, which serve as agenda-setting instruments. And there are others, like the use of decision-making matrices and legislative committee systems which are used at the decision-making stage of the process. Even further, the use of auditors-general and other kinds of expenditure evaluation system are instruments used at the evaluation stage of the policy cycle (Heilman and Walsh 1992; Wu et al. 2010). While all of these tools are important, the foci of design activities, as the discussion in Chapter 2 has shown, are policy formulation and implementation (Hood 1986 and 2007; Linder and Peters 1991; Varone 1998; Varone and Aebischer 2001). It is at these two stages that the possible techniques to be used in realizing policy are first mooted and appraised, and then, finally, executed and put into practice (Goggin 1987).

Policy formulation as a stage of the policy cycle

Policy formulation refers to the stage of generating options about what to do about a public problem (Sidney 2007). Once a government has acknowledged the existence of a public problem and the need to do something about it, that is, once it has entered onto the agenda of government, policy-makers are expected to decide on a course of action to follow in addressing it.

Formulating what this course of action will entail is the subject of policy formulation. It is a stage in which options that might help resolve issues and problems recognized at the agenda-setting stage are identified, refined, appraised and formalized. Although many such alternatives may have already emerged during or prior to agenda-setting (Kingdon 1984), in policy formulation some initial assessment of the feasibility and comparative costs and benefits of different policy options is conducted (May 1981; Forester 1983; Dunn 1986; Weimer 1992; Boardman et al. 2001).). These formulation efforts and dynamics are distinct from the next stage, decision-making, where a course of action is approved by authoritative decision-makers in government (Howlett, Ramesh and Perl 2009).

Thus, as Charles Jones (1984: 7) observed, the distinguishing characteristic of policy formulation is simply that means are proposed in order to see if and how they could resolve a perceived societal problem or government goal. This formulation activity encompasses consideration and discussion of several elements. These include, culminating in considerations of programme design and programme structure:

(a) problem conceptualization
(b) theory evaluation and selection
(c) specification of objectives
(d) programme design
(e) programme structure.

(Wolman 1981: 435)

Policy formulation, therefore, is a process of identifying and assessing possible solutions to policy problems or, to put it another way, exploring the various options or alternatives available for addressing a problem through *policy analysis* (Linder and Peters 1990). This is what Aaron Wildavsky (1979) termed finding and establishing a relationship between 'manipulable means and obtainable objectives' (15–16).

Policy formulation thus involves identifying both the technical and political constraints on state action (May 1981; Sidney 2007). It involves recognizing limitations on state resources such as a lack of credibility, fiscality, capacity or legitimacy, which can limit what is *feasible* in specific circumstances (Majone 1989: 76). Politicians in most societies, for example, cannot do everything they consider would appeal to the public but also cannot ignore popular opinion and public sentiments and still maintain their legitimacy and credibility. Other constraints on policy design can arise from limits on the state's administrative and financial capacity. For example, governments that have an ownership stake in economic sectors such as energy, finance, and transportation may have more policy options open to them than states where the private sector exclusively delivers these goods and services, while states with well-developed and sophisticated administrative apparatuses generally also have a larger range of possible courses of action than those states lacking such resources (Ingraham 1987).

Policy analysis and policy formulation

Harold Thomas (2001) has identified four tasks involved in policy formulation which each involve some element of formal policy analysis and which highlight how some options are carried forward while others are set aside: appraisal, dialogue, formulation or assessment, and consolidation.

In *appraisal* activity, data and evidence are identified and considered. This may take the form of research reports, expert testimony, stakeholder input, or public consultation on the policy problem that has been identified. Here, government both generates and receives input about policy problems and solutions.

Dialogic activity seeks to facilitate communication between policy actors with different perspectives on the issue and potential solutions. Sometimes, open meetings are held where presenters can discuss and debate proposed policy options. In other cases, the dialogue is more structured, with experts and societal representatives from business and labour organizations, for example, getting invited to speak for or against potential solutions.[1]

At the core of deliberations, *formulation* or *assessment* activity sees public officials weighing the evidence on various policy options and drafting some form of proposal that identifies which of these options will be advanced to the ratification stage. This can take the form of draft legislation or regulations, or it could identify the framework for a subsequent round of public and private policy actors' deliberation in order to negotiate a more specific plan of action. This stage often involves formal techniques or instruments such as environmental or regulatory impact assessments designed to focus attention to, and provide data on, certain key considerations of potential policy alternatives (Bregha et al. 1990; Lawrence 2001; Dalal-Clayton and Sadler 2005; Radaelli 2005; Turnpenny et al. 2008; 2009; Franz and Kirkpatrick 2008).

Making recommendations about which policy options to pursue will often yield dissent from those who have seen their preferred strategies and instruments set aside during earlier stages of formulation. These objections can be addressed during the *consolidation* phase, when policy actors often have an opportunity to provide more or less formal feedback on the recommended options and emergent policy design. Some actors who advocated alternative options may come around to joining a consensus on the merits of a particular course of action so that they can stay connected to official policy development efforts (Teisman 2000). Other policy actors may register their continued dissent. Leading policy-makers' rejection of certain types of options need not be based on facts (Merton 1948), but if significant actors in the policy subsystem believe that something is unworkable or unacceptable, this is typically sufficient for its exclusion from further consideration in the policy process (Carlsson, 2000).

Who are the policy designers?

As Thomas' (2001) account of the different sub-stages and activities involved in policy formulation outlined above suggests, different actors are involved in different aspects of policy formulation and policy design. Defining and weighing the merits and risks of various options forms the substance of this second stage of the policy cycle, and more or less formal 'policy analysis' is thus a critical component of policy formulation and policy design activity (Gormley 2007; Sidney 2007; Dunn 2008). The manner in which the *policy advice system* is structured in a particular sector allows us to identify the more or less influential actors involved in design decisions and policy assessments in specific sectoral subsystems or issue networks (James and Jorgensen 2009).

The role of policy advisors and policy advice systems

Given the range of players and sub-stages involved in it, policy formulation is a highly diffuse and often disjointed process whose workings and results are often very difficult to discern and whose nuances in particular instances can be fully understood only through careful empirical case study. Nevertheless, most policy formulation processes do share certain characteristics which are relevant to considerations of policy design. First, and most obviously, formulation is not usually limited to one set of actors (Sabatier and Jenkins-Smith 1993). Second, formulation may also proceed without a clear definition of the problem to be addressed (Weber and Khademian 2008) and may occur over a long period of time in 'rounds' of formulation and reformulation of policy problems and solutions (Teisman, 2000). And third, while formulators often search for 'win-win' solutions, it is often the case that the costs and benefits of different options fall disproportionately on different actors (Wilson 1974). This implies, as Linder and Peters, among others, noted, that the capability of policy designs to be realized in practice remains subject to many political as well as technical variables. However, this does not imply that policy design is impossible, unpredictable or an unworthwhile task, simply that it must be recognized that some possible designs may prove impossible to adopt in practice in given contexts and that the adoption of any design will be a fraught and contingent process as options and various types of policy actors attempt to construct and assess alternative designs (Dryzek 1983).

Politicians situated in authoritative decision-making positions ultimately 'make' public policy. However, they do so most often by following the advice provided to them by civil servants and others whom they trust or rely upon to consolidate policy alternatives into more or less coherent designs and provide them with expert opinion on the merits and demerits of the proposals (MacRae and Whittington 1997; Heinrichs 2005). As such it is useful to think of policy advisors as being arranged in an overall 'policy advisory system' which will differ slightly in every particular issue area but which generally assumes a hierarchical shape moving from the public at large to a small number of key advisors with privileged access to decision-makers.

Recent studies of advice systems in countries such as New Zealand, Israel, Canada and Australia have developed this idea; that government decision-makers sit at the centre of a complex web of policy advisors which include both 'traditional' political advisors in government as well as non-governmental actors in NGOs, think tanks and other similar organizations, and less formal or professional forms of advice from colleagues, friends and relatives and members of the public and political parties, among others (Maley 2000; Peled 2002; Dobuzinskis et al. 2007; Eichbaum and Shaw 2007). As Anderson (1996) noted, 'a healthy policy-research community outside government can play a vital role in enriching public understanding and debate of policy issues, and it serves as a natural complement to policy capacity within government' (486).

Understanding the nature of policy formulation and design activities in different analytical contexts, however, involves discerning how the policy advice system is structured and operated in the specific sector of policy activity under examination (Brint 1990; Page 2010). At their most basic, policy advice systems can be thought of as part of the knowledge utilization system of government, itself a kind of marketplace for policy ideas and information, comprising three separate components: a supply of policy advice, its demand on the part of decision-makers, and a set of brokers whose role it is to match supply and demand in any given conjuncture (Brint 1990; Lindquist 1998). That is, these systems can be thought of as arrayed into three general 'sets' of analytical activities and participants linked to the positions actors hold in the 'market' for policy advice.

The first set of actors at the top of the hierarchy is composed of the 'proximate decision-makers' themselves who act as consumers of policy analysis and advice – that is, those with actual authority to make policy decisions, including cabinets and executives as well as parliaments, legislatures and congresses, and senior administrators and officials delegated decision-making powers by those other bodies. The second set, towards the bottom, is composed of those 'knowledge producers' located in academia, statistical agencies and research institutes who provide the basic scientific, economic and social scientific data upon which analyses are often based and decisions made. The third set in between the first two is composed of those 'knowledge brokers' who serve as intermediaries between the knowledge generators and proximate decision-makers, repackaging data and information into usable form (Lindvall 2009; Page 2010). These include, among others, permanent specialized research staff inside government as well as their temporary equivalents in commissions and task forces, and a large group of non-governmental specialists associated with think tanks and interest groups. Although often thought of as 'knowledge suppliers', key policy advisors almost by definition exist in the brokerage subsystem, and this is where most professional policy analysts involved in policy formulation can be found (Lindvall 2009; Verschuere 2009; Howlett and Newman 2010).

In general, four distinct 'communities' of policy advisors can be identified within the upper levels of any policy advice system depending on their location inside or outside of government, and by how closely they operate to decision-makers: core actors, public sector insiders, private sector insiders, and outsiders (see Table 3.1).

Along with the less knowledgeable public, these sets of actors can also be thought of as existing on a spectrum moving from the abstract to the more practical, and therefore can also be linked to influence and impact on specific policy elements as set out in Table 3.2 (Page 2010). Different types of 'policy advice systems' exist depending on the nature of the knowledge supply and

Table 3.1 The four communities of policy advisors

	Proximate actors	*Peripheral actors*
Public/governmental sector	Core actors:	Public sector insiders:
Executive staff	Central agencies and task forces	Commissions, committees
	Professional governmental policy analysts	Research councils/ scientists International organizations
Non-governmental sector	Private sector insiders:	Outsiders:
	Consultants Political party staff Pollsters Donors	Public interest groups Business associations Trade unions Academics Think tanks Media International non-governmental organizations

Table 3.2 Advisory system actors by policy level

	High-level abstraction	*Programme-level operationalization*	*Specific on-the-ground measures*
Policy goals	General abstract policy aims	Operationalizable policy objectives	Specific policy targets
(normative)	Public, outsiders and insiders	Insiders and core actors	Core actors
Policy means	General policy implementation preferences	Policy instruments	Specific policy tool calibrations
(cognitive)	Public, outsiders and insiders	Insiders and core actors	Core actors

demand in specific policy formulation contexts, which varies not only by national context and institutional design but also by sector (Halffman and Hoppe 2005). What actors do in policy formulation, how they do it, and with what effect, depends in large part on the type of advisory system present in a specific government or area of interest (Brint 1990).[2] However core actors typically, albeit in a constrained fashion, are those most able to influence the construction and selection of policy designs given their ability to influence all aspects of a policy, including the specification of policy targets on the ground, as well as the calibration of policy tools (Page 2010).

The role of policy ideas in policy formulation and policy design

A key aspect of policy design lies in the kinds of ideas held about the feasibility and optimality of alternative possible arrangements of policy tools. Different kinds of actors hold different kinds of ideas and have different levels of influence or impact on policy formulation activities. Not everyone's ideas about policy options and instrument choices are as influential as others when it comes to policy appraisal and design (Lindvall 2009; Marriott 2010) and one has to be very specific about what level of policy and which particular element one is referring to when assessing the influence of specific kinds of actors and ideas on the articulation of policy alternatives. Generally speaking, however, the ideas held by central policy actors play a key role in guiding efforts to construct policy options and assess design alternatives (Ingraham 1987; George 1969; Mayntz 1983; Jacobsen 1995; Chadwick 2000; Gormley 2007).

Different types of ideas, have different effects on different elements of policy-making and hence upon instrument choices and policy designs. Policy goals, for example, consist of a range of ideas from general philosophical and ethical principles to specific causal logics and sociological constructs. And the same is true of policy means, which can embody some knowledge of past practices and concepts of successful and unsuccessful policy implementation, but also extend beyond this to ideological and other ideational structures informing 'practical' choices for goal attainment.

Distinguishing between types of ideas in terms of their level of abstraction and 'practicality' is an important first step in discerning their impact on policy designers. John Campbell (1988) has argued that a small number of distinct and distinguishable idea sets go into public policy-making: distinguishing between cognitive and normative ideas and whether these affect the 'foreground' or 'background' of policy debates and discussions. Or what he calls *programme ideas*, *symbolic frames*, *policy paradigms*, and *public sentiments* (see Table 3.3).

Table 3.3 Ideational components of policy contents

		Level of policy debate affected	
		Background	Foreground
Level of ideas affected	Normative (value)	Public sentiments	Symbolic frames
	Cognitive (causal)	Policy paradigms	Programme ideas

Source: Adapted from John L. Campbell. 1998. 'Institutional Analysis and the Role of Ideas in Political Economy'. *Theory and Society* 27, no. 5: 385.

Ideas such as *symbolic frames* and *public sentiments* tend to affect the perception of the legitimacy or 'correctness' or 'appropriateness' of certain courses of action, while *policy paradigms* represent a 'set of cognitive background assumptions that constrain action by limiting the range of alternatives that policy-making elites are likely to perceive as useful and worth considering' (Campbell 1998; 2002: 385; also Surel 2000). The term *programme ideas* represents the selection of specific solutions from among the set designated as acceptable within a particular paradigm. Thus symbolic frames and public sentiments can be expected to largely influence policy goals (Stimson 1991; Suzuki 1992; Durr 1993; Stimson et al. 1995) while more cognitive aspects such as policy paradigms[3] and programme ideas, on the other hand, can be expected to more heavily influence choices of policy means (Stone 1989; Hall 1993). This helps to capture the manner in which established beliefs, values, and attitudes lie behind understandings of public problems and emphasizes how paradigm-inspired notions of the feasibility of the proposed solutions are significant determinants of policy choices and alternative designs (Hall 1990: 59; also Huitt 1968; Majone 1975; Schneider 1985; Webber 1986; Edelman 1988; Hilgartner and Bosk 1988).

Similarly, in their work on the influence of ideas in foreign policy-making situations, Goldstein and Keohane (1993) and their colleagues noted at least three types of ideas that combined normative and cognitive elements but at different levels of generality: world views, principled beliefs, and causal ideas (see also Campbell 1998; Braun 1999). *World views* or *ideologies* have long been recognized as helping people make sense of complex realities by identifying general policy problems and the motivations of actors involved in politics and policy. These sets of ideas, however, they argued, tend to be very diffuse and do not easily translate into specific views on particular policy problems. *Principled beliefs* and *causal stories*, on the other hand, can exercise a much more direct influence on the recognition of policy problems and on policy content. These ideas can influence policy-making by serving as 'road maps' for action, defining problems, affecting the strategic interactions between policy actors, and constraining the range of policy options that are proposed (Carstensen 2010; Stone 1988; 1989). At the micro-level, 'causal stories' and beliefs about the behaviour patterns of target groups heavily influence choices of policy settings or calibrations (Stone 1989; Schneider and Ingram 1993 and 1994).[4]

These different kinds of policy ideas pitched at different levels of generality and abstraction correlate quite closely with the different elements of policy set out above. The policy ideas found in public sentiments, for example, are generally too broad and normative in nature to have much of a direct impact on programme design. However they serve to set the context within which that design activity occurs. Conversely, policy paradigms have a much greater cognitive component, allowing them to significantly influence the nature of policy means at the policy regime level. These general relationships between idea types and policy elements are set out in Table 3.4 below.

Table 3.4 The relationship between policy ideas and policy design elements

	Governance modes	Policy regimes	Programme aspects
Policy goals	General abstract policy aims	Operationalizable policy objectives	Specific policy targets
Impacting set of ideas	**Ideologies and world views**	**Policy paradigms**	**Causal stories**
Policy means	General policy implementation preferences	Operationalizable policy tools	Specific policy tool calibrations

Such a multi-level analysis of policy ideas helps explain some of the real complexity and difficulties involved in policy formulation and policy design (Bobrow and Dryzek 1987; Bobrow 2006). As Table 3.5 shows, different sets of actors, with different sets of ideas are active at different levels of policy formulation and policy design.

This implies that in a typical design situation the impact of the public and outsiders on formulation is significant but diffused and filtered when it comes to the articulation of causal stories and the design of specific tool selections and calibrations (Lindvall 2009; Page 2010). It also suggests that while very significant in such processes, core actors specifying policy targets and tool

Table 3.5 Ideas, actors and instruments: the general model

	Governance mode	Policy regime	Programme level
Policy level	**High-level abstraction**	**Programme-level operationalization**	**Specific on-the-ground measures**
Policy goals	General abstract policy aims	Operationalizable policy objectives	Specific policy targets
Policy ideas	**World views and ideologies**	**Policy paradigms**	**Causal stories**
Policy actors	**Public, outsiders and insiders**	**Public and private sector insiders and core actors**	**Core actors**
Policy means	General policy implementation preferences	Operationalizable policy tools	Specific policy tool calibrations

calibrations act within a greatly circumscribed landscape of existing world views, and ideologies and policy paradigms (Braun 1999; Maley 2000; Haas 2001; Eichbaum and Shaw 2008; Dunlop 2009; Lindvall 2009).

Conclusion: policy design as constrained expert discourse

It is common policy to find statements such as Halligan's (1995) assertion that a good advice system should consist of:

> at least three basic elements within government: a stable and reliable in-house advisory service provided by professional public servants; political advice for the minister from a specialized political unit (generally the minister's office); and the availability of at least one third-opinion option from a specialized or central policy unit, which might be one of the main central agencies.
>
> (162)[5]

And in all cases a major role in policy formulation and policy design is played by these kinds of core actors, such as professional policy analysts, central agency officials and others (Page 2010; Renn 1995).

However, it is also important to note that their influence becomes more direct, although also more constrained, as the formulation process becomes focused on particular and more precise design dimensions (Meltsner 1976). That is, in a typical policy design situation, not all elements of a policy are at play and the range of choices left to designers at the micro-level of concrete targeted policy tool calibrations is restricted by general policy aims and implementation preferences which, in turn, inform meso-level considerations about alternative policy objectives and policy tool combinations.

Thus in many design situations, general abstract policy aims and implementation preferences can often be taken as given, establishing the context in which design decisions relating to programme-level and on-the-ground specifications are made by policy insiders and core actors. And in many cases, even the goal components of these last two levels of policy may be already established, leaving the designer only the task of establishing specific policy tool calibrations which cohere with these already existing or well-established policy elements. How the macro, meso and micro elements of a policy process fit together, then, is a critical determinant of how key actors view and articulate the range of policy alternatives available to them, and thus a critical component, of policy formulation and policy design (Walker 2000; Walker, Rahman and Cave 2001).

Campbell, J. L. 1998. 'Institutional Analysis and the Role of Ideas in Political Economy'. *Theory and Society* 27, no. 5: 377–409.

Caplan, Nathan and C. H. Weiss. 1977. *A Minimal Set of Conditions Necessary for the Utilization of Social Science Knowledge in Policy Formulation at the National Level*. Lexington, MA: Lexington Books.

deLeon, P. 1992. 'Policy Formulation: Where Ignorant Armies Clash by Night'. *Policy Stud.Rev.* 11, no. 3/4: 389–405.

Eichbaum, Chris and Richard Shaw. 2008. 'Revisiting Politicization: Political Advisers and Public Servants in Westminster Systems'. *Governance* 21, no. 3: 337–63.

Fleischer, Julia. 2009. 'Power Resources of Parliamentary Executives: Policy Advice in the UK and Germany'. *West European Politics* 32, no. 1: 196–214.

Goldstein, J. and R. O. Keohane. 1993. 'Ideas and Foreign Policy: An Analytical Framework'. In *Ideas and Foreign Policy: Beliefs, Institutions and Political Change*, ed. Goldstein, J. and R. O. Keohane. Ithaca, NY: Cornell University Press, 3–30.

Hall, P. A. 1989. *The Political Power of Economic Ideas: Keynesianism across Nations*. Princeton, NJ: Princeton University Press.

—— 1993. 'Policy Paradigms, Social Learning and the State: The Case of Economic Policy Making in Britain'. *Comparative Politics* 25, no. 3: 275–96.

Hansen, R. and D. King. 2001. 'Eugenic Ideas, Political Interests, and Policy Variance: Immigration and Sterilization Policy in Britain and the U.S'. *World Politics* 53 (January): 237–63.

Heinrichs, H. 2005. 'Advisory Systems in Pluralistic Knowledge Societies: A Criteria-Based Typology to Assess and Optimize Environmental Policy Advice'. In *Democratization of Expertise? Exploring Novel Forms of Scientific Advice in Political Decision-Making*, ed. S. Maasen and P. Weingart. Dordrecht: Springer, 41–61.

Jacobs, Alan M. 2008. 'How Do Ideas Matter? Mental Models and Attention in German Pension Politics'. *Comparative Political Studies* 42, no. 2: 252–79.

James, Thomas E. and Paul D. Jorgensen. 2009. 'Policy Knowledge, Policy Formulation, and Change: Revisiting a Foundational Question'. *Policy Studies Journal* 37, no. 1: 141–62.

Lindvall, Johannes. 2009. 'The Real but Limited Influence of Expert Ideas'. *World Politics* 61, no. 4: 703–30.

Maley, Maria. 2000. 'Conceptualising Advisers' Policy Work: The Distinctive Policy Roles of Ministerial Advisers in the Keating Government, 1991–96'. *Australian Journal of Political Science* 35, no. 3: 449–449.

Nilsson, Mans, Andrew Jordan, John Turnpenny, Julia Hertin, Bjorn Nykvist and Duncan Russel. 2008. 'The Use and Non-Use of Policy Appraisal Tools in Public Policy Making: An Analysis of Three European Countries and the European Union'. *Policy Sciences* 41: 335–55.

O'Faircheallaigh, Ciaran. 2010. 'Public Participation and Environmental Impact Assessment: Purposes, Implications and Lessons for Public Policy Making'. *Environmental Impact Assessment Review* 30: 19–27.

Radaelli, C. M. 2005. 'Diffusion without Convergence: How Political Context Shapes the Adoption of Regulatory Impact Assessment'. *Journal of European Public Policy* 12, no. 5: 924–43.

Schmidt, Vivien A. 2010. 'Taking Ideas and Discourse Seriously: Explaining Change Through Discursive Institutionalism as the Fourth New Institutionalism?' *European Political Science Review* 2, no. 1: 1–25.

Sidney, Mara S. 2007. 'Policy Formulation: Design and Tools'. In *Handbook of Public Policy Analysis: Theory, Politics and Methods*, ed. Frank Fischer, Gerald J. Miller and Mara S. Sidney. New Brunswick, NJ: CRC/Taylor & Francis, 79–87.

Turnpenny, John, Claudio M. Radaelli, Andrew Jordan and Klaus Jacob. 2009. 'The Policy and Politics of Policy Appraisal: Emerging Trends and New Directions'. *Journal of European Public Policy* 16, no. 4: 640–53.

Walker, Warren E., S. Adnan Rahman, and Jonathan Cave. 'Adaptive Policies, Policy Analysis, and Policy-Making.' *European Journal of Operational Research* 128, no. 2 (January 16, 2001): 282–289.

Weible, Christopher M. 2008. 'Expert-based Information and Policy Subsystems: A Review and Synthesis'. *Policy Studies Journal* 36, no. 4: 615–35.

Zito, A. R. 2001. 'Epistemic Communities, European Union Governance and the Public Voice'. *Science and Public Policy* 28, no. 6: 465–76.

Chapter 4

Policy design and implementation tool choices

A significant part of policy design activity, as we have seen, involves matching policy goals with the ideas formulators hold about policy means or tools. Understanding policy instrument choices and the range of possibilities present in any design situation requires both an understanding of what kinds of instrument options exist, which subset of those is generally considered feasible or possible in a given context, and which among that smaller subset of all possible tools is deemed by policy experts to be the most appropriate to use at a given time. In the effort to help deal with these questions, students of policy formation and policy instruments in a variety of academic disciplines have over the years developed several models or conceptual schemes which help to explain how policy designers go about their tasks.

The origins of policy design as an academic field of study

Fields interested in studying public policy, such as political science and political sociology, have traditionally been concerned with studying policy 'inputs' or the dynamics of public policy formation. For example, in political science a key focus has been upon the role played by public opinion, political party activities, elections and similar phenomena in affecting policy-making processes and defining policy content, while, in the case of political sociology, a key focus has been on understanding the roles played by social structure in defining actor 'interests' and positions in policy-making processes (Mayntz 1983).

Studies in these disciplines revealed a great deal about policy formation but tended to neglect the implementation component of policy-making. Studies in other fields such as public administration and management and organization studies, on the other hand, following the admonitions of early students of the field such as the US president and political scientist Woodrow Wilson

(1887) traditionally focused their efforts on the study of the inner workings of government – especially upon the study of behavioural and management issues involved in such tasks as financial administration and budgeting, ministerial responsibility and accountability, the operation of the merit principle and human resources/personnel administration – and purposely avoided considering the more political aspects of policy processes.

In his pathbreaking early works on public policy-making, Harold Lasswell drew on both these literatures not only to define public policy, clarify important aspects of policy-making such as the number and type of stages involved in policy deliberations, and emphasize the importance of context to its workings (Torgerson 1985 and 1990), but also to think about the main instruments of policy-making. Lasswell (1954) noted the extent to which governments could affect policy-making through manipulations involving, among other things, 'symbols, signs and icons', and argued that a principal task of the policy sciences must be to understand the nuances of these actions and their effects (Lasswell 1954; 1971).

Like others of Lasswell's insights, this orientation was retained by many later students of policy-making who developed very flexible notions of the multiple means by which governments could affect, or give effect to, policy. In these early works, 'policy instruments' were defined very broadly so as to include a wide range of tools or techniques of governance used at different stages of the policy process. However, in the 1970s as the effort to improve policy-making through improved policy designs took shape, work turned to focus on the evaluation of the impact on policy outcomes of specific kinds of implementation-related tools, primarily economic ones like subsidies and taxes (Mayntz 1983; Woodside 1986; Sterner 2002).[1] This work eventually resulted in a specific approach to policy analysis which had as its central focus the evaluation of the characteristics, merits and demerits of particular policy instrument choices.

Bardach (1980) and Salamon (1981), for example, both argued in the early 1980s that policy studies had 'gone wrong' right at the start by defining policy in terms of 'issues', 'areas' or 'fields' rather than in terms of 'instruments'. As Salamon put it:

> The major shortcoming of current implementation research is that it focuses on the wrong unit of analysis, and the most important theoretical breakthrough would be to identify a more fruitful unit on which to focus analysis and research. In particular, rather than focusing on individual programs, as is now done, or even collections of programs grouped according to major 'purpose,' as is frequently proposed, the suggestion here is that we should concentrate instead on the generic tools of government action, on the 'techniques' of social intervention.
>
> (1981: 256)

Following these injunctions, other scholars began to investigate the links between implementation failures and policy success (Mayntz 1979; Goggin et al. 1990; O'Toole 2000) and turned their gaze directly on the subject of how implementation alternatives were crafted and formulated. Studies in economics and law which focused on the 'ex-post' evaluation of the impact of policy outputs (Bobrow 1977; Stokey and Zeckhauser 1978) began the more systematic appraisal of implementation alternatives and, ultimately, insights gleaned from a wide body of interdisciplinary literature concerning policy inputs and governmental processes were combined in the 1980s and 1990s in the explicit study of policy design. Many lessons about policy instruments and policy design were drawn from legal studies, for example, which revealed a great deal about how tools such as laws, regulations and other mechanisms involved in the delivery of various kinds of goods and services operate; and upon procedural aspects of formulation and implementation activities such as the passage of legislation and forms of administrative rule-making, while organization, management and administrative studies provided insights into the links between administrative systems and governance modes, among others (Peters and Pierre 1998; Pierre and Peters 2005).

Scholarly attention in the early 1980s was focused on the need to more precisely categorize types of policy instruments in order to better analyze the reasons for their use (Salamon 1981; Tupper and Doern 1981; Trebilcock and Hartle 1982; Bressers and Honigh 1986; Bressers and Klok 1988). Careful examination and systematic classification of implementation instruments and instrument choices, it was argued, would not only lead to insights into the factors driving the policy process and the characterization of long-term patterns of public policy-making, as Lasswell had hoped, but would also allow practitioners to more readily draw lessons from the experiences of others with the use of particular techniques in specific circumstances and hence improve policy designs and outcomes (Mayntz 1983; Linder and Peters 1984; Woodside 1986).

During this period studies in Europe and North America shed a great deal of light on the construction and establishment of regulatory and other political and administrative agencies and enterprises; traditional financial inducements, and the 'command-and-control' measures adopted by administrative agencies, during this period (Tupper and Doern 1981; Hood 1986; Howlett 1991; Vedung 1997; Landry et al. 1998). And this new emphasis upon the systematic study of policy instruments quickly generated a sizable academic literature and resulted in immediate application in the design of many new policy initiatives in emerging areas such as pollution prevention and professional regulation (Trebilcock 1983; Hippes 1988). Significant subjects such as the reasons behind shifts in patterns of instrument choices associated with the waves of privatization and deregulation which characterized the period also received attention (Howlett and Ramesh 1993).[2]

Soon the field of instrument studies had advanced enough that Salamon (1989) could argue that the 'tools approach' had become a major approach to policy studies in its own right, bringing a unique perspective to the policy sciences with its focus on policy outputs.[3] At this point he framed two important research questions to be addressed in future analyses of the tools of government action: 'What consequences does the choice of tool of government action have for the effectiveness and operation of a government program?' and 'What factors influence the choice of program tools?' (265). These questions were taken up by the 'tools approach' and the policy design literature in the 1990s.

The development of taxonomies and models in the study of policy design

Assessing and answering Salamon's questions required scholars interested in policy design to engage in a lengthy process of social scientific analysis and model-building related to the study of implementation tools. These efforts expanded the number of preliminary questions which needed to be answered before Salamon's queries could be addressed (Salamon 1981; Timmermans et al. 1998; Hood 2007) to include:

1   What potential tools does any government have?
2   How can these be classified?
3   How have these been chosen in the past?
4   Is there a pattern for this use?
5   If so, how can we explain this (or these) pattern(s)?
6   Can we improve on past patterns of use?

In order to answer these questions, policy scientists pursuing the tools approach followed, not necessarily as systematically as might be hoped, a five-stage research and analytical model-building strategy; one quite typical of the social sciences (see Figure 4.1 below).[4] Each of the stages in this process is set out and described below.

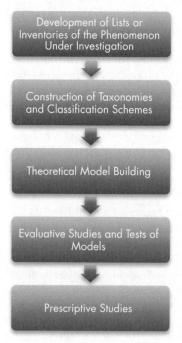

Figure 4.1 Analytical steps in social science model-building
Source: Modified from McKelvey, Bill.1982. *Organizational Systematics: Taxonomy, Evolution, Classification*. Berkeley, CA: University of California Press.

The construction of empirical inventories

As Figure 4.1 shows, the first step in the systematic study of policy instruments, as in any other similar endeavour in the social sciences, is the establishment of an inventory of the dependent variable. While there were many scholars who had looked at specific tools in the past (such as Cushman's 1941 study of regulatory agencies which was often cited by early students of the field), the first efforts to systematically define the range of possible instruments which could be used in a policy design originated in the post-World War II planning exercises undertaken by the United Nations and the Organization for Economic Co-operation and Development (OECD) in Europe.

Key figures in this research included Nobel Prize winning development economists such as E. S. (Etienne) Kirschen and Jan Tinbergen, who published groundbreaking studies including *Economic Policy in Our Times* (1964) dealing with the instruments for economic policy they had viewed in operation in the process of post-war European reconstruction. One of the first inventories of instruments was Kirschen et al.'s (1964) identification of well over forty different types of implementation instruments then prevalent in European economic policy-making activities, ranging from public enterprises to various forms of government procurement and tax incentive and subsidy schemes. Such studies were followed by many others examining the instruments prevalent in other areas, such as banking and foreign policy (Hermann 1982), adding to the list tools such as interest rate determination and other monetary and fiscal tools. These were pathbreaking studies which, although they did not make any distinctions between general implementation preferences, policy mechanisms or calibrations, and very often confused implementation tools and instruments used at other stages of the policy process, laid the groundwork for such future refinements by providing the raw data required for later classification efforts.

The development of taxonomies

Once a fairly exhaustive inventory has been created, the next major step in theory construction is to move towards taxonomy. That is, examining the list of the phenomena under consideration and attempting to classify or categorize the subject matter into a smaller number of mutually exclusive categories which, together, retain the exhaustive character of the original lists. Many such schemes were developed in the policy instruments literature of the 1960s to 1980s.

Kirschen and his fellow authors (1964), for example, utilized a resource-based taxonomy of governing instruments to group instruments into five general 'families' according to the 'governing resource' they used: public finance, money and credit, exchange rates, direct control, and changes in the institutional framework (16–17). However, this scheme was very sectorally specific and focused on the specific problem of achieving economic development goals. More generic schemes were developed such as that put forward by Theodore Lowi (1966; 1972), which heavily influenced later thinking on the subject. Lowi

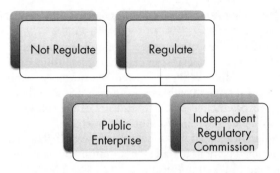

Figure 4.2 Cushman's three types of policy tools
Source: Cushman, R. E. 1941. *The Independent Regulatory Commissions*. London: Oxford University Press.

developed the insight first put forward by students of public administration in the USA like Cushman (see Figure 4.2), that governments had only a small number of alternative choices in any given regulatory situation, depending on the amount of coercion they wished to employ in that situation – in Cushman's case, choosing either to regulate or not and, if so, to regulate either by the use of public enterprises or regulatory commissions. This analysis, among other things, introduced the idea that instrument choices were multi-level and nested, an insight which would be further developed in the years to come.

In his own work, however, Lowi argued that a four-cell matrix based on the specificity of the target of coercion and the likelihood of its actual application would suffice to distinguish all the major types of government implementation activity. The original three policy types he developed included the weakly sanctioned and individually targeted 'distributive' policies; the individually targeted and strongly sanctioned 'regulatory' policy; and the strongly sanctioned and generally targeted 'redistributive' policy. To these three Lowi later added the weakly sanctioned and generally targeted category of 'constituent' policy (see Table 4.1).

This was a significant advance, since it attempted to reduce the complexity of instrument choice to a single two-dimensional framework. However, Lowi's categories of tools – distributive, redistributive, constituent and regulatory – did not fit well with existing tool inventories and hence were difficult to operationalize and test (Roberts and Dean 1994). As a result, many other classification schemes emerged in the literature in the mid-to-late 1980s.

Table 4.1 Lowi's matrix of policy implementation activities

		Specificity of target	
		Specific	*General*
Likelihood of sanctions	*High*	Regulatory	Re-distributive
	Low	Distributive	Constituent

Many of these efforts, but not all, followed Lowi and Cushman's lead in focusing on some aspect of coercion as the key element differentiating policy instrument types. In a key development, however, some also introduced a greater number of differentiating criteria. Balch (1980), for example, talked about both 'carrots' (inducements or incentives) and 'sticks' (coercion or disincentives), while Bardach (1980) argued that government had three 'technologies' which they could utilize in any given choice situation: enforcement, inducement, and benefaction; and that these strategies required different combinations of four critical governmental resources: money, political support, administrative competency, and creative leadership. Elmore (1987) identified four major classes of instruments: mandates, inducements, capacity-building, and system-changing.

Further studies moving in the design direction refined this idea of only a limited number of 'governing resources' lying behind each tool. Christopher Hood (1983; 1986) generated a major work on the subject in 1986 which was heavily influenced by detailed studies of the British and German policy implementation processes undertaken previously by Dunsire (1978) and Mayntz (1975). It involved the elaboration of a fourfold resource-based categorization scheme for policy instruments which served as an admirable synthesis of the other, earlier, models.

Hood argued that governments have essentially four resources at their disposal which they can use to either effect changes in their environment or detect them: *nodality*, meaning the resource that existed simply by nature of the fact that government's existed at the 'centre' of social and political networks but which can also be thought of as 'information' or 'knowledge'; *authority*; *treasure*; and *organization* (or 'NATO' in Hood's terminology). In Hood's scheme, implementation instruments are grouped together according to which of the NATO resources they *most* or *primarily* relied upon for their effectiveness, fully recognizing that most used some combination of these resources in practice (Anderson 1977; Hood 1986).[5]

This taxonomy proved useful in providing a limited number of eight clearly differentiated categories of instruments (see Table 4.2).

Table 4.2 Hood's 1986 taxonomy of substantive policy instruments

		Governing resource			
		Nodality	Authority	Treasure	Organization
Principle use	Detectors	Surveys	Licencing	Policing	Record-keeping
	Effectors	Public information campaign	Regulation	Subsidies	Government agencies

Source: Adapted from Christopher Hood. 1986. *The Tools of Government.* Chatham: Chatham House Publishers.

Models of instrument choice

As Linder and Peters (1990: 307) noted, once the tools of government have been inventoried and classified, 'the need to do something more becomes irresistible'. The next logical step was 'to explore functional connections' involving 'matching instruments to goals, policy problems, social impact and organizations'. Taking this next step towards the idea of policy design, as we have seen, requires clarifying the nature of the criteria by which experts assess policy tools and the nature of the contexts in which they can reasonably be anticipated to perform as expected.

Kirschen et al., in their early 1964 work, had already gone some distance towards that goal by arguing that the key determinants of policy choice in the case of the economic instruments they had identified were the economic objective or goal pursued and the structural and conjunctural context of the choice. The economic objectives, they argued, were determined by the interaction of political parties and their representatives in government, administrators, and interest groups (1964: 224–36), while the structural and conjunctural context, in turn, was affected by the influence of long-term economic processes and structures, and current economic conditions (236–38). They argued that the actual choice of instrument from within the set that fit these epistemic and contextual constraints should be made on essentially technical grounds, according to efficiency and cost criteria; although the political preferences of interest groups and governments – including sociological and ideological constraints – and the institutional limitations of the political system itself had to be taken into account as factors influencing key decision-makers (238–44).

This was a prescient analysis of the overall set of factors affecting instrument choices (Majone 1976; 1989), combining as it did both technical and political factors. However, it was also one which was not adequately grounded in a classification of instruments so as to be able to produce specific recommendations or hypotheses concerning appropriate instrument selections and policy designs in different circumstances or times.

The first models of instrument choices which were so grounded attempted to identify a limited number of criteria upon which policy tools varied; creating single or multiple 'spectrums' or 'continuums' of instrument characteristics which it was hoped could then be associated with specific government preferences among these criteria. Dahl and Lindblom, for example, as early as 1953 had argued that the number of alternative politico-economic instruments is virtually infinite, and proposed five long continua as a method of assessing tool preferability in specific contextual situations (Dahl and Lindblom 1953). Their first continuum ranged instruments according to whether they involved public or private enterprises or agencies; the second according to whether they were persuasive or compulsory; the third according to whether they involved direct or indirect controls over expenditures; the fourth according to whether they involved organizations with voluntary or compulsory membership; and the fifth according to whether government agencies were autonomous or directly responsible to legislators or executive members. Although Dahl and Lindblom did not pursue any further the question of whether and to what extent governments actually used these criteria in order to choose a particular instrument, their idea of arranging instruments on a continuum in order to better clarify the reasons behind their choice was adopted by many authors.[6]

A simplified version of this model was put forward by a group of Canadian scholars including Bruce Doern, Richard Phidd, Seymour Wilson and others,[7] who published a series of articles and monographs in the late 1970s and early 1980s that turned Lowi's two-dimensional matrix of policy choices into a single continuum of policy instruments based on the 'degree of government coercion' each instrument choice entailed. They first placed only self-regulation, exhortation, subsidies, and regulation on this scale (Doern 1981) but later added in categories for 'taxation' and public enterprise (Tupper and Doern 1981) and finally, an entire series of finer 'gradiations' within each general category (Phidd and Doern 1983) (see Figure 4.3 below).

For Doern and his colleagues, the development of their coercion spectrum model led to the hypothesis of a twofold rationale of instrument choice; one that fitted very well with the notion of a 'continuum' of choices, and which offered a great deal of explanatory power in the context of liberal-democratic states. This rationale was based on an appreciation of the ideological preferences of liberal-democratic governments for limited state activity and on the difficulties posed to this principle by the relative political 'strength' of the societal actors in resisting government efforts to shape their behaviour. Assuming that all instruments were more or less technically 'substitutable' – or could perform any task although not necessarily as easily or at the same cost – they argued that in a liberal-democratic society, governments, for ideological reasons, would prefer to use the least coercive instruments available and would only 'move up the scale' of coercion as far as was necessary in order to overcome societal resistance to attaining their goal. As Doern and Wilson put it:

> politicians have a strong tendency to respond to policy issues, (any issue) by moving successively from the least coercive governing instrument to the most coercive. Thus they tend to respond first in the least coercive fashion by creating a study, or by creating a new or reorganized unit of government, or merely by uttering a broad statement of intent. The next least coercive governing instrument would be to use a distributive spending approach in which the resources could be handed out to constituencies in

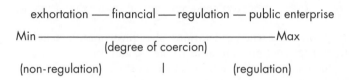

Figure 4.3 The Doern continuum
Source: Doern, G. B. and R. W. Phidd. 1983. *Canadian Public Policy: Ideas, Structure, Process.* Toronto: Methuen.

such a way that the least attention is given as to which taxpayers' pockets the resources are being drawn from. At the more coercive end of the continuum of governing instruments would be a larger redistributive programme, in which resources would be more visibly extracted from the more advantaged classes and redistributed to the less advantaged classes. Also at the more coercive end of the governing continuum would be direct regulation in which the sanctions or threat of sanctions would have to be directly applied.

(Doern and Wilson 1974: 339)

This model was lauded for its simplicity and elegance but, as critics pointed out, was still problematical in its application to policy design decisions since 'coercion' appears to be indivisible,[8] or at best, still very difficult to operationalize with the degree of precision required by the model (Trebilcock et al. 1982: 22–23).[9]

Contemporary conceptions of instrument choice

While groundbreaking, these studies were fairly preliminary and in some cases somewhat rudimentary. However, they provided clear directions for future studies to take. Hood's taxonomy of policy instruments or design elements, for example, failed to distinguish between procedural and substantive uses, or between different levels of policy means, but was a valuable start to consideration and development of more comprehensive and accurate taxonomies of these instruments in later years.[10] And Doern and his colleagues did not deal with the subject of policy mixes, or the selection and design of not just a single instrument, but rather a 'package' or 'bundle' of different types. However, what Doern and his colleagues had actually discovered was a link between the basic tool types set out in Hood's NATO model and the willingness of governments to use these different resources against specific target groups (Woodside 1986; Baxter-Moore 1987). That is, the Doern model centred on the relationship existing between policy tool choice and a specific kind of governance arrangement which predetermined, among other things, an 'appropriate' mode of co-ordinating state and societal actors. And, third, both sets of studies tended to ignore the 'micro-level' of the specific reasons why some permutation within a general tool category – such as the setting of a specific level of tariff or subsidy, or the use of a loan rather than a grant, would occur.

Fortunately, however, earlier generations of implementation scholars had not completely neglected procedural instruments, and other works, like those of Gunningham and his colleagues (Gunningham et al. 1998) had begun to deal with the problem of the design of policy mixes.[11] And others, like those of Schneider and Ingram, developed more sophisticated notions of the inter-relationships existing between governance modes and target group behaviour (Schneider and Ingram 1997). Meanwhile other scholars such as

Salamon had also turned their attention to the issue of micro-calculations and calibrations, and developed ideas about the sets of factors policy formulators take into account in fine-tuning their instrument choices (Salamon 1989; 2002).

Improving on Hood's taxonomy of policy instruments: adding in procedural tools

In the case of procedural instruments, several works dealing with aspects of the subject provided a broad sense of which direction to pursue in attempting to elevate this area of instrument studies to the level that substantive implementation instrument research had attained through taxonomy construction and model-building (Walker 1983; 1991; Qualter 1985). In their 1988 work, for example, Bressers and Klok (1988) had noted the ways in which 'subjective rational actors' can be influenced by manipulation of the alternatives placed before them and that different instruments can affect the number of policy options developed in the policy process, or the calculations of costs and benefits of alternative courses of action made by policy actors. While some of the instruments they examined were 'substantive' (for example, the use of licences to affect the cost of certain activities), most of the instruments captured by their scheme were procedural; especially those dealing with the selective creation, provision and diffusion of information to policy actors.[12]

Taken together, the works of Bressers and Klok, along with that of Schneider and Ingram, and others in the U.S. and Europe, identified a large number of procedural instruments; their inventory, like that in the case of substantive tools, being accompanied by several ideas about how to classify them (Chapman 1973; Weiss and Tschirhart 1994). These authors identified, among others, tools involved in education, training, institution creation, the selective provision of information, formal evaluations, hearings, and institutional reform (Wraith and Lamb 1971; Chapman 1973; Kernaghan 1985; Peters 1992; Weiss and Tschirhart 1994; Bellehumeur 1997). Research into the tools and mechanisms used in intergovernmental regulatory design also identified several other such instruments, including intergovernmental 'treaties' and a variety of 'political agreements' that can affect target-group recognition of government intentions and vice versa (Bulmer 1993; Doern and Wilks 1998; Harrison 1999). Other research into interest-group behaviour and activities highlighted the existence of tools related to group creation and manipulation, including the role played by private or public sector patrons in aiding the formation and activities of such groups (Burt 1990; Phillips 1991; Pal 1993; Finkle et al. 1994; Nownes and Neeley 1996; Lowry 1999). Still other specialized research into aspects of contemporary policy-making highlighted the use of procedural techniques such as the provision of research funding for, and access to, investigative hearings and tribunals (Salter and Slaco 1981; Gormley 1989; Cairns 1990; Jenson 1994).

While most researchers focused on the manner in which these instruments were used to enhance 'desirable' traits in public policy-making such as enhanced participation and the wider dissemination of policy-relevant knowledge, some scholars like Saward (1992) also emphasized that procedural tools were also used to 'negatively' affect interest groups' and other actors' behaviour: that is, to restrict their freedom to associate and engage in policy-influencing activities. This latter research highlighted the role such tools have played on the 'dark side' of politics and policy-making; for example, suppressing government enemies and rewarding friends via punishment, exclusions and denial of information (Goodin 1980; Saward 1990; 1992). Examples of 'negative' procedural policy tools identified at this time included co-opting opponents through provision of funds and other privileges; denying information; keeping opponents' views from the public; penalizing opponents by denying funding or recognition; fragmenting opposition – divide and conquer – by selective rewarding; rewarding 'neutrals'; adding administrative hurdles and costs to opponents; and many more. These latter studies, however, all existed outside the mainstream of policy instrument research, which continued to focus almost exclusively on substantive implementation tools but were ready to be used when policy design and implementation studies moved in a procedural direction in the late 1990s.

Hood's taxonomy of substantive instruments could be modified to help make sense out of this disparate list of procedural tools and this task was undertaken in the late 1990s in several quarters. Classifying procedural instruments just as Hood had done for their substantive counterparts, that is in accordance with the type of 'governing resource' on which they primarily rely for their effectiveness, generated a useful preliminary taxonomy of procedural tools. Drawing a distinction between 'positive' and 'negative' uses of governing resources in terms of whether they encourage or discourage actor participation in policy processes further parallels the 'effector–detector' distinction made in Hood's original discussion of substantive tools (Howlett 2000) (see Table 4.3).

Table 4.3 A resource-based taxonomy of procedural policy instruments

		Governing resource			
		Nodality	Authority	Treasure	Organization
Principle use	'Positive'	Freedom of information	Mandated participatory processes	Interest-group funding	Conferences and commissions
	'Negative'	Propaganda	Preferential access to policy-makers	Targeted campaign funding	Red tape

Source: Howlett, M. 2000. 'Managing the "Hollow State": Procedural Policy Instruments and Modern Governance'. *Canadian Public Administration* 43, no. 4: 412–31.

As was the case with Hood's discussion of substantive instruments, this taxonomy is useful in so far as it highlights a small number of different basic resources used by different types of procedural tools and therefore allows a virtually unlimited number of such instruments to be placed in a limited number of general categories, preparing the ground for the development of improved understandings of the basic contours and possibilities of tool selection and of policy designs.

This insight allows a simplified NATO model to be set out in Table 4.4, which includes both procedural and substantive tools as well as a clearer idea of what constitutes a basic governing resource. It is this model which is used in Chapters 5–8 below to set out and describe the basic subtypes and most common individual kinds of implementation instruments used in contemporary policy designs.

Table 4.4 A simplified taxonomy of substantive and procedural implementation tools

		Governing resource			
		Information	Authority	Treasure	Organization
Purpose of tool	Substantive	Public information campaigns	Independent regulatory agencies	Subsidies and grants	Public enterprises
	Procedural	Official secrets acts	Administrative advisory committees	Interest-group funding	Government reorganizations

Improving on Doern's model of implementation instrument choice: analyzing policy mixes

In the late 1990s, work on instrument selection began to assess the question of the potential to develop optimal policy mixes and to move away from a focus on single instrument choices (Grabosky 1994; Gunningham and Young 1997). Studies such as Gunningham, Grabosky and Young's work on 'smart regulation' led to the development of efforts to identify complementarities and conflicts within instrument mixes or tool 'portfolios' involved in more complex and sophisticated policy designs (Barnett et al. 2008; Shore 2009; Buckman and Diesendorf 2010). For them, the key question was no longer 'why do policy-makers utilize a certain instrument?' as it was for earlier generations of students of policy instrument choice, but rather 'why is a particular combination of procedural and substantive instruments utilized in a specific sector?' (Dunsire 1993; Howlett 2000; Salamon 2002; Cubbage et al. 2007; Gleirscher 2008; Gipperth 2008; Taylor 2008; Clark and Russell 2009; McGoldrick and Boonn 2010).[13]

This new generation of design scholars began to develop what may be described as a 'scalpel' – as opposed to the more blunt 'hammer' – approach to instrument use; one that emphasizes the importance of designing policies that employ a mix of policy instruments carefully chosen to create positive interactions with each other (Sinclair 1997).[14] Proponents of 'smarter' regulation, for example, proposed the development of sophisticated policy instrument mixes in which government's combined a range of market solutions and public and private orderings in order to overcome societal resistance and effectively attain their policy goals in an expeditious and efficient manner (Gunningham et al. 1998; Santos, Behrendt and Teytelboym 2010; Gossum, Arts and Verheyen 2010).

In their 1990 study of policy targets and their behaviour, Schneider and Ingram also began to systematically pursue Doern's insight that the extent of a government's willingness to alter the underlying behaviour of key policy actors was a major factor affecting its choice of policy implementation tool. They argued that policy-making 'almost always attempts to get people to do things that they might not otherwise do' and noted that:

> If people are not taking actions needed to ameliorate social, economic or political problems, there are five reasons that can be addressed by policy: they may believe that law does not direct them or authorize them to take action; they may lack incentives or capacity to take the actions needed; they may disagree with the values implicit in the means or ends; or the situation may involve such high levels of uncertainty that the nature of the problem is not known, and it is unclear what people should do or how they might be motivated.
>
> (Schneider and Ingram 1990: 513–14)

That is, they recognized that each of Hood's 'statecraft' resources required not only state capacity in that area – that is, a plentiful supply of the 'resource' – but also a corresponding belief or endowment on the part of target groups which would allow that capacity to be utilized effectively (Schneider and Ingram 1990a; 1990b; 1993; 1994; 1997).

Thus, the effective use of 'nodality' for example, requires the transmission of information to targets, 'authority' requires the enforcement capability to coerce or force targets to do something they might not otherwise wish to do, 'treasure' requires having the fiscal capacity to provide targets with incentives or disincentives to act in certain ways, and 'organization' requires the administrative capacity to provide them with some good or service directly. But in order to be effective not only must governments have an adequate 'supply' of these resources, but targets must also be susceptible to their deployment: effective information transmission requires *credibility* or the belief among targets that a government is telling the truth; the effective use of authority requires *legitimacy* or the belief among the target population that the use of authority is legally and morally appropriate; the effective use of treasure resources requires *cupidity* or the willingness on the part of actors to accept payments or make them; and the effective use of organization requires

Figure 4.4 State and societal components of 'governing resource' effectiveness

trust on the part of the target group that an administration is competent and capable of actually delivering the promised goods or services. The relationships between government organizational capacity, resource availability and target beliefs are set out in (creating Figure 4.4). That is, as Schneider and Ingram noted, each 'resource' is not an absolute entity but a relationship, composed of both a state capacity and a target group belief creating a 'governance' relationship between the two parties to a policy arrangement.

This is an important insight in policy design studies as it links instrument choices to governance modes, since each of the four governance modes identified in Chapter 1 – legal, market, network and corporatist – is premised on the existence of one of these four arrangements.

Thus legal governance relies on a combination of authority and legitimacy, market governance on treasure and cupidity, network governance on information and credibility and corporatist governance on organization and trust. Policy designs are sustained and constrained by these basic relationships, which help establish longer-term tool preferences, and hence policy alternative preferences, in the minds of policy designers (Jochim and May 2010).

Developing a micro-level model of tool calibrations: Linder and Peters' clarification of the attributes of instruments choice

While helpful, however, these insights remain firmly at the 'meso' level of tool preferences and need to be applied to the 'micro' level of the choice of specific tool calibrations. In 1989, Linder and Peters first described eight 'attributes of instruments' which they argued affected specific micro-level tool choices. These were: complexity of operation, level of public visibility, adaptability across uses, level of intrusiveness, relative costliness, reliance on markets, chances of failure, and precision of targeting (1989: 56). In his later work, however, Peters (2000) reduced this number to seven and altered their content so that they became: directness, visibility, capital/labour intensity, automaticity or level of administration required, level of universality, reliance on persuasion versus enforcement, and their 'forcing vs enabling' nature (39). This was no doubt due to the conclusion he drew from further study that drawing a sharp distinction between 'market-based' and 'state-based' tools is less useful than thinking about these as 'modes of governance; while 'chances of failure' is also a highly contextual item which does not 'adhere' to an instrument as a fundamental characteristic. The other difference between the two lists is the addition of several sub-elements to 'level of intrusiveness' which, if removed, leaves five main instrument characteristics or appraisal criteria: *automaticity, visibility, intrusiveness, cost*, and *precision of targeting*. The first four criteria are linked to specific tool choices from within a resource category and all deal with the level of resource intensiveness of an instrument choice: that is, to the degree to which it utilizes, respectively, organizational, nodality, treasure or authority resources. Precision of targeting, on the other hand, is a key criterion related to tool calibrations or 'settings'.

Putting these considerations together with those found at the governance mode and policy regime lever generates a set of nested implementation tool criteria involved in a typical design situation, as set out in Figure 4.5.

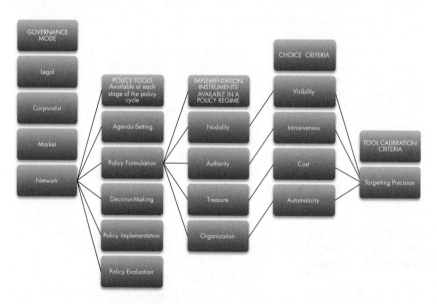

Figure 4.5 Final model of implementation tool selection process involved in policy design

Conclusion: the multi-level and nested nature of policy designs

As this discussion has shown, over the course of the past thirty years, the study of policy implementation instruments has advanced through the various stages of social scientific theory construction and now contributes a great deal of knowledge to policy formulation and policy design (Hood 2007; Lascoumes and Le Galès, 2007).

Current policy design theory is based on the insights developed during this period that while policy goals are manifold and alter over time, and while the choice of policy means is context driven and resource contingent, the toolbox with which designers must work is essentially generic (Majone 1989). That is, as Hood, Lowi and others noted, the reasons behind the actual choice a government may make to implement its policy goals may be complex, but the set of possible choices is limited in nature, bound as they are to the limited number of types of different governing resources they have at their disposal. Understanding the basic types of instruments available to policy-makers and establishing the criteria that policy experts use for assessing the advantages and disadvantages of their use is essential knowledge required to understand how designs emerge and thus to aid in the creation of new ones as well as the assessment and improvement of existing ones (Gibson 1999). That is, as Renate Mayntz (1983) argued, 'to approach the problems of effective programme design', it was 'necessary first to identify the relevant programme elements and characteristics which are the object of decision in a process of programme design' (126).

The next four chapters use the statecraft-resource model developed here to address the role that specific kinds of implementation instruments play in policy design. Several of the major or best known implementation tools that fall into each of the four major categories of resources (information, authority, treasure and organization) identified in the modified Hood model set out above are examined in terms of their specific characteristics and strengths and weaknesses as related to the key criteria of intrusiveness, cost, visibility, automaticity and precision of targeting. Chapter 9 then discusses the patterns or trends present in contemporary governments with respect to their use, while Chapter 10 reflects on the implications of these trends for policy design and policy designers.

Readings

Bemelmans-Videc, Marie-Louise and Evert Vedung. 1997. 'Conclusion: Policy Instrument Types, Packages, Choices and Evaluation'. In *Carrots, Sticks and Sermons: Policy Instruments and Their Evaluation* (eds) M. L. Bemelmans-Videc, R. C. Rist and E. Vedung. New Brunswick, NJ: Transaction Publishers, 249–73.

Cushman, R. E. 1941. *The Independent Regulatory Commissions*. London: Oxford University Press.

de Bruijn, Johan A. and Ernst F. ten Heuvelhof. 1995. 'Policy Networks and Governance'. In David L. Weimer (ed.) *Institutional Design*. Boston, MA: Kluwer Academic Publishers, 161–79.

—— 1997. 'Instruments for Network Management'. In W. J. M. Kickert, E.-H. Klijn and J. F. M. Koppenjan (eds) *Managing Complex Networks: Strategies for the Public Sector*. London: Sage, 119–36.

Doern, G. B. and V. S. Wilson. 1974. 'Conclusions and Observations'. In *Issues in Canadian Public Policy*. ed. G. B. Boern and V. S. Wilson Toronto: Macmillan, 337–45.

Goodin, Robert E. 1980. *Manipulatory Politics*. New Haven, CT: Yale University Press, 1–36.

Hood, C. 1983. 'Using Bureaucracy Sparingly'. *Public Administration* 61, no. 2: 197–208.

—— 2007. 'Intellectual Obsolescence and Intellectual Makeovers: Reflections on the Tools of Government after Two Decades'. *Governance* 20, no. 1: 127–44.

Howlett, Michael. 1991. 'Policy Instruments, Policy Styles, and Policy Implementation: National Approaches to Theories of Instrument Choice'. *Policy Studies Journal* 19, no. 2: 1–21.

—— 2000. 'Managing the "Hollow State": Procedural Policy Instruments and Modern Governance'. *Canadian Public Administration* 43, no. 4: 412–31.

—— 2004. 'Beyond Good and Evil in Policy Implementation: Instrument Mixes, Implementation Styles and Second Generation Theories of Policy Instrument Choice'. *Policy and Society* 23, no. 2: 1–17.

Howlett, Michael and Jeremy Rayner. 2007. 'Design Principles for Policy Mixes: Cohesion and Coherence in "New Governance" Arrangements'. *Policy and Society* 26, no.4: 1–18.

Issalys, Pierre. 2005. 'Choosing among Forms of Public Action: A Question of Legitimacy'. In *Designing Government: From Instruments to Governance* (eds) P. Eliadis, M. Hill and M. Howlett. Montreal: McGill-Queen's University Press, 154–81.

Kickert, W. J. M. and J. F. M. Koppenjan. 1997. 'Public Management and Network Management: An Overview'. In *Managing Complex Networks: Strategies for the Public Sector*, ed. W. J. M. Kickert, E.-H. Klijn and J. F. M. Koppenjan. London, Sage, 35–61.

Kirschen, E. S., J. Benard, H. Besters, F. Blackaby, O. Eckstein, J. Faaland, F. Hartog, L. Morissens and E. Tosco. 1964. *Economic Policy in Our Time*. Chicago, IL: Rand McNally.

Linder, Stephen H. and B. Guy Peters. 1989. 'Instruments of Government: Perceptions and Contexts'. *Journal of Public Policy* 9, no. 1: 35–58.

Lowi, T. J. 1972. 'Four Systems of Policy, Politics and Choice'. *Public Administration Review* 32, no. 4: 298–310.

Peters, B. Guy. 2005 '.The Problem of Policy Problems'. In P. Eliadis, M. Hill and M. Howlett (eds) *Designing Government: From Instruments to Governance*. Montreal: McGill-Queen's University Press, 77–105.

Rathgeb-Smith, Steven and Helen Ingram. 2002. 'Policy Tools and Democracy'. In L. M. Salamon (eds) *The Tools of Government: A Guide to the New Governance*. New York: Oxford University Press, 565–84.

Salamon, L. M. 1981. 'Rethinking Public Management: Third-Party Government and the Changing Forms of Government Action'. *Public Policy* 29, no. 3: 255–75.

Saward, Michael. 1990. 'Cooption and Power: Who Gets What from Formal Incorporation'. *Political Studies* 38: 588–602.

Schneider, A. L. and H. Ingram. 1990 'Policy Design: Elements, Premises and Strategies'. In *Policy Theory and Policy Evaluation: Concepts, Knowledge, Causes and Norms*, ed. S. S. Nagel. New York: Greenwood Press, 77–102.

—— 1993. 'Social Construction of Target Populations: Implications for Politics and Policy'. *American Political Science Review* 87, no. 2: 334–47.

—— 1994. 'Social Constructions and Policy Design: Implications for Public Administration'. *Research in Public Administration* 3: 137–73.

Woodside, K. 1986. 'Policy Instruments and the Study of Public Policy'. *Canadian Journal of Political Science* 19, no. 4: 775–93.

Part III

THE ELEMENTS OF POLICY DESIGN

Chapter 5

Organizational implementation tools

Organizational implementation instruments include a broad range of governing tools which rely upon the use of government institutions and personnel to affect policy output delivery and policy process change. There is a wide variety of *substantive organizational tools* available to affect both the production and consumption/distribution of goods and services in society. However, these generally fall into two main types depending on the proximity of their relationship to government and hence the ability of government to control the effects of their utilization: direct government and quasi-governmental tools. *Procedural organizational tools* generally involve the organization and reorganization of government agencies and processes in order to affect key parameters of the policy communities governments face in making public policies.

Each type of tool is closely associated with a different mode of governance. Direct government tools, for example, are a principle component of legal modes of governance, while quasi-governmental tools are a feature of corporatist modes, and procedural organizational tools are commonly used to construct network governance arrangements and architectures. Market modes generally eschew or discourage the use of these kinds of tools.

Substantive organizational instruments

There are many types of substantive instruments which rely for their effectiveness upon the organizational resources of governments. All involve (and rely primarily) on the use of government personnel to achieve government goals, usually operating in structures created and controlled by governments. Most of these are 'direct' government organizations, but can also include 'indirect' or quasi- or parastatal ones; the best known example of which is the state-owned or 'public enterprise' – which itself comes in many shapes, sizes, colours and flavours.

Direct government

The direct use of government agencies for substantive policy purposes involves the 'delivery of a good or service by government employees, funded by appropriations from government treasury' (Leman 1989 and 2002). Within this general type of direct government organizational tool, there are several common forms or subtypes found in many jurisdictions. These include the following:

Line departments

In most countries government agencies undertake a wide variety of tasks on a direct basis. These include, but are certainly not limited to, those listed in (Table 5.1).

These services are provided at all levels of government (central or federal, provincial, state or regional, as well as urban or local) in slightly different configurations in different countries. Unemployment, welfare or social security payments, for example, can be the task of central governments in some countries and eras, and of provincial or local governments in others.

Typically modern government agencies follow what is known in the public administration literature as a Weberian 'monocratic bureaucracy' form of organization (Brubaker 1984; Beetham 1987). This is a type of organizational structure first systematically described and analyzed by the German political sociologist Max Weber in his early twentieth-century work, *Economy and Society*. Weber argued that although bureaucratic forms of organization had a long history, a significant change had occurred in the modern era as such organizations had come to be viewed as providing services to the public rather than being the property of a monarch or emperor to do with as he or she pleased. The main characteristics of a modern government agency, in Weber's view, were:

- Personnel are appointed on the basis of a merit system of appointment, retention and recruitment.
- Office holders do not own the office in which they work, but hold it subject to the provisions of the merit system.
- That offices tend to be organized in a hierarchical fashion with a relatively small span of control and multiple levels.
- That all activities in the agency operate according to the rule of law – that office holders are not above the law and must operate within its limits (including provisions for their accountability – via some form of 'chain of accountability' – to representative assemblies in modern liberal democracies who actually establish and promulgate laws).

(Albrow 1970; Weber 1978)

Table 5.1 Tasks typically undertaken by government agencies

Task	Examples
Facilitating commerce	Mint, standards of weights and measures bureaus
Managing public lands	Commissioners of public lands, ministries of lands and parks or environment or natural resources
Constructing public works	Departments of public works – airports, highways
Research, testing and statistics	National statistical agencies
Law and justice	Courts, solicitor-general or attorney-general offices, corrections and prisons, policing
Technical assistance, record-keeping and libraries	Farm extension, ministries of agriculture, national archives, national libraries
Health care	Ministries of health – hospitals. clinics, dentists, nursing, home care.
Social services	Ministries of welfare and social, family or community services
Education and training	Ministries of education, post-secondary education colleges and universities, technical and training institutes
Labour relations	Ministries of labour and labour relations.
Marketing	Tourism, ministries of small business, ministries of trade and commerce
Defence	Ministries of defence, army, navy, air force, coast guard
Supplying internal government needs	Ministries of supply and services, Queen's printers
Finance	Ministries of finance and treasury boards
International affairs	Ministries of external or foreign affairs

Source: Hodgetts, J. E. 1973. *The Canadian Public Service: A Physiology of Government 1867–1970.* Toronto: University of Toronto Press.

What are commonly referred to as 'line' departments (in order to distinguish them from central, headquarters or 'staff' units) have this 'classic' hierarchical Weberian monocractic bureaucractic form and are thoroughly embedded in legal forms of governance. Such units are typically organized in a pyramidal shape linking offices of civil servants in various branches and sections to a single department head, such as a department of health or a department of highways. A sub-variation of this is the 'ministry'; a form in which, typically multiple pyramids of departments culminate in a single head (e.g. a ministry of lands, parks, and housing) or an 'agency', which operates separately from the policy-making level of managerial control (Verhoest et al. 2010).[1]

These forms of government organization are the 'workhorses' of publicly provided goods and service delivery in most modern states. Although many modern states originally practised legal modes of governance in most sectors, establishing legal rules and forms of legitimation through the rule of law, they have grown dramatically through the creation and expansion of ministries, departments and agencies in areas such as defence, transportation and, later, social welfare, education and health provision. This has resulted in the conversion of many sectors from legal modes of governance to more corporatist ones featuring larger and active state organizations, often with a monopoly over the goods and services they provide. These kinds of organizations can be very large (the US Department of Defense, for example, has over two million employees, including approximately 650,000 civilians) and can be subdivided into hundreds of separate branches, bureaus, sections and agencies. They employ the most personnel and deliver by far the largest percentage of state-provided goods and services in liberal-democratic, and virtually all other, forms of modern government.

The 'government employees' employed in line departments are typically civil or public servants. In most liberal-democratic countries these are unionized and well-paid positions, and although this is not the case in many other countries where officials may supplement their wages illegally through various forms of corruption ('kickbacks', bribes, 'service' payments, expediting 'fees' and so on), in either case the use of public servants to directly deliver public services is an expensive proposition, which in itself discourages its use. How well these officials are educated and trained and what kinds of facilities and information they have to work with also affects their capacity and perceived competence and, along with cost, can pay a significant role in their placement within a policy design (Brunsson 2006). Countries or sectors with well-resourced administrative systems regarded as highly efficient and competent by their citizenry are more likely to feature direct government service provision in their policy designs than countries with corrupt or inefficient civil services, given the advantages the former often hold for governments in terms of cost and ease of program administration.

Central support agencies

These are agencies which are similar in appearance to line departments, but often act more like private companies; delivering services within governments rather than to external constituencies. Some of these are very old (like government stationers and printers) while others (like government systems and information technology units) are much more recent. Many of these agencies are quite large and since they often serve functions similar to private companies they are, and have often been, primary targets for government efforts to develop market modes of governance in some sectors through contracting out or privatizing government services – that is, they are simply turned into 'firms' supplying government services by severing their funding through general appropriations revenue and establishing autonomous boards of directors. Cost issues are typically a major factor influencing their inclusion in policy designs.

Social and health insurance and pension plans

Social and health insurance and pension schemes like those used in many countries for unemployment insurance, elderly income support and health care are other such government organization-based schemes, ones in which all individuals in certain categories are mandated to make payments with a government agency which acts, usually, as a monopoly insurance provider for that group (Katzman 1988; Moss 2002). Some of these schemes, of course, are among the largest areas of government expenditure and are virtually identical in organizational form to direct government organizational tools given their universal and mandated nature – with the main difference being that programme funds come from dedicated insurance payments rather than general tax revenue. These schemes are generally very high profile and targeted to specific kinds of outputs. They are often intended to be revenue-neutral, although any short-term shortfalls in these schemes typically have to be made up by governments. They also can provide large pools of capital which governments can use to finance infrastructure and other kinds of investments. As such, they are very popular and found throughout the world, although their configuration and extent of private sector involvement varies greatly from country to country. Countries which do not have such schemes typically cite reasons related to costs or intrusiveness in already existing private sector programmes.

Quasi-governmental organizational forms

All of these second type of government agencies have an essentially bureaucratic organizational structure and also exist largely as Weberian forms of administration – although most are structured in a more 'business-like' fashion with fewer rules and regulations guiding their behaviour than government departments and agencies. These include the following main types.

Public enterprises and other corporate forms

Public enterprises or 'state-owned enterprises' (SOEs) are the most common and well-known type of quasi-governmental substantive organizational tool. SOEs undertake or have undertaken a wide variety of tasks in many jurisdictions (see Table 5.2).

There are many different definitions of public enterprises with different levels of public ownership ascribed to these organizations.[2] Perry and Rainey (1988) developed an exhaustive typology by examining the different types of ownership, sources of funding and mode of social control exercised over these organizations. The key feature of these organizations, however, is that they have a corporate form and are not administrative agencies. That is, they operate under separate legislation or under general corporate legal principles, and government control is exercised indirectly as a function of government share ownership; typically through voting control over appointments to the company board of directors – who usually can be removed 'at pleasure' by the government. The board of directors then hires and fires senior management so that government control is indirect and 'arm's-length', unlike the management and control of direct government administrative agencies. Some public enterprises can raise and borrow money on their own authority, while others are limited in their sphere of independence and must seek funding or permission to borrow from governments. Similarly some are free to set whatever prices they would like for their products while others must seek government permission to alter prices and may be subsidized to provide a good or service at below market value. While government share ownership can drop below 50 per cent and still exercise control if the remainder of the shares is widely held, it is more common for a government to own 50 per cent or more of voting shares (in fact it is very common for them to own 100 per cent). However, there is a growing number of 'mixed' enterprises with joint public-private or multiple government ownership.

These companies can be exceedingly large, although they can also be much smaller, in some cases limited to one or two factories or offices. Sovereign-wealth funds, holding the proceeds of oil and gas or pension revenues in countries like Singapore and Dubai, for example, are among the largest firms in terms of assets and can control hundreds of billions of dollars in investments (Elson 2008), while large public hydroelectrical or petrochemical utilities in countries like Canada, Norway, Mexico, Iran and Venezuela also rank first among companies in those countries based on size of assets controlled (Laux and Molot 1988).

The use of state-owned enterprises is common in corporatist forms of governance which prize their high levels of automaticity, intrusiveness and visibility as well as their generally low cost and ability to be precisely targeted

Table 5.2 Examples of tasks undertaken by public enterprises

Task	Example (Canada, twentieth century)
Housing	Canadian Mortgage and Housing Corporation
Finance	Bank of Canada, Small Business Development Bank, Caisse de Depot et Placement de Quebec
Wartime production	Canadian Arsenals
Transportation	Canadian National Railways, Via Rail, Air Canada/Trans-Canada Airlines, St Lawrence Seaway Co., BC Ferries, Northern Transportation Company Ltd.
Strategic industries	Atomic Energy of Canada Ltd, Petro-Canada
Communications	Canadian Broadcasting Corporation, Radio-Canada
Cultural industries	Canadian Film Development Corporation, National Film Board, National Museum Corps
Utilities	SaskTel, Hydro Quebec, Ontario Hydro, BC Hydro
Infant industries	Petrosar, Athabaska Tar Sands, Canadian Development Corporation
Sick industries	Skeena Cellulose, BCResources Investment Corporation
Property management	British Columbia Building Corporation
Regional development	Prince Rupert Coal Corporation, DEVCO, Cape Breton Development Corp.
Lotteries and vice	BC Liquor Stores, Société des Alcools de Quebec, Casino Nova Scotia, Lotto-Canada
Local utilities	Translink, Edmonton Telephones
Marketing boards	Canada Wheat Board, Britsh Columbia Egg and Milk Marketing Board, Freshwater Fish Marketing Board

Source: Vining, A. R., and R. Botterell. 1983. 'An Overview of the Origins, Growth, Size, and Functions of Provincial Crown Corporations'. In *Crown Corporations: The Calculus of Instrument Choice*, ed. J. R. S. Pritchard. Toronto: Butterworths, 303–68.

in different sectors and policy areas. However, there have been many efforts to privatize these companies, or move their ownership from the government to the private sector as some governments have attempted to shift from corporatist to more market modes of governance or cut costs (Savas 1989). These efforts have been successful in sectors where competition exists, such as marketing boards, product producing companies, and property management (Savas 1987; Laux 1993) but have generally foundered in other areas where the privatized corporation has simply become a monopoly service provider. This has often been the case with large-scale utilities such as water, electricity or public transportation providers where natural monopoly conditions often exist (Chapman 1990; Gayle and Goodrich 1990; Bos 1991). In these cases they have often been re-nationalized or re-regulated through the creation of regulatory oversight agencies and mechanisms (see Chapter 6 below) (Mees 2005; Leland and Smirnova 2009). Policy designers now very much take these contextual circumstances into account in proposing or recommending either the creation or privatization of SOEs.

Organizational hybrids (alternative service delivery)

In recent years, numerous hybrid forms of indirect government organizations have also been developed and implemented in many jurisdictions. These have often been proposed in situations where governments would like to privatize or contract out government services but where there is not a competitive market; thereby limiting the utility of outright sale or divestment by a government (Mathur and Skelcher 2007).

Examples of these types of tools include so-called 'special operating agencies' (SOAs) (Koppell 2003; Birrell 2008) which were established in many countries in the 1980s and 1990s in the effort to grant more autonomy to central service agencies and remove them from day-to-day government control. This was typically done by 'outsourcing' whatever services could be secured from a competitive external marketplace, while allowing agencies providing those goods and services which could not be so relocated to charge real prices to purchasers and to retain their earnings and make their own reinvestment decisions (Aucoin 2006; Flumian et al. 2007).

A second type of hybrid is the 'quasi-autonomous non-governmental organization' or *quango*, an organizational form in which a non-governmental agency is established and given a grant of authority by a government to provide a particular good or service (Hood 1986). These can be precisely targeted and many airports, ports and harbours are run by such 'independent authorities' which rely on governments for their monopoly position but which are answerable to their own boards for their activities rather than to the government itself (Kickert 2001). These agencies are usually then able to charge their own prices for the good or service they provide, retain their earnings, and raise funds on capital markets for investments, removing these items from government books (Flinders and McConnel 1999; Lovink 1999; Advani and Borins 2001).

There can be serious principle-agent problems with these kinds of agencies, however, which can affect their use in fields with legal or corporatist modes of governance (Koppell 2003). Maintaining the arm's-length nature of the relationship of public enterprises and quangos to government is difficult, and such agencies may not have enough autonomy for governments to avoid the consequences of scandals or other problems associated with them. That is, these relationships can be either too close (day-to-day interference) or too distant (agencies become distant and aloof powers unto themselves). Utilizing this form of substantive organizational tool can be also very expensive and linked to unpopular actions with political and economic consequences for governments – like tax increases, political scandals and high profile financing and operational issues. Many public agencies also do not have to face the discipline of the market in terms of meeting shareholder or investor expectations for profitability and hence lack at least this incentive to operate in a cost-efficient manner, raising difficulties for many governments practising market forms of governance in specific sectors (Kernaghan 1993; Ford and Zussman 1997; Flumian et al. 2007). These kinds of visibility and cost issues generally discourage the inclusion of these agencies in policy designs.

Partnerships and contracting out

More recent efforts on the part of some governments to shift some sectors from legal or corporatist to market modes of governance – that is, to offload legal and financial responsibility for goods and service delivery and have existing goods and services delivered through the private or quasi-governmental sector – have evolved into several distinct forms of organization which are more private than public, with the public sector acting mainly as a purchaser of goods and services provided by private companies (Grimshaw et al. 2001; Grimsey and Lewis 2004; Greener 2006).

One typical form of such activity is 'contracting out' or outsourcing, in which internal provision of some good or service is simply replaced with a source external to government (Zarco-Jasso 2005). This can be more complicated if a non-governmental provider does not exist for a particular product or service, so that a government must first, or simultaneously, create a non-governmental provider (Brown et al. 2008). Outsourcing of highway and railway maintenance in many countries in the 1980s and 1990s, for example, involved government managers creating their own firms, which then bid on, and received government contracts to provide maintenance services; those companies then immediately hired former government workers, and in some cases used former government equipment, to provide the same service (McDavid and Clemens 1995).

More recently this form of activity has moved to the capital goods sector with the development of so-called 'P3s' or 'public-private partnerships' in which governments encourage private sector firms to build and operate public infrastructure such as schools, office buildings, hospitals and sports facilities, and even transportation infrastructure such as bridges and roads, in return for a government guarantee of a long-term lease or use agreement with the provider (English and Skellern 2005). The net effect of this activity is to remove capital costs from government budgets while retaining the service (Rosenau 1999; Boase 2000).

Different kinds of these partnerships exist, such as collaborative partnerships with NGOs to control hospital admissions for the disabled, operational partnerships with companies and other governments, to share costs for many of the items discussed above; and contributory partnerships where governments may provide funding without necessarily controlling the use of such funds, as occurs when matching funds are provided for local or community-based environmental improvement projects (Kernaghan 1993; Daniels and Trebilcock 1996; Hodge and Greve 2007).

Although popular in some countries and sectors in recent years as examples of 'collaborative' or 'joined-up' government, such schemes often stretch the resources of non-profit or volunteer organizations and can result in inefficient or incompetent goods and services delivery (Evans et al. 2005; Riccucci and Meyers 2008; Smismans 2008; Tsasis 2008). These kinds of cost and reliability issues increasingly have affected considerations of such tools and their inclusion in policy designs.

Procedural organizational instruments

Substantive tools, of course, are only one half of the uses towards which government organizational resources can be put. The second use is procedural. This involves the use of the organizational resources of government (personnel, staffing, institutionalization and internal procedures, etc.) to alter or affect policy processes in order to better achieve general government aims or specific programme activities.

It bears repeating that these are not direct or indirect goods and service delivery mechanisms, as are their substantive counterparts, but procedural activities, generally efforts aimed at creating or restructuring policy community structure and/or behaviour through government leadership or 'network management' efforts.

According to Agranoff and McGuire (1999: 21), this latter activity involves 'network managers' in 'selecting appropriate actors and resources, shaping the operating context of the network and developing ways to cope with strategic and operational complexity'. The key dimensions or tasks involved in these kinds of network management activities include the identification of potentially compatible network actors, given the issue at hand; limiting potential conflicts that would hinder flexibility; recognizing legal requirements; balancing political objectives/conflicts with policy objectives; and assigning costs in implementation.

In any policy process, policy managers need to work with the structure and operation of any network which already exists in the area; recognize potential new actors, limit the role of ineffective actors; balance their time and resource commitments (money, technology, expertise, etc.); maintain the focus of the network in achieving goals; and build trust between actors/reduce possible conflicts (Mandell 1994; 2000; Agranoff 1998; Agranoff and McGuire 1999; Koppenjan and Klijn 2004; Wu et al. 2010). In order to achieve these ends, various kinds of organizational network management tools can be used. Several of the most common of these are set out below.

Network management tools

There are many different types of procedural tools linked with the use of specific government organizational resources which can affect various aspects of policy subsystem behaviour in policy processes. Interest in these tools has grown as many governments, as discussed in Chapter 1, have moved in the direction of more overt network management in some sectors in recent years.

Staff or central (executive) agencies

This is an old form of government organization, one in which a small, co-ordinating government agency, rather than one which directly delivers services to the public, is created to centralize agency initiatives in some area. Such 'staff or 'central' agencies are generally created as a means to control other administrative agencies and are often linked very closely to the political executive (Bernier, Brownsey and Howlett 2005). In Westminister-style parliamentary systems, for example, older examples include privy council offices and treasury board secretariats, while newer ones include presidential, premier and prime minister's offices, ministries of state, communication units, intergovernmental secretariats, and various kinds of implementation units (Chenier 1985; Savoie 1999; Lindquist 2006).

Although small (even most prime minister's offices until recently had less than 100 personnel, most of whom handled correspondence) these are central co-ordinating units which exercise a great deal of control over other bureaucratic agencies through their links to the executive and to the budgetary and policy processes in government. They have seen much growth in recent years as political executives have sought to re-establish control over far flung administrative apparatuses (Campbell and Szablowski 1979; Rhodes and Weller 2001; Bevir et al. 2003; Bernier et al., 2005). Unlike line departments, these staff or central agencies are less, or non-hierarchical, flatter organizations typically staffed by political appointees, although others also employ permanent officials as well. Key officials are chiefs of staff, principle secretaries and specialized positions such as a clerk of the privy council or cabinet secretary. These agencies play a major and increasing role in designing and co-ordinating policies and policy-making, ensuring accountability to legislatures and controlling the budgets, activities and plans of line departments and ministries. Their small cost is a major design consideration although this is often offset by their high visibility and high level of intrusiveness in the affairs of the government agencies they control or co-ordinate.

Tribunals and other quasi-judicial bodies

These are created by statute and perform many administrative functions, hearing appeals concerning licencing (e.g. of pesticides), certification (of personnel or programmes), and permits (e.g. for disposal of effluents). Appointed by government, they usually represent, or purport to represent, some diversity of interests and expertise.

Administrative hearings are conducted by tribunals in a quasi-judicial fashion, often in order to aid tribunals in their activities. These hearings are bound by rules of natural justice, and procedures may also be dictated by statutory provisions. The decisions of tribunals are designed to be binding on the ministry in question but may be subject to various political, administrative, and judicial appeals. Public hearings may be statutorily defined as a component of the administrative process.

In the framework of administration, tribunals are directed toward securing compliance with administrative edicts and the achievement of identified standards of behaviour by both governmental and non-governmental actors. They may act as a mechanism with which to appeal administrative decisions, but in most cases proceedings are held at the discretion of a decision-making authority and public hearings are often 'after the fact' public information sessions rather than being true consultative devices (Grima 1985; Stewart and Sinclair 2007). They can be precisely targeted and are an important component of legal modes of governance which are generally low cost and nearly invisible. However, in other forms of governance, like market or corporatist modes, their relatively high levels of intrusiveness can diminish their appeal in the eyes of policy designers.

Creating or reorganizing government agencies

Another fairly commonly used procedural organizational tool is to establish new government agencies or reform existing institutions in order to focus or re-focus state and societal activities on specific problems or issue areas (Goetz 2007; Durant 2008). Setting up a new government ministry for technology or a new research council to promote advanced technologies like biotechnology, e-technologies, or other high technology sectors, for example, is a common action on the part of governments wanting to target a new area of activity for further development (Hood 2004; Lindquist 2006; van Thiel 2008). However, such actions are highly visible and, if repeated too often, quite costly. They are also quite intrusive and, as a result, are proposed, and used, only infrequently.

Establishing analytical units

Some governments have also set up internal think tanks or research institutes in order to provide policy advice to governments (Dobuzinskis et al. 2007; Marchildon 2007). Many government departments and agencies also have established specialized policy units designed to generate studies and reports which can influence or help to persuade both government officials and non-governmental actors of the merits of government plans. These agencies also often employ outside consultants to bring additional expertise and knowledge to policy formation, implementation and evaluation (Schwartz 1997; Perl 2002; Speers 2007). The knowledge they generate is used to inform internal policy-making processes and also to garner support for government positions from outside groups (Whiteman 1985 and 1995).

New analytical units such as those policy shops created in many juris-dictions in the 1970s and 1980s in order to promote formal policy analysis and what is now referred to as 'knowledge-based' or 'evidence-based' policy-making are good examples of procedural organizational tools (Prince 1979; Prince and Chenier 1980; Chenier 1985; Hollander and Prince 1993; Lindquist 2006). These agencies can be precisely targeted and are generally low cost and have low visibility. However their impact on policy-making can raise the ire of stakeholders and others in market, corporatist and network forms of governance, while other agencies in more legal modes also find them to be rivals. Such considerations have dampened enthusiasm for such units in many jurisdictions and sectors and reduced their appeal in policy designs in recent years.

Establishing clientele units

New administrative units in areas like urban affairs, science, technology and other areas flourished in the 1970s, as did new environmental units in many countries in the 1970s and 1980s; they were joined by units dealing with areas such as youth and small business in the 1990s; while in the post-1990 period other new units were developed in countries like Canada and Australia to deal with aboriginal affairs, and in many countries to promote multiculturalism, women's and human rights. Human rights units dealing with minorities and the disabled are good examples of network mobilization and activation occasioned by government organizational (re)engineering (Malloy 1999; 2003; Teghtsoonian and Grace 2001; Teghtsoonian and Chappell 2008; Osborne et al. 2008).

In general these agencies can be precisely targeted in order to undertake the management functions set out in Table 5.3. They are very popular in network governance modes given their generally low cost, high visibility and high levels of automaticity. They are also popular in policy designs in legal governance given their relatively high levels of intrusiveness.

Table 5.3 Analytical agency network managerial tasks

1	Vertical and horizontal co-ordination
2	Overcome institutional blockages like federalism and divisions of power
3	'Mainstreaming'
4	Building commitments
5	Building legitimacy/developing visions and agreement on alternatives
6	Building coalitions
7	Structuring NGO activity, e.g. lobbying activities

Source: Mandell, M. P. 2000. 'A Revised Look at Management in Network Structures'. *International Journal of Organizational Theory and Behavior* 3, nos.1/2: 185–210.

Establishing government reviews, ad hoc task forces, commissions, inquiries and public hearings

A sixth common procedural organizational tool used by governments is the establishment of a government review. These range from formal, mandated, periodic reviews of legislation and government activity by congressional or parliamentary committees and internal administrative bodies to 'ad hoc' processes such as task forces or inquiries designed to activate or mobilize network actors to support government initiatives (Gilmore and Krantz 1991; Bellehumeur 1997; Marchildon 2007; Sulitzeanu-Kenan 2007, 2010; Rowe and McAllister 2010).

Ad hoc task forces and inquiries are typically temporary bodies, much shorter term and often more issue related than institutionalized advisory committees. Ad hoc commissions are also created as instruments to consult a variety of interests with regard to economic and other areas of planning activity. These range from the presidential or royal commissions to those created at the departmental level. Presidential and royal commissions are the most formal and arm's length, and therefore, are the most difficult for governments to control and predict, and therefore are used less often (Maxwell 1965; Doern 1967; Clokie and Robinson 1969; Wilson 1971; Chapman 1973; Flitner 1986; Salter 1990; Jenson 1994).

Task forces have been created in many jurisdictions for planning, consultation, or conflict resolution concerning many specific issues. The task force may be invoked by a government when there is an area of conflict in which different groups have different interests and perspectives or where they require information in order to arrive at a decision or judgement (Marier 2009; Rowe and McAllister 2006).

The subject matter of an ad hoc commission is typically urgent, of concern to more than one ministry and level of government, and is the subject of some controversy (Resodihardjo 2006; Sulitzeanu-Kenan 2010). It is invoked at the discretion of government and is subject to political, economic, and social pressures. Indeed, the very initiation of the commission is likely to be the product of pressure by public interest groups. But, as Chapman (1973: 184) noted 'Commissions may also play a significant political role and are often used as a method for postponing to an indefinite future decision on questions which appear to be embarrassing but not urgent'. Employment of these instruments for this purpose can result in serious legitimation problems for governments utilizing these policy tools, however, given their high level of visibility (Heinrichs 2005; Hendriks and Carson 2008; Stutz 2008; Marier 2009).

Public participation through hearings is the most common type of public or network consultation in many sectors (Rowe and Frewer 2005). Hearings vary by degree of formalization and when they occur in a policy process. The most effective and influential are often flexible processes that are geared towards policy formulation such as project reviews or environmental assessments, but the most common are rigid processes that take place in or after the implementation stage of a process, such as a formal policy evaluation exercise (Dion 1973; Baetz and Tanguay 1998; Edelenbos and Klijn 2005). Public hearings are often mandated by legislation and most often occur after a decision has been taken – that is, purely as information and/or legitimation devices. Actual instances of open, truly empowered public hearing processes are very rare (Riedel 1972; Grima 1985; Torgerson 1986).

Although sometimes used for other purposes such as information collection or blame attribution, these tools are often also used to overcome institutional 'blockages' and veto points such as those which are commonly found in federal–state or intergovernmental relations or in interdepartmental jurisdictional struggles (Ben-Gera 2007). They can also help bolster the capacity of groups to become more involved in the policy process if funding is extended to their participants, thereby promoting network governance (Robins 2008). They can be precisely targeted and are generally low cost. However, their high level of visibility can cause problems for governments and results in their less frequent appearance in policy designs than would otherwise be the case (Rowe and Frewer 2005).

Legislative and executive oversight agencies

This category of organizational tools also includes specialized agencies with very different policy-making functions, like arm's-length independent auditors-general or access to information commissioners, which are units typically attached to legislatures, providing some oversight or control over executive branch activities (Campbell-Smith 2008). Many principle-agent problems can also be overcome through administrative procedures mandating over-sight agency reviews of government actions (McCubbins and Lupia 1994; McCubbins et al. 1987), especially if these are linked to funding and budgetary issues (Hall 2008). These latter units are usually fairly small, inexpensive and highly visible, and there has been a proliferation of such units in recent years dealing with areas such as corruption, human rights and the promotion of ethnic and gender equality (Malloy 2003). They often represent an effort to promote legal governance in sectors typically configured in other modes.

Conclusion

Organization-based implementation tools are generally costly and high visibility. This is because they rely on government personnel funded by appropriations from general revenue raised through taxes or royalties, although some are also funded from market revenue stemming from the sale of goods or services. The use of tax-based funding makes the use of public servants expensive in the sense that governments tend to have a limited capacity to tax citizens to pay for services and incur opportunity costs no matter which activity they choose to adopt. It can also lead to governance failures, as the link between system outputs and inputs (expenditures and revenues) is usually not clear, providing the opportunity for funds to be misallocated and effort misspent, all in the fishbowl environment of public government (Le Grand 1991).

However in some countries additional sources of revenue – such as those accruing from natural resources rents or 'royalties' – especially from oil and natural gas activities in many states in the contemporary era – can make the expenses involved in direct delivery appear less onerous for the public at large and in such circumstances such tools are much easier for governments to establish and maintain. It is also the case that some publicly delivered goods and services can be charged for – for example through highway or bridge tolls, or publicly run electricity, fuel or food services, among many others – and can be priced like any other private good or service, helping to explain why many resource-rich countries have large public sectors and why many countries of all types have large public sectors and state-owned enterprises.

Despite their real or perceived cost, and in spite of many efforts to create or replace them with other forms of service and goods delivery, direct delivery of goods and services by public agencies remains what Christopher Leman (1989) has called 'the forgotten fundamental' of implementation instruments and policy designs. That is, much attention has been focused in the past three decades on the privatization of public goods and service production and distribution facilities and organizations, and many efforts have been made to replace chargeable publicly provided goods ('toll' or 'club' goods such as toll bridges or publicly run recreational facilities) (Potoski and Prakash 2009) with privately supplied ones, largely in the effort to improve productivity or reduce the burden on taxpayers and governments of the wages of public servants involved in direct government provision (Dunleavy 1986; Ascher 1987; Cook and Kirpatrick 1988; Donahue 1989; Finley, 1989; Cowan 1990; Hanke and Walters 1990; Heald 1990; Connolly and Stark 1992). However, these efforts have generally been less successful than often thought or alleged.

Such practices were a key component of 'New Public Management' (NPM) thinking in the 1980s and 1990s in many countries and are a key component of contemporary efforts to promote 'public-private partnerships' and 'collaborative government' (Linder 1999). However, it is sometimes overlooked that 'old-fashioned' government agencies are still the most common and pervasive policy instrument in most sectors (Leman 1989; Aucoin 1997; Olsen 2005). Even in the ostensibly most private sector-oriented market governance systems (like the USA or, more recently, New Zealand), direct government goods and service production usually reaches close to 50 per cent of gross national product (GNP) – that is, half of the dollar value of all goods and services produced in a country in one year – while direct civil service employment typically hovers in the area of 15–20 per cent of the labour force but can also be much higher (Christensen and Pallesen 2008; Derlien 2008; Busemeyer 2009).[3]

This organizational activity is somewhat sectorally focused, due to large publicly provided expenditures on direct government activities like defence and the military which cannot be delivered by the private sector and/or items such as health care, social security, education and pensions associated with the development of modern welfare states and the extension of legal rights to these services to members of the public. It also includes what statistical agencies refer to as the 'MUSH' sector – municipalities, universities, schools and hospitals – which in many countries are established as autonomous or semi-autonomous operating agencies of more senior levels of government. In many countries MUSH sector agencies are among the largest employers since the activities they undertake – such as education and health care, as well as sewer, road and parks maintenance – are very labour intensive.

Many of the recent innovations in organizational forms, from special operating agencies, to quangos, private-public partnerships and various kinds of hybrid organizations, have emerged largely in the effort to reduce the size of existing organizations and transform some sectoral activities from legal and corporatist to market modes of governance (Hardiman and Scott 2010). This is done in the name of improving the efficiency of service delivery, or in order to try to reduce the resource burden large public service delivery agencies place on budgets and taxpayer loads (Verhoest et al. 2007; O'Toole and Meier 2010).

Either way, it has promoted the frequent appearance of experiments in alternate instruments and policy designs, although much less often their realization in practice. And even where they have been implemented, many of these efforts have proved unsuccessful in either improving the efficiency of goods and service delivery or reducing tax burdens. Significant areas of public expenditure and effort such as health care and education, for example, have generally proved immune to privatization efforts given their overall cost structures, mandatory service delivery nature and high levels of citizen support (Le Grand 2009). Most successes have come in either small-scale direct service privatizations or in single-industry company privatizations which have generally not altered earlier governance modes (Verhoest et al. 2010).

Procedural organizational instruments have also been growing in frequency of appearance, but for different reasons: under efforts to shift sectoral activity undertaken through older legal forms of governance to more corporatist or network forms. Government reorganizations are increasingly common and these reorganizations and the new agencies often created alongside them are intended to use government organizational resources to refocus government efforts and interactions with policy community/network members rather than directly improve the delivery of particular types of goods and services (Herranz 2007; Bache 2010).

As Peters (1992) noted, re-organization of existing departments and agencies serves to refocus government efforts and reposition government administration within policy networks, bringing together policy community members to reconsider the effectiveness of network management activities (Banting 1995; de la Mothe 1996), improving management of complex areas by restructuring relationships (May 1993; Metcalfe 2000) and can insert government actors between competing private actors in networks by, for example, creating consumer departments to sit between producers and (un)organized consumers (Bache 2010). These moves are often accompanied by the increasing use of government reviews and inquiries, as well as consultative conferences and other similar organizational forms for stakeholder and public consultation (Crowley 2009; Lejano and Ingram 2009).

Readings

Bellehumeur, Robert. 1997. 'Review: An Instrument of Change'. *Optimum* 27, no. 1: 37–42.

Cantor, R., S. Henry and S. Rayner. 1992. *Making Markets: An Interdisciplinary Perspective on Economic Exchange*. Westport, CT: Greenwood Press.

Goldsmith, Stephen and William D. Eggers. 2004. 'Designing the Network'. In *Governing by Network: The New Shape of the Public Sector*. Washington, DC: Brookings Institution Press, 55–92.

Hood, Christopher. 2004. 'Controlling Public Services and Government: Towards a Cross-National Perspective'. In *Controlling Modern Government; Variety, Commonality and Change* (eds) C. Hood, O. James, B. G. Peters and C. Scott. Cheltenham: Edward Elgar, 3–21.

Kernaghan, Kenneth. 1993. 'Partnership and Public Administration: Conceptual and Practical Considerations'. *Canadian Public Administration* 36, no. 1: 57–76.

Leech, Beth L., F. R. Baumgartner, T. La Pira and N. A. Semanko. 2005. 'Drawing Lobbyists to Washington: Government Activity and the Demand for Advocacy'. *Political Research Quarterly* 58, no. 1: 19–30.

Leman, Christopher K. 2002 'Direct Government'. In *The Tools of Government: A Guide to the New Governance* (ed.) L. M. Salamon. New York: Oxford University Press, 48–79.

Lowndes, Vivien and Chris Skelcher. 1998. 'The Dynamics of Multi-Organizational Partnerships: An Analysis of Changing Modes of Governance'. *Public Administration* 76, Summer: 313–33.

McCubbins, Mathew D., Roger G. Noll and Barry R. Weingast. 1987. 'Administrative Procedures as Instruments of Political Control'. *Journal of Law, Economics, and Organization* 3, no. 2: 243–77.

Olsen, Johan P. 2005. 'Maybe It Is Time to Rediscover Bureaucracy'. *Journal of Public Administration Research and Theory* 16, no. 1: 1–24.

Peters, B. Guy. 1992. 'Government Reorganization: A Theoretical Analysis'. *International Political Science Review* 13, no. 2: 199–218.

Posner, Paul L. 2002. 'Accountability Challenges of Third-Party Government'. In L. M. Salamon (ed.) *The Tools of Government: A Guide to the New Governance*. New York: Oxford University Press, 523–51.

Riccucci, Norma M. and Marcia K. Meyers. 2008. 'Comparing Welfare Service Delivery Among Public, Nonprofit and For-Profit Work Agencies'. *International Journal of Public Administration* 31: 1441–54.

Savas, Emmanuel S. 1989/90. 'A Taxonomy of Privatization Strategies'. *Policy Studies Journal* 18, no. 2: 343–55.

Stanton, Thomas H. and Ronald C. Moe. 2002. 'Government Corporations and Government-sponsored Enterprises'. In *The Tools of Government: A Guide to the New Governance* (ed.) L. M. Salamon. New York: Oxford University Press, 80–116.

Tupper, Allan and G. Bruce Doern. 1988. 'Canadian Public Enterprise and Privatization'. In *Privatization, Public Policy and Public Corporations in Canada*. (eds) A. Tupper and G. B. Doern: Montreal Institute for Research on Public Policy, 1–50.

Vining, Aidan R., Anthony E. Boardman and Finn Poschmann. 2005. 'Public-Private Partnerships in the US and Canada: "There are No Free Lunches"'. *Journal of Comparative Policy Analysis*. 7, no. 3: 199–220.

Chapter 6

Authoritative implementation tools

Substantive authoritative instruments

There are many types of 'authoritative' instruments. All involve, and rely primarily on, the ability of governments to direct or steer targets in the directions they would prefer them to go through the use of the real or perceived threat of state-enforced sanctions. While treasure resources, discussed in the next chapter, are often used to encourage 'positive' behaviour – that is, behaviour which is aligned with government goals – authoritative actions can be used for this purpose, but are often also used in a 'negative' sense, that is, to prevent or discourage types of behaviour which are incongruent with government expectations (Ajzen 1991).

The use of the coercive power of the state to achieve government goals through the control or alteration of societal (and governmental) behaviour is the essence of *regulation*, the most common type of governing instrument found in this category and the one most compatible with legal forms of governance. In general, all types of regulation involve the promulgation of more or less binding rules which circumscribe or alter the behaviour of particular target groups (Hood 1986a; Kiviniemi 1986). As it has been succinctly described by Barry Mitnick, this invoves the 'public administrative policing of a private activity with respect to a rule prescribed in the public interest' (Mitnick 1978). Rules take various forms and include standards, permits, prohibition, and executive orders. Some regulations, like ones dealing with criminal behaviour, are *laws* and involve the police and judicial system in their enforcement. Most regulations, however, are *administrative edicts* created under the terms of enabling legislation and administered on a continuing basis by a government department or a specialized, quasi-judicial government agency (Rosenbloom 2007). In relatively rare cases the authority to enact, enforce or adjudicate regulations can also be delegated to NGOs in various forms of 'voluntary' or 'self-regulation'.

With regulation, the government does not provide goods and service delivery 'directly' through the use of its organizational resources but rather allows this to occur in a controlled fashion through an intermediary – usually a private company or market enterprise, but also sometimes state-owned enterprises or, more commonly, NGOs such as churches, voluntary organizations and association, trade unions and professional bodies. Depending on how this is done, this can be compatible with either market or corporatist types of governance (Mitnick 1978; Scott 2001). Other procedural authoritative tools are also compatible with network governance.

Direct government regulation

Regulation is a fundamental technique or tool of legal governance. Although citizens may not always be aware of their presence, among other things regulations govern the price and standards of a wide variety of goods and services they consume, as well as the quality of water they drink and the air they breathe.

There are numerous definitions of regulation, but a good general one is offered by Michael Reagan (1987), who defines it as 'a process or activity in which government requires or proscribes certain activities or behaviour on the part of individuals and institutions, mostly private but sometimes public, and does so through a continuing administrative process, generally through specially designated regulatory agencies'. Thus, in this view, regulation is a prescription by the government which must be complied with by the intended targets; failure to do so usually involves a penalty, sometimes financial but also often involving incarceration and imprisonment.

This type of instrument is often referred to as 'command and control' regulation since it typically involves the government issuing a 'command' to some target group in order to 'control' their behaviour. 'Control' also sometimes refers to the need for governments to monitor and enforce target group activity in order for a 'command' to be effective.

This type of regulation is very common in both social and economic spheres in order to encourage 'virtues' and discourage 'vices', however those are defined at the time. Thus criminal law, for example, is a kind of regulatory activity, as are common laws and civil codes, which all countries have and which states develop and implement, usually relatively non-controversially (May 2002; Cismaru and Lavack 2007). Although much less significant in terms of the day-to-day lives of many citizens, much more attention is paid in the policy tools literature to economic regulation which affects aspects of established markets for goods and service production, and is often resisted by target companies and industries if they feel it undermines their competitive position either domestically or internationally (Baldwin and Cave 1999; Crew and Parker 2006).

It is sometimes difficult for governments to 'command and control' their targets if these targets resist regulatory efforts (Scholz 1991) or if governments do not have the capacity or legitimacy required to enforce their orders. As a result of these difficulties other types of regulation exist in which rules are more vague and the threat of penalties may be, at best, remote. These different types of regulation are discussed below.

Laws

Law is an important tool of modern government and the very basis of legal modes of governance (Ziller 2005). Several different types of laws exist, however. These include distinctions often drawn by legal scholars between private and public law; private civil or tort law and common law; public criminal and administrative law; and hybrids such as class action suits which combine features of public and private law. These different types of law vary substantially in terms of what kinds of situations they can be applied to, by whom and to what effect (Keyes 1996; Scheb and Scheb 2005).

All of these laws can be thought of as 'regulations' since all involve the creation of rules governing individual behaviour (Williamson 1975; 1996; Ostrom 1986). However, in the form it is usually discussed by policy scholars, 'regulation' is typically thought of as a form of public law; although even then it can also involve criminal and individual or civil actions (Kerwin 1994; 1999; West 2005).

Keyes (1996) has usefully described the six types of legal instruments which can be used by governments when they wish to invoke their authority to try to direct societal behaviour (see also Brandsen et al. 2006). These are shown in Table 6.1.

While laws can prohibit or proscribe many kinds of behaviour (and encourage others either by implication or overtly), in order to move beyond the symbolic level, they all require a strong enforcement mechanism, which includes various forms of policing and the courts (Edelman 1964; 1988). And even here a considerable amount of variation and discretion is possible since inspections and policing can be more or less onerous and more or less frequent, can be oriented towards responding to complaints or actively looking for

Table 6.1 Six types of legal instruments

1	Statutes
2	Delegated legislation between levels of government
3	Decisions of regulatory bodies and courts
4	Contracts or treaties
5	Quasi-legislation such as tax notices and interpretative bulletins
6	Reference documents such as background papers, other legislation, standing orders, etc.

Source: Keyes, J. M. 1996. 'Power Tools: The Form and Function of Legal Instruments for Government Action'. *Canadian Journal of Administrative Law and Practice* 10: 133–74.

transgressions ('police patrols' vs 'fire alarms', and can be focused on punishment of transgressions or prevention, in the latter case often with a strong educational component designed to persuade citizens and others to adopt modes of behaviour more congruent with government aims and objectives (McCubbins and Schwartz 1984; Hawkins and Thomas 1989; McCubbins and Lupia 1994; May and Winter 1999). A desire for 100 per cent compliance on the part of governments requires a high level of scrutiny and thus some kind of ongoing, institutionalized, regulatory presence within a government organization or agency: typically a line department such as a police department or some other similar administrative bureau with investigatory and policing powers.

All laws are intrusive and many are highly visible. A significant problem with the use of laws in policy designs, however, pertains to cost, automaticity and precision of targeting. With respect to the first two, while passage of a law is usually not all that costly, the need for enforcement is. Laws have a low degree of automaticity as they rely upon citizen's goodwill and perceptions of legitimacy for them to be obeyed. Inevitably this will not ensure 100 per cent compliance and will thus require the establishment of an enforcement agency, such as the police, customs agencies, immigration patrols, coastguards and the courts. Precision of targeting is also an issue since most laws have general applicability and often cannot single out specific groups or targets for differential treatment. These problems have led to the use of alternate forms of regulation expected to reduce these costs and allow for improved targeting of specific actors.

Independent regulatory commissions

Direct administrative implementation of legislative rules is very common in legal modes of governance. However, in the economic realm, especially, it often raises concerns about corruption and patronage, that is, in the abuse of administrative discretion to either ease enforcement in certain cases or administer it capriciously in others. Checks on administrative discretion usually exist through the court system, whereby those who feel they have been unfairly treated can often appeal administrative decisions and seek their overturn (Jaffe 1965; Edley 1990). This can be a very time-consuming and expensive process, however, and several distinct forms of regulatory agencies with semi-independent, quasi-judicial status have been developed in order to avoid governance problems associated with direct departmental regulation.

The most well-known of these is the *independent regulatory commission* or IRC used in corporatist modes of governance. Although some early exemplars of this instrument can be found in canal authorities in Great Britain and other European railway, highway and transportation regulatory authorities of the eighteenth and nineteenth centuries, the IRC as it is currently known stems mainly from concerns raised in the post-Civil War USA about unfair practices in railway transportation pricing and access. These led to the creation of an innovative organizational regulatory form in the 1887 US Pendleton Act which established the US Interstate Commerce Commission, a quasi-judicial body operating at arms length from government which was intended to act autonomously in the creation and enforcement of regulations and which remained in operation for over 100 years (until 1995) (Cushman 1941).

Independent regulatory commissions evolved from the transportation sector to become common in many other sectors, not limited to those dealing with economic issues. They are 'semi-independent' administrative agencies in the sense that, as was the case with public enterprises, government control is indirect, and exercised via the appointment of commissioners who are more or less difficult to remove from office (Stern 1997; Gilardi 2005b and 2005c; Jacobzone 2005; Majone 2005; Christensen and Laegreid 2007). Irene Wu has listed eleven aspects of their organization, staffing and function which makes such agencies 'independent' (Wu 2008) (see Table 6.2).[1]

IRCs are quasi-judicial in the sense that one of their main activities is adjudicating disputes over the interpretation and enforcement of rules – a task taken away from the courts in order to ensure that expertise in the specific activities regulated is brought to bear on a case in order to have more expert, timely and predictable results. Decisions of independent regulatory commissions are still subject to judicial review, although often this is only in terms of issues relating to procedural fairness, rather than the evidentiary basis of a decision (Edley 1990; Berg 2000; Laegreid et al. 2008; Lehmkuhl 2008).

IRCs are relatively inexpensive, specialized bodies that can remove a great deal of the routine regulatory burden in many areas of social and economic life from government departments, and are quite popular with governments wishing to simplify their agendas and reduce their need to supervise specific forms of social behaviour on a day-to-day basis. In the contemporary period independent regulatory commissions are involved with all aspects of market behaviour, production, distribution and consumption, as well as many areas

Table 6.2 Requisites for regulatory agency independence

1 An independent leader
2 Exclusive licencing authority
3 Independent funding
4 Private sector regulatees
5 Little movement of staff between industry and regulator
6 Consumer offices
7 Universal service offices
8 Notice and comment decision-making
9 Rules against gifts
10 Rules against conflicts of interest
11 Post-employment rules

Source: Wu, Irene. 2008. 'Who Regulates Phones, Television, and the Internet? What Makes a Communications Regulator Independent and Why It Matters'. *Perspectives on Politics* 6, no. 4: 769–83.

of social life. Many specialized forms of IRCs exist, such as the use of 'marketing boards', or arm's-length regulatory bodies often staffed by elected representatives of producers and granted specific rights to control prices and/or supply, thereby creating and enforcing pricing and supply regimes on producers. This has occurred primarily in areas affected by periodic bouts of over- or under-supply and can be found in areas such as bulk agricultural commodities like wheat or milk which are very sensitive to price fluctuations, but also in areas, such as liver and heart transplants, subject to chronic supply shortages (Weimer 2007; Royer 2008). These boards typically act as rationing boards charged with allocating supply quotas and setting prices in order to smooth out supply fluctuations in the activity involved.

Although it began with regulation of trade, commerce and distribution, primarily railways and transport, the IRC instrument quickly moved to production, and in the post-World War I era in many countries were implemented in areas such as labour and industrial disputes regulation, as well as the commodity-based marketing boards mentioned above. In the post-World War II era they were used to cover a range of emerging consumer and consumption issues such as consumer rights, landlord–tenant interactions, human rights disputes and others (Hodgetts 1973).

As Berg (2000) and Stern and Holder (1999) noted, in addition to questions related to their level of independence or autonomy, additional design criteria include the clarity of their roles and objectives; their degree of accountability of governments or the public; their level and type of participation and transparency; and ultimately their predictability in terms of being bound by precedents either of their own making or through judicial review (see also Berg et al. 2000).

IRCs, like more direct government regulation, have been the subject of efforts at deregulation as some governments attempted to move some sectors away from legal and corporatist governance forms towards more market modes of operation. Some high profile privatization and deregulation in transportation, telecommunication and financial industries in many countries occurred as a result of these effort (Levi-Faur 2003). The reality, however, is that there has been no across-the-board reduction in the use of more directive tools (Drezner 2001; Vogel 2001; Wheeler 2001). Like privatization, deregulation is nowhere as widespread as claimed by both enthusiasts and critics (Iacobucci et al. 2006).[2] Indeed, regulations have been expanded in many sectors to compensate for the loss of state control following privatization of public enterprises (Jordana and Levi-Faur 2004; Braithwaite 2008) and IRCs are among the most favoured means of re-regulating deregulated or privatized industries and activities (Ramesh and Howlett 2006).

With respect to targeting, including precision and selectivity among groups and policy actors, the information needed to establish regulation is less than with many other tools because a government need not know in advance the subject's preferences, as is necessary in the case of some other instruments. It can just establish a standard, for example a permitted pollution level, and expect compliance. This is also unlike the situation with financial incentives, for example, which will not elicit a favourable response from regulatees unless their intended subjects have a preference for them (Mitnick 1980).

There are still some concerns about the use of this instrument in policy designs, however, linked to considerations of cost and visibility. The cost of enforcement by regulatory commissions can be quite high depending on the availability of information, and the costs of investigation and prosecution in highly legalistic and adversarial circumstances can also be very large. Regulations also are often inflexible and do not permit the consideration of individual circumstances, and can result in decisions and outcomes not intended by the regulators (Bardach 1989; Dyerson and Mueller 1993). They quite often distort voluntary or private sector activities and can promote economic inefficiencies. Price regulations and direct allocation, for example, restrict the operation of the forces of demand and supply and affect the price mechanism, thus causing sometimes unpredictable economic distortions in the market. Restrictions on entry to and exit from industrial sectors, for example, can reduce competition and thus have a negative impact on prices. Regulations can also inhibit innovation and technological progress because of the market security they afford existing firms and the limited opportunities for experimentation they might permit. For these and other reasons, they are often labelled as overly intrusive by many firms and actors.

Indirect government regulation

A third form of regulation is 'indirect regulation' which is very compatible with corporatist modes of governance. There are several different types of such regulation, however, which vary in terms of their design attributes.

Delegated professional regulation

This is a relatively rare form of regulatory activity which occurs when a government transfers its authority to licence certain practices and discipline transgressors to non-governmental or quasi-governmental bodies whose boards of directors, unlike the situation with independent regulatory commissions, they typically do not appoint (Elgie 2006; Kuhlmann and Allsop 2008).

Delegated regulation typically involves legislatures passing special legislation empowering specific groups to define their own membership and regulate their own behaviour. Brockman (1998) defines it as:

> the delegation of government regulatory functions to a quasi-pubic body that is officially expected to prevent or reduce both incompetence (lack of skill, knowledge or ability) and misconduct (criminal, quasi-criminal or unethical behaviour) by controlling the quality of service to the public through regulating or governing activities such as licencing or registration – often involving a disciplinary system (fines, licences, suspension or revocation) and codes of conduct/ethics, etc.

This occurs most commonly in the area of professional regulation where many governments allow professions such as doctors, lawyers, accountants, engineers, teachers, urban planners and others to control entrance to their profession and to enforce professional standards of conduct through the grant of a licencing monopoly to an organization such as a bar association, a college of physicians and surgeons, or a teachers' college (Tuohy and Wolfson 1978; Trebilcock et al. 1979; Tuohy 1992; 1999; Sinclair 1997). Typically, appeals of the decisions of delegated bodies may also be heard by the courts or specialized administrative tribunals (Trebilock 2008).

The idea behind delegated regulation, as with independent regulatory commissions, is that direct regulation through government departments and the courts is too expensive and time-consuming to justify the effort involved and the results achieved. Rather than tie up administrators and judges with many thousands of cases resulting from, for example, professional licencing or judicial or medical malpractice, these activities can be delegated to bodies composed of representatives of the professional field involved who are the ones most knowledgeable about best practices and requirements in the field. Governments have neither the time nor expertise required to regulate multiple interactions between lawyers and their clients, teachers and students, or doctors and patients, for example, and a form of 'self-regulation' is more practical and cost efficient.

Scandal in areas such as business accounting in many countries in recent years, however, can undermine confidence in a profession's ability or even willingness to police itself, and can lead to a crisis in confidence in many aspects of delegated self-regulation (Vogel 2005; Bernstein and Cashore 2007; Tallontire 2007). Of course, any delegation of government regulatory authority can be revoked if misbehaviour ensues.

Voluntary or incentive regulation

Another form of indirect or 'self-regulation' has a more recent history than delegated regulation and has been extended to many more areas of social and economic life. This is typically a form found in market governance systems in which, rather than establish an agency with the authority to unilaterally direct targets to follow some course of action with the ability to sanction those actors who fail to comply, instead a government tries to persuade targets to voluntarily adopt or conform to government aims and objectives.

Although these efforts often exist 'under the shadow of hierarchy' (Heritier and Lehmkuhl 2008) – that is, where a real threat of enhanced oversight exists should voluntary means prove insufficient to motivate actors to alter their behaviour in the desired fashion – they also exist in realms where hierarchies don't exist, such as the international realm when a strong treaty regime, for example, cannot be agreed upon (Dimitrov 2002; 2005; 2007). A major advantage often cited for the use of voluntary standard-setting is cost savings, since governments do not have to pay for the creation, administration, enforcement and renewal of such standards, as would be the case with traditional command

and control regulation whether implemented by departments or independent regulatory commissions. Such programmes can also be effective in international settings, where establishment of effective legally-based governmental regimes can be especially difficult (Schlager 1999; Elliott and Schlaepfer 2001; Cashore et al. 2003; Borraz 2007).

Moffet and Bregha set out the main types of voluntary regulation (see Table 6.3) found in areas such as environmental protection.

These tools attempt such activities as inducing companies to exceed pollution targets by excluding them from other regulations or enforcement actions; establishing covenants in which companies agree to voluntarily abide by certain standards; establishing labelling provisions or fair trade programmes; providing favourable publicity and treatment for actors exceeding existing standards; promoting co-operation over new innovations; and attempting to improve standards attainment by targeted actors through better auditing and evaluation. These are all forms of what Sappington (1994) has termed 'incentive regulaton'.

The role played by governments in voluntary regulation is much less explicit than in traditional regulation, but is nevertheless present. Unlike the situation with command and control or delegated regulation, in these instances governments allow non-governmental actors to regulate themselves without creating specific oversight or monitoring bodies or agencies or empowering legislation. As Gibson (1999: 3) defined it:

> By definition voluntary initiatives are not driven by regulatory requirements. They are voluntary in the sense that governments do not have to order them to be undertaken . . . [but] governments play important roles as initiators, signatories, or behind-the-scenes promoters.

While many standards are invoked by government command and control regulation, others can be developed in the private sphere, such as occurs in situations where manufacturing companies develop standards for products or where independent certification firms or associations guarantee that certain standards have been met in various kinds of private practices (Gunningham

Table 6.3 Types of voluntary regulation

1	Legislated compliance plans
2	Regulatory exemption programs
3	Government–industry negotiated agreements
4	Certification
5	Challenge programs
6	Design partnerships
7	Standards auditing and accounting

Source: Moffet, J., and F. Bregha. 1999. 'Non-Regulatory Environmental Measures'. In *Voluntary Initiatives: The New Politics of Corporate Greening*, ed. R. B. Gibson. Peterborough: Broadview Press.

and Rees 1997; Andrews 1998; Iannuzzi 2001; Cashore 2002; Eden 2009; Eden and Bear 2010).

These kinds of self-regulation, however, are often portrayed as being more 'voluntary' than is actually the case. That is, while non-governmental entities may, in effect, regulate themselves, they typically do so, as Gibson notes, with the implicit or explicit permission of governments, which consciously refrain from regulating activities in a more directly coercive fashion (Gibson 1999; Ronit 2001). As long as these private standards are not replaced by government enforced ones, they represent the acquiescence of a government to the private rules, a form of delegated regulation (Haufler 2000; 2001; Knill 2001; Heritier and Eckert 2008; Heritier and Lehmkuhl 2008).

That is, as a 'public' policy instrument, self-regulation still requires some level of state action – either in supporting or encouraging development of private self-regulation or retaining the 'iron fist' or the threat of 'real' regulation if private behaviour does not change (Cutler et al. 1999; Gibson 1999; Cashore 2002; Porter and Ronit 2006). This is done both in order to ensure that self-regulation meets public objectives and expectations (see for example, Hoek and King's (2008) analysis of the ineffective self-regulation practiced by TV advertisers in New Zealand) and to control the kinds of 'club' status which self-regulation can give to firms and organizations which agree to adhere to 'voluntary' standards (Potoski and Prakesh 2009). Certification schemes, for example, can closely approximate cartel-like arrangements which allow premiums to accrue to club members rather than to the public. As Delmas and Terlaak (2001) noted, joining or participating in voluntary schemes entails both costs and benefits to companies, which undertake detailed cost–benefit calculations about whether or not to join voluntary associations. This is one of the 'limits of virtue' which David Vogel (2005) noted in his studies of various corporate social responsibility (CSR) schemes in the late 1990s and first decade of the twenty-first century (see also Tallontire 2007; Steurer 2010; and Natural Resources Canada 2003).

It is also the case that any possible savings in administrative costs over more direct forms of legal regulation must be balanced against additional costs to society which might result from ineffective or inefficient administration of voluntary standards, especially those related to non-compliance (Gibson 1999; Karamanos 2001; Henriques and Sadorsky 2008).

Market creation and maintenance

Paradoxically as it might seem from its title, another form of indirect regulatory instrument used by government is the use of co-called 'market-based' instruments (Hula 1988; Fligstein 1996). These refer to a particular type of regulatory tool in which governments establish property rights frameworks or regimes which establish various kinds of limits or prices for certain goods and services and then allow market actors to work within these 'markets' to allocate goods and services according to price signals (Averch 1990; Cantor et al. 1992).

Such schemes have often been proposed mostly in the area of environmental and resource policy, from land and water use (Murphy et al. 2009) and bio-conservation (ecosystem services) (Wissel and Watzold 2009), but have also been used in the fisheries, such as individual tranferable quotas (ITQs) (Pearse 1980; Townsend et al. 2006), and with respect to the control of greenhouse gas regulation, such as the 'cap and trade' systems created in the European Union and other countries associated with the Kyoto Protocol and climate change mitigation efforts (Heinmiller 2007; Voss 2007; Hahn 2008; Toke 2008; Pope and Owen 2009).

However, despite much publicity, few of these schemes have been implemented given the difficulties of setting prices and limits on items such as pollutants, problems with leakage and poor enforcement in the system and dangers associated with market failures, as well as the inability of governments to bear the blame for problems with these systems, despite their ostensibly arm's length character (Stavins 1998; 2001; Mendes and Santos 2008; Keohane et al. 2009). Unlike traditional regulation, these designs can be higher cost and less automatic than expected, and also are very difficult, if not impossible, to target towards specific actors and groups (Krysiak and Schweitzer 2010; Mickwitz et al 2008).

Procedural authoritative instruments

Procedural authority-based instruments typically involve the exercise of government authority to recognize or provide preferential treatment access or treatment to certain actors – and hence to fail to recognize others – in the policy process, or to mandate certain procedural requirements in the policy-making process in order to ensure it takes certain views or perspectives into account. These instruments perform a wide variety of network management functions (Agranoff and McGuire 1999), very often in order to gain support or marginalize policy opponents but also to ensure certain standards and standard practices are followed in policy choices (Goodin 1980; Saward 1992).

Policy network activation and mobilization tools

In terms of network management activities, many procedural authoritative tools are involved largely in the 'selective activation' of policy actors and/or their 'mobilization' through the extension of special recognition in a policy process. The key use of authority is in the extension of preferential access to decision-makers or regulators for certain views and actors and not others, or at least to a lesser extent (Doerr 1981).

Procedural authoritative tools attempt to ensure efficiency and effectiveness of government actions through activation of policy actor support. Networks may be structured, for example, through the creation of various advisory processes which all rely on the exercise of government authority to

Table 6.4 Actions undertaken by procedural authoritative instruments

Problem identification
Mobilizing interest
Spanning and bridging activities
Claims-making
Knowledge acquisition
Convening and deliberating
Community capacity-building
Transparency, evaluation and feedback

Source: Phillips, S. D., and M. Orsini. 2002. 'Mapping the Links: Citizen Involvement in Policy Processes'. Ottawa: Canadian Policy Research Networks.

recognize and organize specific sets of policy actors and give them preferential access to government officials and decision-makers (Pierre 1998; Hall and O'Toole 2004). These include advisory councils, ad hoc task forces and inquiries, consultations, and public hearings (Hall and O'Toole 2004). Phillips and Orsini (2002) list the types of policy process activities which advisory committees undertake (see Table 6.4).

Several distinct types of authoritative network management tools can be identified. Prominent ones include the following.

Advisory councils

Advisory councils are the best example of procedural authoritative instruments and are very common in market and corporatist governance arrangements. These are more or less permanent bodies established to provide advice to governments – either political-executive or administrative – on an ongoing basis. They are often established on a sectoral (e.g. industry specific such as an automobile trade advisory committee) basis, but also can be topical (e.g. biomedical ethics) (Gill 1940; Brown 1955; Smith 1977). These committees play a major role in many areas but are especially prominent in areas of new technologies where they play a significant role in linking governments to various kinds of expert or 'epistemic' communities (Haas 1992; Jasanoff 1998; Heinrichs 2005; Dunlop 2009).

The archetypal advisory council is a more or less permanent body used to institutionalize interest group members in government deliberations (Heinrichs 2005). They are at least partially if not fully co-optive in nature and intended to align the ideas and actions of the regulated group and the government ministry to which they are attached. However, they can also be more standalone and independent sources of expert advice to governments such as science and technology councils, councils of economic advisors, and others (Phidd 1975; Doern 1971).

Smith (1977) and Brown-John (1979) identify eight main types of advisory committees commonly found in modern liberal-democratic governments. These are set out in Table 6.5.

Table 6.5 Types of advisory committees

1	General advisory committees – to discuss policy alternatives generated by government, comment on current policies, examine trends and needs, and suggest alternatives to status quo
2	Science and technology advisory committees – to provide expert advice in narrow specialist areas
3	Special clientele advisory committees – to assist governments to make and implement policies in special sectors of the economy or society
4	Research advisory committees – lengthy, research oriented to tackle large questions
5	Public conferences – e.g. citizens' assemblies, national forest congresses, etc.
6	Geographic-based advisory committees – to deal with geographic particularities, e.g. in agriculture
7	Intergovernmental advisory committees – to co-ordinate between government levels
8	Interdepartmental committees – to achieve vertical and horizontal coordination in government

Sources: Smith, T. B. 1977. 'Advisory Committees in the Public Policy Process'. *International Review of Administrative Sciences* 43, no. 2:153–66; Brown-John, C. L. 1979. 'Advisory Agencies in Canada: An Introduction'. *Canadian Public Administration* 22, no. 1: 72–91.

Brown (1955) lists several purposes of such bodies which stress their network nature (see Table 6.6).

These boards are generally very inexpensive and almost invisible. They can be precisely targeted and enhance the automaticity of government. They are also viewed, generally, as non-intrusive. As a result they have proliferated in all governments in recent years. This proliferation has led in some countries to the passage of legislation to control and standardize the number of advisory

Table 6.6 Purposes of advisory boards

1	Source of advice
2	A source of support for regulators
3	A means of popularizing a regulatory regime
4	A 'listening post' for industry and government to listen to each other
5	A means of reaching agreement and resolving conflicts between government and interests
6	An agency for special inquiries
7	A device for patronage
8	A set of ambassadors for an administrative agency

Source: Brown, D. S. 1955. 'The Public Advisory Board as an Instrument of Government'. *Public Administration Review* 15: 196–201.

committees and their behaviour. The US Advisory Committee Act (1972), for example, specifies membership and guidelines and standard operating procedures for these types of committees (Brown 1955; Cronin and Thomas 1970; Brown 1972; Smith 1977; Heinrichs 2005) (see Table 6.7).

Public consultation, stakeholder and consensus conferences

In addition to more permanent bodies, governments can also organize short-term and long-range mechanisms to provide input and legitimate government policy-making (Leroux et al. 1998). Increasingly, the role of the public in these processes has been expanded to include participation in the design of the consultation process as well as in making policy recommendations to government (Abelson et al. 2003; Dryzek and Tucker 2008). Sometimes mandated by legislation, appropriate levels of government will often elicit public involvement in administrative activities such as regulatory monitoring and environmental impact assessment.

Abelson et al. (2003) has noted that these participation efforts can be classified by looking at the procedures, representation, and information involved and by looking at their outcomes. Key issues in the design of consultative processes are (1) who is involved and who is not (for example, whether elites or the public are involved; or whether only stakeholders rather than the public, per se, are consulted);[2] (2) who makes this determination, for example, government or representative groups (Howlett 1990); (3) what resources they have, such as access to funding; access to staff; access to politicians; access to information; or access to witnesses (Salter and Slaco 1981); and (4) whether or not their recommendations are binding (Webler and Tuler 2000; Margerum 2008). Dion lists several of these design criteria on several conjoint continua in Table 6.8.

These consultations can cover an extraordinarily wide range of topics – from constitutional issues related to voting systems and the like (Kogan 2010)

Table 6.7 US Advisory Committee Act (1972) criteria

1	Written charter explaining role of committee
2	Timely notice of committee meetings in Federal register
3	Fair and balanced representation on committees
4	Sponsoring agencies prepare minutes of meetings
5	Open committee meetings to the public wherever possible
6	Provide public access to information used by the committee
7	Government given sole authority to convene and adjourn meetings
8	Committees terminated in two years unless renewed or otherwise provided by statute

Source: Smith, T. B. 1977. 'Advisory Committees in the Public Policy Process'. *International Review of Administrative Sciences* 43, no. 2: 153–66.

Table 6.8 Types of public consultation – design criteria

1   From the point of view of publicity: how private and secret these consultations are, versus public, open and transparent.
2   From the point of view of official status: whether consultations are unofficial, semi-official or official.
3   From the point of view of origin: whether the consultations are 'organic' (traditional) or 'inorganic' (imposed).
4   From the point of view of imperiousness: whether participation is optional or compulsory.

Source: Dion, L. 1973. 'The Politics of Consultation.' *Government and Opposition* 8, no. 3: 332–53.

to much more mundane ones such as city zoning changes. They are typically organized by private government agencies, although in some jurisdictions, like Australia, consultants specializing in the organization and delivery of consultation exercises have become much more prominent in recent years (Hendriks and Carson 2008).

Conclusion

The evolution of regulation as a key policy instrument in the toolbox of modern government is a well-known story. From the development of the principle of delegated legislation in the early years of the evolution of the modern state (Page 2001; Gilardi 2002; Thatcher and Stone-Sweet 2003) to the first creation of specialized quasi-judicial independent regulatory commissions in the United States after the Civil War (Huntington 1952; Eisner 1994a; 1994b), the gradual development of bureaucratic expertise and capacity in the social and economic realms is a defining characteristic of the legal and corporatist modes of governance found in many policy sectors and a central feature in many policy designs (Berg 2000; Howlett 2002; Howlett 2004; Scherer 2008).

Debates about the merits of this development continues in many areas, however, especially those sectors which could be organized along market lines. For example, a large literature exists on whether or not regulations serve the public or the private interest (Posner 1974; Stigler 1975) and whether or not they contribute to economic efficiency by correcting market failures (Croley 2007) or instead create new government failures (Wolf 1979 and 1987; Le Grand 1991; Zerbe and McCurdy 1999). The discussion has generated a plethora of studies about the merits of particular types of regulation over others (Hawkins and Thomas 1989; Williams 2000; Ringquist et al. 2003), the problems of regulatory capture (Laffont and Tirole 1991) and the difficulties of legislative and judicial oversight of regulatory activities (de Smith 1973; Angus 1974; McCubbins and Schwartz 1984; McCubbins and Lupia 1994; Gilardi 2005a).[3]

The early 1980s was a turning point in the debate on regulation in many countries, as the idea that regulations were conceived and executed solely in the public interest came under heavy attack from a wide range of critics. Much of this criticism relied heavily on works by authors and economists of the Chicago (Stigler 1971; Peltzman 1976; Becker 1983) and Virginia (Posner 1974; Landes and Posner 1975; Buchanan and Tollison 1984; Tollison 1991) schools of political economy who argued that many regulations were inefficient as well as inequitable. Governments led by right-wing politicians in many countries, like Ronald Reagan in the USA and Margaret Thatcher in the UK, but also Labour governments in New Zealand and elsewhere, further fanned popular sentiment against regulations by putting deregulation and the search for alternatives to traditional 'command and control' regulation at the centre of policy reform agendas designed to address declines in productivity and persistent inflation and high unemployment present at the time (Howlett and Ramesh 2006). Many governments began at this time to experiment with forms of 'voluntary regulation'.

Many 'deregulation' measures, however, are commonsense reforms intended to iron out shortcomings, anomalies and obsolescence in existing regulations rather than a response to any particular systemic pressure (Wilson 2003). The nature and extent of problems change, as do solutions available to deal with them (Frischtak 1995). The campaign for removal or at least weakening of such regulations is often led by businesses which find complying with them in new technological environments to be onerous. Their efforts find ready support among voters who have their own reasons for disaffection with outdated, inappropriate and seemingly meaningless regulations which can impose costs on them for various services – like telephony – which seem unwarranted. The regulators' frustration with the costs of their implementation further reinforces the calls for reform.[4]

However, it must also be noted that at the same time that some deregulation has occurred, re-regulation of many sectors has also taken place. And, as the discussion in this chapter has shown, an explosion of the use of procedural authoritative implementation tools has also occurred. While some of this activity can be traced to attempts to shift governance modes in various sectors, it is also the case that changes have occurred as policy design ideas have changed, given different configurations of costs and other instrument attributes in some sectors.

Readings

Bryson, John M. and Barbara C. Crosby. 1993. 'Policy Planning and the Design and Use of Forums, Arenas, and Courts'. In *Public Management: The State of the Art* B. Bozeman. (ed.) San Francisco, CA: Jossey-Bass.

Cook, Dee. 2002. 'Consultation, for a Change? Engaging Users and Communities in the Policy Process'. *Social Policy and Administration* 36, no. 5: 516–31.

Crew, M. A. and C. K. Rowley. 1986. 'Deregulation as an Instrument in Industrial Policy'. *Journal of Institutional and Theoretical Economics* 142: 52–70.

Doern, G. Bruce. 2004. 'Institutional and Public Administrative Aspects of Voluntary Codes'. In *Voluntary Codes: Private Governance, the Public Interest and Innovation* K. Webb (ed.), Ottawa: Carleton Research Unit on Innovation, Science and Environment, 57–76.

Eisner, Marc Allen. 1994. 'Economic Regulatory Policies: Regulation and Deregulation in Historical Context'. In *Handbook of Regulation and Administrative Law* D. H. Rosenbloom and R. D. Schwartz (eds) . New York: Marcel Dekker, 91–116.

Hall, Thad E. and Laurence J. O'Toole. 2004. 'Shaping Formal Networks through the Regulatory Process'. *Administration and Society* 36, no. 2: 186–207.

Heinrichs, Harald. 2005. 'Advisory Systems in Pluralistic Knowledge Societies: A Criteria-Based Typology to Assess and Optimize Environmental Policy Advice'. In *Democratization of Expertise? Exploring Novel Forms of Scientific Advice in Political Decision-Making* S. Maasen and P. Weingart (eds). Dordrecht: Springer, 41–61.

Keyes, John Mark. 1996. 'Power Tools: The Form and Function of Legal Instruments for Government Action'. *Canadian Journal of Administrative Law and Practice* 10: 133–74.

Mitchell, Ronald K., Bradley R. Agle and Donna J. Wood. 1997. 'Toward a Theory of Stakeholder Identification and Salience: Defining The Principle of Who and What Really Counts'. *Academy of Management Review* 22, no. 4: 853–86.

Pierre, Jon. 1998. 'Public Consultation and Citizen Participation: Dilemmas of Policy Advice'. In *Taking Stock: Assessing Public Sector Reforms* B. G. Peters and D. J. Savoie (eds). Montreal: McGill-Queen's Press, 137–63.

Salamon, Lester A. 2002. 'Economic Regulation'. In *The Tools of Government: A Guide to the New Governance* L. M. Salamon (ed.) . New York: Oxford University Press, 117–55.

Stutz, Jeffrey R. 2008. 'What Gets Done and Why: Implementing the Recommendations of Public Inquiries'. *Canadian Public Administration* 51, no. 3: 502–21.

Townsend, Ralph E., James McColl and Michael D. Young. 2006. 'Design Principles for Individual Transferable Quotas'. *Marine Policy* 30: 131–41.

Walters, Lawrence C., James Aydelotte and Jessica Miller. 2000. 'Putting More Public in Policy Analysis'. *Public Administration Review* 60, no. 4: 349–59.

West, William. 2005. 'Administrative Rulemaking: An Old and Emerging Literature'. *Public Administration Review* 65, no. 6: 655–68.

Wu, Irene. 2008. 'Who Regulates Phones, Television, and the Internet? What Makes a Communications Regulator Independent and Why It Matters'. *Perspectives on Politics* 6, no. 4: 769–83.

Chapter 7

Financial
implementation tools

Substantive financial instruments

Financial substantive tools are not synonymous with all government spending, since much of this goes to fund direct service delivery and also support regulatory agencies (as well as to provide information, which will be discussed in Chapter 8 below). Rather, such tools are specific techniques of governance involved in transferring treasure resources to or from other actors in order to encourage them to undertake some activity desired by governments through the provision of financial incentives, or to discourage them through the imposition of financial costs.

Like organizational and authoritative tools, there are many different permutations of these instruments and mechanisms. In fact, they can be calibrated down to the decimal point, since they involve the transfer of money, or goods and services with a calculable dollar value, between governments and between governments and non-governmental actors and organizations. And, as such, their exact configuration is virtually infinite in variety. Nevertheless, like organizational and authority-based tools, their basic types are few and categorizable according to what kind of treasure resource they rely upon to extract expected behaviour from targeted organizations, groups and individuals. Transfers can be either in cash or tax-based but also can be made through a wide range of 'cash equivalents', for example procurement, loans guarantees, insurance, or vouchers among others. Both principal types and some of the many alternate means are discussed below.

The use of these treasure resources in policy designs to allow states to obtain their substantive goals is very common and is compatible with several modes of governance, but especially market-based ones. Modern liberal-democratic states spend billions annually on many different programmes involving the use of these tools. However, in some areas, such as industrial activity, some efforts have been made in recent years – through provisions of free trade treaties and the like – to restrict their use. These efforts have been only partially successful, though, often resulting in the transformation of cash-based incentives and disincentives to other forms of financial tools rather than their complete abandonment.

Cash-based financial tools

Grants, subsidies and user fees

Haider defines grants as 'payments in cash or in kind (or charges) to lower units of government, non-profits or profit-seeking companies, NGOs (and individuals) to support public purposes' (Haider 1989: 94). All substantive grants are subsidies or 'unearned savings to offset production costs' and are one of the oldest forms of financial tool through which governments pay companies, organizations or individuals to do (or not to do – like agricultural subsidies for not growing corn or wheat, etc.) some (un)desired form of activity (Lybecker and Freeman 2007). This is the 'carrot' in instrument and imple-mentation models based on the idea of the use of 'carrots and sticks' (regulations or penalties by governments in their efforts to influence non-governmental actors).

User fees are the most straightforward financial disincentive (one of the 'sticks' available to governments) as they, too, simply affect target behaviour by increasing the cost of doing some action. While straightforward in principle, however, in practice their design can be quite complex depending on exactly what it is that governments wish to accomplish through their imposition, for example, revenue generation, goods or service rationing or some combination of the two and how non-governmental actors are likely to react to such charges (Deber et al. 2008).

These kinds of cash-based tools use the direct transfer of treasure resources from governments to some other actor in the form of monetary payments. They vary along several dimensions. They can, to cite only a few examples, be large or small; a single instance or multi-year in nature; tax deductible (which increases their size) or not; used alone or in combination with other instruments (for instance in conjunction with the use of public enterprises in regional development programmes); matched or not by recipients; or linked to some other item (e.g. a per capita grant) (Woodside 1979; Leeuw 1998; Haider 1989). They typically can be very precisely targeted down to the level of the individual and individual firm or plant, and can be very precisely calibrated. They are also quite visible as they appear in public accounts and are considered to be more intrusive than information-based tools, but less so than authority- or organization-based ones. They can also be designed in such a way as to enhance their automaticity, although this is more the case with tax- and royalty-based payments, as discussed below.

Tax- or royalty-based financial instruments

The second main type of substantive treasure-based instrument involves those which are based not on direct cash transfers, but rather on indirect transfers mediated through the tax system, or in some countries, through the use of royalty systems designed to capture natural resource rents. In these systems, a government can forego tax or royalty income they would otherwise have collected from an individual, organization or firm, which serves as an incentive to targets to undertake the activity receiving favourable tax treatment; or, in the case of tools which increase taxes on certain kinds of activity, to not undertake that activity or to undertake less of it.

Tax- and royalty-based expenditures

Tax expenditures or 'tax incentives' come in many kinds. Maslove defines them as 'special provisions in the tax law providing for preferred treatment and consequently resulting in revenue losses (or gains)' (Maslove 1978; Surrey 1979). These can be 'paid in advance' and can be carried forward for numbers of years and, like cash-based schemes, can be 'matched' by other sources of funds, range in size and significance, and can be used in conjunction with other instruments.

Different subtypes exist depending on 'where' government tax revenue is forgone. *Tax incentives* generally involve deductions from corporate or personal income, meaning their actual effect on a target group is determined by the marginal rate of taxation individual persons or firms must pay. Their effect therefore varies from group to group. *Tax credits* on the other hand are direct deductions from taxes owed and therefore their size is the same regardless of the tax rates individual taxpayers face. Tax credits are typically the only ones which can be 'negative', in the sense that they can be used to push a taxpayer's tax load beyond zero so that a refund (or real cash transfer) may ensue. However, most tax expenditures will only push a taxpayer's taxes to zero, meaning their effect also remains conditional on the amount of taxes targets pay.

These same schemes can also be developed with transfers from non-tax-based revenue in mind, such as resource royalty payments or other forms of economic rents. Governments can, for example, promote oil and gas exploration by allowing energy companies to write off some portion of their exploration costs against royalties they would otherwise have to pay.

Excise taxes

Excise taxes are another treasure-based tool, one that acts as a disincentive to individuals, organizations and groups to undertake specific actions and activities. Cnossen (2005: 2) defines these as 'all selective taxes and related levies and charges on goods and services'. They have several general purposes: (1) to raise revenue for general purposes, (2) to offset 'external costs', (3) to discourage consumption, and (4) to pay for public goods (Nowlan 1994).

Raising revenue through taxes is, of course, the oldest technique of government practised, from taxes placed on road use by the Romans to the tea tax US colonists rebelled against at the Boston Tea Party. In this form, excise taxes typically supported legal modes of governance. Using taxes to offset costs of production – to pay for pollution clean-up or health consequences of tobacco use in order to correct production or consumption 'externalities' like pollution or carbon emissions which otherwise would be passed onto the general public – is a much newer form and is more compatible with market governance modes (Mandell 2008; Toke 2008; Pope and Owen 2009). A similar effort involves so-called 'vice taxes' for activities such as gambling, alcohol consumption, lotteries, or, more frequently in recent years, various forms of 'virtuous' 'green' taxes such as those designed to cover the cost of recycling car batteries or used oil or paint, or even returnable bottle deposits, all designed to offset the costs of the activities concerned (Cnossen 2005; Eloi 2009). The use of motor fuel taxes to cover the cost of road construction or mass transit is an example of the fourth of Nowlan's purposes.

Such taxes generally discourage the taxed activity by raising its price. This, of course, can be a mixed blessing for activities such as public transit and can often result in unintended consequences for items taxed in order to raise revenues, both in terms of taxpayer resistance and upset, and in the unintended encouragement of the increased use of non-taxed items or substitute goods and services. They are generally inexpensive to establish, although they require an extensive revenue collection and enforcement presence to avoid evasion, and can be either highly visible, if added onto prices, or almost invisible, if included with posted prices. They can be targeted to specific kinds of goods and services and set up to be highly automated. They are generally considered to be quite intrusive by those paying them, however, which is the main reason they are often excluded from policy designs.

Cash or tax-equivalent financial tools

Both cash and tax or royalty-based transfers provide financial incentives and disincentives to policy actors to undertake or refrain from undertaking specific activities encouraged or discouraged by governments. However, such encouragement and discouragement does not always require a direct or indirect cash transfer. Governments are also able to provide financial incentives through the much less direct use of their spending powers to offset costs or provide additional benefits to policy targets. Several of the more prominent of these tools are discussed below.

Preferential procurement

Preferential procurement involves the use of government purchases to subsidize companies or investors which agree to abide by specific provisions of government contracts. These can extend to preferential treatment for firms which, for example, employ the disabled or women, or ethnic or linguistic minorities, but also often extend to special favourable treatment for small business; national defence contractors; and regional development schemes in which investors receive government contracts if they agree to locate factories or distribution or other services in specially designated regions (Bajari and Tadelis 2001; Rolfstam 2009).

Procurement schemes play a major part in efforts by governments to promote 'third sector' or volunteer and community group-based delivery of public services and are often a part of corporatist governance arrangements. In many cases it may be illegal or unconstitutional for a government to directly deliver funding to such groups, especially since many have a religious or 'faith base' which can violate constitutional limits separating church and state activities (Dollery and Wallis 2003; Black et al. 2004; Kissane 2007; Hula et al. 2007; Zehavi 2008). However, these groups may still be able to receive favourable treatment such as in bidding for government contracts, making procurement an important part of their funding base and of efforts to enhance their policy delivery capacity (Carmel and Harlock 2008; Chapman et al. 2008; Diamond 2008; Hasan and Onyx 2008; Walsh et al. 2008).

Like direct cash subsidies, many trade agreements attempt to ban procurement plans which favour national over international suppliers but these provisions do not extend to favourable treatment for marginalized groups or individuals. Such procurement schemes, of course, by extending favourable treatment to some contractors also act as a disincentive to non-favoured groups and firms which are discouraged from bidding for contracts and other services to the extent of the subsidy provided (McCrudden 2004). The main advantage of such forms of subsidy over other forms of payments is their low visibility profile, which encourages their use.

Favourable insurance and loan guarantees

Insurance or loan guarantees also act as a subsidy to the extent that government backing helps to secure loans thereby raising the reliability of borrowers, altering the types of borrowers who might otherwise not qualify for loans, or reducing interest payments and charges that individuals and companies would otherwise have to pay (Maslove 1983). The difference in cost constitutes a subsidy. Such guarantees are very common in areas such as student loans, for example, in which governments agree to serve as the guarantor of loans to banks which otherwise would reject most students as too risky. They are also common in areas such as export development, whereby a government may provide insurance to a domestic firm to help it offset the risk of undertaking some action in a foreign country, or provide a foreign company or government with assurance that a contract will be fulfilled by the supplying firm. Some loans can also be made directly to individuals and firms on a 'conditionally repayable' basis; that is, whereby a loan turns into a grant if the conditions are successfully met, for example, in making housing payments. These tools are almost invisible, can be precisely targeted and are often considered to be less intrusive than grants and direct cash or tax transfers, making them a popular choice for policy designs in sectors in which governments are pursuing market modes of governance.

Vouchers for public services

Vouchers are 'money replacements' provided by governments to certain groups in order to allow them to purchase specified goods and services in specific amounts. These are typically used when a government does not trust someone to use a cash transfer for its intended purpose, for example with vouchers for food (food stamps), child care or welfare hotel/housing payments. Some governments like Denmark and Sweden, however, also use these to provide some freedom of choice for consumers to select particular kinds of public services (usually education) in order to promote competition within monopoly provision systems or to allow equitable funding arrangements between providers based on specific attributes – such as schools provided by different religious denominations (Le Grand 2007; Andersen 2008; Klitgaard 2008). These can lead to grey markets (when food stamps, for example are sold at a discount to 'undeserving' recipients) and may not improve service delivery if there is little choice provided in the supply of goods and services for which vouchers are issued (Valkama and Bailey 2001). As a result, although often mooted, vouchers appear only rarely in policy designs.

Sales of state assets at below market prices

Governments can also sell off or 'rent out' certain items – from the TV and radio spectrum to old or surplus equipment, buildings and land. If prices are set below market rates then this is a subsidy to investors and businesses, etc. (Sunnevag 2000). Many privatizations of formerly state-owned firms in collapsed socialist countries in the 1990s, for example, involved this kind of sale, including for lucrative mineral and oil and gas rights, which made billions of dollars for the many former officials who were favoured in these deals (Newbery 2003). Given the costs involved, and their generally high profile, however, this tool also does not feature very often in policy designs in countries which are stable and solvent.

Procedural financial instruments

Treasure resources, of course, like organizational and authoritative ones, can also be used to alter the nature of policy processes. Procedural financial tools are generally used to attempt to alter or control aspects of the interest articulation and aggregation systems in contemporary states by creating or encouraging the formation of associations and groups where this activity might not otherwise occur, or, more prosaically, by rewarding government friends and punishing enemies through various kinds of payment schemes or penalties.

Phillip Schmitter, in his comparative studies of European systems, argued that the interest articulation systems in different countries form a spectrum from 'free market', 'competitive' pluralism to 'state-sponsored oligarchic corporatism' (see Figure 7.1).

In Schmitter's (1977; 1985) view pluralism is a system of interest articulation in which interest groups are 'free-forming', have voluntary membership, and are multiple and non-monopolistic/competitive. That is, more than one group can represent individual members. This closely approximates the situation with network and market governance regimes at the sectoral level. Corporatist regimes are the opposite – they require state licencing, have compulsory membership, and are monopolistic.[1] Neo-pluralism is a modern version of pluralism which takes into account some state activity in this area (e.g. the USA, Canada, Great Britain) and can be considered the analogue of legal governance at the sectoral level.[2]

Olson's (1965) view of the 'collective action problems' interest groups face in these different governance contexts is an important insight helpful to understanding the rationales for the government use of procedural financial instrument in these situations. Olson argued that in any political system, some individuals have fewer incentives and more disincentives to form and join interest groups than others – for example, someone benefiting from some proposed government action might have a stronger motivation to lobby for it, than would someone who stood neither to gain nor suffer from it. As a result, in a 'free association' system, there would be a tendency for specific affected interests –

Pluralism............. Neo-pluralism............. Societal corp . ... State corp.

(freely associational).............>>>........................(State sanctioned)

Figure 7.1 Spectrum of interest articulation systems
Source: Schmitter, P. C. 1977. 'Modes of Interest Intermediation and Models of Societal Change in Western Europe'. *Comparative Political Studies* 10, no. 1: 7–38.

for example, businesses negatively affected by regulation – to form groups and pressure governments, while other more general interests – for example, to retain tough environmental standards on industry – would be poorly represented. Due to this unequal distribution of the costs and benefits of political action, in many issue areas, Olson argued, in pluralist systems 'general interest' groups were unlikely to form, or if they did would be quickly captured by 'special interests' who had more to gain from their existence and activities (Strolovitch 2006).[3]

Governments, however, can play a major, though little studied, role in affecting this general pattern of interest group behaviour by either encouraging or discouraging interest group formation and activity. These activities are little known, but quite common in many countries. Governments can do this, for example, by creating (or not) systems of associational rights which allow groups to form, using their actions and resources to publicize events and issues, and providing funds for the creation and maintenance of groups. Procedural financial tools are key ones used to affect these kinds of interest group system behaviour.

These tools generally fall into two types, those which are used to create or help support the formation of interest groups and those which help to activate or mobilize them. The latter can be thought as 'network creation tools' while the latter can be considered as 'network mobilization tools'.

Policy network creation tools

Although their activities in this domain are often hidden from view, governments practising network and corporatist governance modes are very often actively involved in the creation and organization of policy networks and many key policy actors. An important activity in this regard is the use of government financial resources to create either the organizations themselves which go into the establishment of a policy network – research institutes, think tanks, government departments and the like – or to facilitate the interaction of already existing but separate units into a more coherent network structure (Hudson et al. 2007).

Funding is very often provided to think tanks and other policy research units and brokers by governments, either in the form of direct funding or as contracts (Rich 2004; Abelson 2007). More controversial, however, and at the same time not very well understood, is the role governments play in funding interest groups (Anheier et al. 1997).

Interest group creation

Provision of seed money is a key factor in interest group creation (Nownes 2004). King and Walker (1991), for example, found that the percentage of groups that received aid from outside groups in startups in the United States was 34 per cent for profit sector groups, non-profit 60 per cent, and citizens'

Table 7.1 Average percentage of "Seed Money" obtained by groups from each source by group type

| Source | Type of group% | | | | |
	Patronage	Societal disturbbance	Personal disturbance	Splinter	Genenric entrepreneurial
Foundations	38	38	0	23	19
The Government	0	0	0	0	0
Corporations	0	1	17	3	2
Other					
Associations	32	11	3	0	2
Individuals	19	18	3	28	29
Personal Funds	0	31	60	43	43
Other**	11	1	17	3	5
Total	100	100	100	100	100
n	10	12	6	16	16

Note: ** Includes loans, merchandise sales, fees for service, and special events.

Source: Nownes, A., and G. Neeley. "Toward an Explanation for Public Interest Group Formation and Proliferation: "Seed Money", Disturbances, Entrepreneurship, and Patronage." Policy Studies Journal 24, No. 1 (1996): 74–92.

groups 89 per cent. Nownes and Neeley (1996) surveyed 121 national pubic interest groups in the USA in the mid-1990s and uncovered the a pattern of extensive foundation support in terms of how their origin was financed (Table 7.1). While this survey revealed no direct government involvement, it did show that Foundations provided a large percentage of the funding for pressure group creation, and since these operate under special tax treatment in the USA, this gives the US federal government a substantial indirect role in interest group creation in that country (Lowry 1999; Carmichael 2008).

In other countries however, a much more direct role is played by governments, sometimes also with a substantial indirect role through foundations, but sometimes not. In Canada, for example, Pal (1993) noted that many of the prominent national interest groups in specific sectors, such as the Canadian Day Care Advocacy Association, the Canadian Congress for Learning Opportunities among Women, the Canadian Ethnocultural Council and others had emerged from conferences and workshops organized by federal government departments in the 1980s and 1990s (see also Finkle et al. 1994). Similar results can be found in many other jurisdictions. This activity is generally low profile and inexpensive, but can be considered intrusive and is not all that easily targeted, making it a less popular instrument in policy designs than network mobilization (see below). However, where interest groups do not exist, governments may have little choice but to facilitate their creation if they wish to practise a network or corporatist form of governance.

Network mobilization tools

A second key type of activity undertaken by governments through the use of procedural financial policy tools relates less to the creation of new groups and networks than to the reorientation of older, already existing ones. Again, in the case of think tanks and other such actors, this can be accomplished through various forms of government contracting and procurement, notably consulting (Speers 2007). A significant target for this kind of funding, however, is interest groups.

Interest group alteration/manipulation/co-optation

Cash funds or the tax system are used in many countries to alter interest group behaviour. The aim may be simply to neutralize or co-opt a vocal opponent of government (Kash 2008), but can also be a more broad-based effort to 'even out the playing field' for groups which lack the kinds of resources available to other groups (such as business) to mobilize and pressure governments to adopt policies of which they approve (Furlong and Kerwin 2004; Boehmke 2005).[4] Governments often use this tool to counterbalance, for example, lobbying on the part of business interests.

Lowry (1999) found that two main types of foundations exist in the USA – company sponsored and independent – and both take active roles not only in interest group creation (discussed above) but also in funding interest group activities. In the United States in 1992 for example, he uncovered 463 grants made by 37 company foundations and 125 independent foundations just to environmental groups, $32.6 million from independent foundations versus only $1.5 million from company-sponsored foundations. Again, given the favourable tax treatment foundations enjoy in the USA, this gives the US government a substantial indirect role in interest group activity as well as their creation.

In other countries, as with interest group creation, foundations are less important and governments also provide 'sustaining' funding after groups are created. Stanbury, for example, examined the Canadian federal public accounts for 1986–87 and found 17 federal departments gave $185 million to over 500 groups (excluding non-policy groups like those providing shelters for battered women).[5] One hundred and sixty of these groups were defined only as 'public interest groups' (or classical pressure groups) and received $24 million from federal departments alone that year. Burt (1990) similarly surveyed the sources of funding received by 144 women's groups (24 per cent of the estimated 686 such groups in Canada at the time) in the early 1980s and found the government was the single largest donor by far for most types of groups, far outstripping membership dues (see Table 7.2).

In Europe Mahoney and Beckstrand (2009) identified 1,164 civil society groups that received funding from the European Commission in 2003–7. They shared in 120 million euros of funding at the EU level and another 75 million

Table 7.2 Source of funding for women's groups (Canada)

Most important source of funds	Type of group, %			
	Traditional	Status of women	Service	Shelter
Government	33	40	38	52
Dues	8	20	9	0
Fund-raising	17	7	2	11
Other n/a	42	33	51	37
	100	100	100	100

Source: Burt, Sandra. 1990. 'Canadian Women's Groups in the 1980s: Organizational Development and Policy Influence'. *Canadian Public Policy* 16, no. 1: 17–28.

in international, national and sub-national-level funding. These were primarily groups operating at the EU level in areas such as youth, sports, education and cultural activities in support of the EC mandate to develop a supra-national EU civil society.

This funding is almost invisible, can be precisely targeted, and although often considered intrusive in legal and market governance modes, is quite compatible with network and corporatist activities. As a result it is a growing area and a prominent feature of many contemporary policy designs.

Conclusion

The use of financial resources is one of the oldest forms of government activity and instrument use. The use of substantive financial instruments is quite common in designs and in terms of size and impact, it is as significant as direct government service delivery or regulation.

The use of this resource, as Hood (1983; 1986) noted, is sometimes restricted by a lack of treasure resources, either because a country is poor and simply cannot generate revenue or, as has happened in jurisdictions like California, for example, because of various measures which prevent or limit government access to substantial taxpayer wealth. However, notwithstanding these limitations, in general all governments spend considerable sums encouraging certain activities and discouraging others through the use of various kinds of fiscal and monetary tools and techniques. An important trend in this area, noted by Howard (1993; 1995; 1997), is towards the increased use of tax-based incentives rather than subsidies. This is due to a number of reasons but often reflects concerns with visibility and automaticity.

As for procedural financial tool uses, as mentioned above, the use of these techniques in sectors employing corporatist and network modes of governance is also increasing at a substantial rate, although the exact mechanisms used vary from country to country, such as the use of indirect foundations in the USA, compared to more direct government allocations in many other jurisdictions.

Readings

Beam, David A. and Timothy J. Conlan. 2002. 'Grants'. In *The Tools of Government: A Guide to the New Governance* L. M. Salamon (ed.). New York: Oxford University Press, 340–80.

Cairns, Ben, Margaret Harris and Patricia Young. 2005. 'Building the Capacity of the Voluntary Nonprofit Sector: Challenges of Theory and Practice'. *International Journal of Public Administration* 28: 869–85.

Cnossen, Sijbren. 2005. 'Economics and Politics of Excise Taxation'. In *Theory and Practice of Excise Taxation: Smoking, Drinking, Gambling, Polluting and Driving*. S. Cnossen (ed.) Oxford: Oxford University Press, 1–19.

Cordes, Joseph J. 2002. 'Corrective Taxes, Charges and Tradable Permits'. In *The Tools of Government: A Guide to the New Governance* L. M. Salamon (ed.) New York: Oxford University Press, 255–81.

Deber, Raisa, Marcus J. Hollander and Philip Jacobs. 2008. 'Models of Funding and Reimbursement in Health Care: A Conceptual Framework'. *Canadian Public Administration* 51, no. 3: 381–405.

Howard, Christopher. 2002. 'Tax Expenditures'. In *The Tools of Government: A Guide to the New Governance* L. M. Salamon (ed.). New York: Oxford University Press, 410–44.

Juillet, Luc, Caroline Andrew, Tim Aubry and Janet Mrenica. 2001. 'The Impact of Changes in the Funding Environment on Nonprofit Organizations'. In *The Nonprofit Sector and Government in a New Century* K. L. Brock and K. G. Banting (eds). Montreal: McGill-Queens University Press, 21–62.

Kelman, Steven J. 2002. 'Contracting'. In *The Tools of Government: A Guide to the New Governance* L. M. Salamon (ed.). New York: Oxford University Press, 282–318.

Klitgaard, Michael Baggesen. 2008. 'School Vouchers and the New Politics of the Welfare State'. *Governance* 21, no. 4: 479–98.

Leeuw, Frans L. 1998. 'The Carrot: Subsidies as a Tool of Government' In *Carrots, Sticks and Sermons: Policy Instruments and Their Evaluation* Marie-Louise Bemelmans-Videc, Ray C. Rist and Evert Vedung (eds). New Brunswick, NJ: Transaction Publishers, 77–102.

Maddison, Sarah. 2005. 'Democratic Constraint and Embrace: Implications for Progressive Non-Government Advocacy Organisations in Australia'. *Australian Journal of Political Science* 40, no. 3: 373–89.

Nownes, Anthony and Grant Neeley. 1996. 'Toward an Explanation for Public Interest Group Formation and Proliferation: "Seed Money", Disturbances, Entrepreneurship, and Patronage'. *Policy Studies Journal* 24, no. 1: 74–92.

Pal, Leslie A. 1993. *Interests of State: The Politics of Language, Multiculturalism, and Feminism in Canada*. Kingston: McGill-Queen's University Press.

Phillips, S. D. 1991. 'How Ottawa Blends: Shifting Government Relationships with Interest Groups'. In *How Ottawa Spends 1991–92: The Politics of Fragmentation*, F. Abele (ed.). Ottawa: Carleton University Press, 183–228.

Sharpe, David. 2001. 'The Canadian Charitable Sector: An Overview'. In *Between State and Market: Essays on Charities Law and Policy in Canada* J. Phillips, B. Chapman and D. Stevens (eds). Toronto: University of Toronto Press,.

Stanton, Thomas H. 2002. 'Loans and Loan Guarantees'. In *The Tools of Government: A Guide to the New Governance* L. M. Salamon (ed.). New York: Oxford University Press, 381–409.

Young, Lisa and Joanna Everitt. 2004. *Advocacy Groups*. Vancouver: UBC Press, 67–86.

Chapter 8

Information-based implementation tools

Information-based tools are those based on the last of the four categories of resources set out by Hood (1986): 'nodality' or 'centrality' or, as we have defined it, communicating 'knowledge' or 'information' to target groups. These are the 'sermon' in the 'carrots, sticks and sermons' formulation of policy instruments.

Exactly what is meant by the term 'information' or 'communication', varies from author to author, ranging from its association with all forms of political activity (Deutsch 1963; Bang 2003) to a very specific focus on one type of action, like political advertising (Firestone 1970; Young 2007). These different foci make classifying and analyzing the wide range of activities and tasks more difficult than it should be (Ledingham 2003).

As Evert Vedung defines them, information-based policy tools are efforts to use the knowledge and data available to governments to influence consumer and producer behaviour in a direction consistent with government aims and wishes and/or gather information in order to further their aims and ambitions' (Vedung and van der Doelen 1998). This definition, however, while useful, is limited in that it conceals or elides the two different general purposes to which these tools can be put to use (Howlett et al. 2010). These are the familiar procedural versus substantive distinction used throughout this book – whether these activities are intended to serve as devices primarily oriented towards the manipulation of policy actors and policy processes (Edelman 1988; Saward 1992; Mikenberg 2001; Sulitzeanu-Kenan 2007) or social and economic ones involved in the production of goods and services (Hornik 1989; Salmon 1989a; 1989b; Jahn et al. 2005; Howlett 2009). Disentangling the two is necessary for a clear analysis of the role each plays in policy designs.

It is also important to note that many new communication practices have emerged in recent years, at least in part due to the development of new information technologies, notably computerization and the internet (Feldman and Khademian 2007) which have broadened the range and menu of government nodality tools. These include the development and use of instruments which promote citizen empowerment such as freedom of information (FOI) legislation, the use of public performance measures, various forms of e-government and the increased use of government surveys and advertising among others (Hood and Margetts 2007). Some of these tools – like FOI legislation – are compatible with legal forms of governance, while others – like the increased use of government advertising campaigns – are more compatible with market-based modes.

Substantive informational instruments

Following Vedung's lead we can define substantive government communication policy instruments as those policy techniques or mechanisms which rely on the use of information to directly or indirectly affect the behaviour of those involved in the production, consumption and distribution of different kinds of goods and services in society.

The most high profile and thus most commonly observed and chronicled type of substantive tool is the instrument focused on the effort to alter consumer behaviour: the *government information campaign*. This includes various campaigns waged by governments to encourage citizens to, for example, eat well, engage in fewer vices and otherwise behave responsibly which are common especially in market modes of governance. However, communication activities aimed at altering producer behaviour through provision of product and process information to customers (*labelling and product information*) are also very prominent in legal and other modes. As Hood (1986) noted, these kinds of tools can be targeted at different levels of society – individuals, groups and populations as a whole and according to whether they are intended to collect or disseminate information.

Information dissemination tools

Adler and Pittle defined 'persuasion instruments' as those 'persuasion schemes [which] convey messages which may or may not contain factual information which overtly seek to motivate target audiences to modify their behaviour' (Adler and Pittle 1984: 160). These tools are used often, as they are fairly inexpensive. However, they remain controversial as the line between communications and intrusive propaganda is one which is easily blurred (Gelders and Ihlen 2009 and 2010).

Exhortation and moral suasion

The most prominent type of substantive information tool designed to persuade is the appeal from political leaders to various social actors, urging them to follow a government's lead in some area of social or economic life. Stanbury and Fulton (1984) provide a list of 'exhortation' and 'moral suasion' activities which include 'pure political leadership such as appeals for calm, better behaviour, high principles and whereby voluntary action is urged under threat of coercion if refused' (304).

Such forms of moral suasion are usually aimed at individual producers or sectors and are typically used within the context of an already existing regulatory regime. That is, governments can regulate in the event of failure without necessarily creating new legal instruments. Many countries, for example, administer important aspects of their financial systems in this fashion, asking banks, taxpayers and other financial institutions to act in a certain way (e.g. keep interest rates low, or allow certain groups to borrow funds) with the implicit or explicit threat of direct government regulation if such requests are ignored or go unfulfilled (Bardach 1989). Government requests are often very focused and can be quite secretive (for example, in the immediate aftermath of the 9/11 airline hijackings when the US government urged credit card companies to provide records of suspicious activities by suspected hijackers).

Information campaigns

Mass media and targeted information campaigns, on the other hand, are much more visible, by definition, and tend to be aimed less at producers than at consumers. Adler and Pittle (1984) describe these tools as 'notification instruments' which:

> Convey factual information to the intelligent target. Implicit in the notification approach is the belief that the target, once apprised of the facts, will make the appropriate decision.

Some notification tools do attempt to be purely factual, ongoing and passive in nature, such as nutritional labelling on foodstuffs or health warnings on cigarettes (Padberg 1992; Baksi and Bose 2007). They are usually enacted in regulations (i.e. disclosure is mandatory) and are aimed at providing information to consumers allowing them to make better decisions, or overcome information asymmetries between producers and consumers, with the expectation that they will change their behaviour in some way consistent with government goals – for example, reducing smoking or eating nutritional foods (Jahn et al. 2005). Although the evidence of the effectiveness of such campaigns is mixed (Mann and Wustemann 2009; Barreiro-Hurlé et al 2010), this has not dampened their growth.

Other information campaigns are more active and less factual, but have the same intent; that is, providing social actors with more information about aspects of their behaviour and its advantageous or deleterious quality, urging enhancement of the former and a diminishment of the latter. The information often transmitted through such information instruments is not always so factual, however, but can be used to 'sell' a government's policies in the same way that other products are marketed. Such campaigns are often conducted at the mass level and use a variety of mass-media delivery mechanisms (commercials, broadcasts, newspaper advertisements and the like). High profile campaigns in many countries to prevent drinking and driving or encourage the purchase of war bonds during wartime are good examples of the use of this kind of instrument.

This kind of mass campaign began with the emergence of mass media and is now common in most countries. Many national governments are now the largest purchasers of advertising in their countries and far outstrip national brands well known for their advertising overkill, such as alcoholic beverage and soft drink companies, as well as fast food chains.[1]

Although they can be costly, such campaigns are generally less expensive than many other alternatives, although the costs of non-compliance must also be taken into account (Pellikaan and van der Veen 2002). Generally governments will tend to include information tools and government communications in policy designs only when:

1   100 per cent compliance is not required for a policy to be effective;
2   government and public interests coincide (e.g. on health awareness) so that government appeals are likely to be favourably received; and
3   only in relatively short-term crisis situations when other tools may require too much lead time to be effective; where
4   it is otherwise difficult to impose sanctions and where
5   the issue in question is not very complex (technological or legal) in nature but can be reduced to the level of advertising slogans.

(See Rose 1993; Romans 1966; Vedung and van der Doelen 1998.)

Information and knowledge collection tools

Information collection is the key to many and better policies (Nutley et al. 2007) and, as Hood (1986) pointed out, many implementation instruments exist to collect information and can contribute to enhanced 'evidence-based' policy-making. This extends to the use of licensing provisions in which information may be collected before or after a licence is granted, but can also involve the use of research and generation of new policy-relevant knowledge.

Judicial inquiries and executive commissions

One fairly common and high-profile means by which governments collect information is the judicial inquiry or executive commission. These exist on a spectrum depending on their relationship to government agencies and according to their functions. Some inquiries and task forces are largely internal to government and intended to mobilize network actors. These have been discussed in Chapter 5 above in the context of procedural organizational tools. Other kinds of commissions, however, are designed primarily to collect information (Sulzeabu-Kenan 2010; Rowe and McAllister 2006). Many judicial inquiries fall into this category and have a great deal of autonomy from governments. They are a common feature of legal modes of governance. Presidential and royal commissions are independent and autonomous but still depend on government for budgets and resources. All of these devices can be used to summarize existing knowledge or generate new data on a subject (Chapman 1973; Bulmer 1981; Sheriff 1983; Clark and Majone 1985; d'Ombrain 1997; Elliott and McGuinness 2001; Montpetit 2003; 2008; Salter 2003; Prasser 2006).

National statistical agencies

Another such tool is the use of statistical agencies which are specifically tasked with collecting data on a wide variety of social activities of individuals, groups and firms. These typically operate using internationally recognized standards for classifying these activities and may rely more or less heavily on voluntary disclosure of information. These agencies, or those like them, may conduct surveys on specialized topics and/or periodic censuses of national or sub-national populations.

This information is often used to determine such factors as the level of per capita grants transferred between governments, or the number and types of hospitals and medical facilities which should be built and where these, and other public institutions like schools and offices, should be located. They are expensive to establish and maintain but once in operation can be used to collect information on many subjects at relatively low cost.

Surveys and polling

In many countries governments are now the largest purchasers of surveys (Hastak et al. 2001) and many government agencies now undertake surveys on a regular basis, both as environmental scans in order to try to anticipate issues, but also in order to determine public opinion on agency performance (Rothmayr and Hardmeier 2002; Page 2006).

Procedural informational instruments

In order to pursue their preferred policy initiatives, governments often use procedural tools based on government information resources in order to attempt to alter the behaviour of policy network members involved in policy-making processes (Burris et al. 2005), just as they attemp to alter consumer and producer behaviour through the employment of substantive information-based tools.

Information-based procedural policy tools are those designed to affect policy processes in a way consistent with government aims and ambitions through the control and selective provision of information. As Hood suggested, these are 'nodality' instruments because the information exchanged is valuable largely as a function of the government's position as a key nodal link in a policy network. Some of these efforts are aimed at promoting information release while others are aimed at preventing it.

Both European and American studies have found that governments have increasingly employed a variety of procedural information-based instruments to indirectly affect the outcomes of the policy process in a way that is consistent with their aims and objectives (Kohler-Koch 1996; Johansson and Borell 1999; Hall and O'Toole 2000). The most commonly observed and chronicled category of procedural tool is the type which focuses on the use of *general information prevention or disclosure laws and other tools* – such as access to information laws – in order to provide policy network actors with the knowledge required to effectively filter and focus their demands on government for new policy measures or reforms to older ones. However, governments are also very much involved in the use of communications on government websites and through other means (Gandy 1982; Hood and Margetts 2007) to provide additional information to policy network members in specific sectoral or issue areas.

Information release tools

Stanbury and Fulton (1984) describe two common types of procedural information release or disclosure tools: *information disclosure* (through freedom of information and privacy laws) and *consultation/co-optation tools*, like public hearings; the discreet use of confidential information such as planned leaks to the press; or planned public disclosure of government intentions.

Freedom of information legislation

These provisions allow access to an individual's own records and those of others – with numerous exemptions – many benign (to protect other individuals from unnecessary disclosure) and allowing access to documents and records of others – with numerous exemptions – again many benign and intended to protect individuals from unnecessary disclosure. These legislative arrangements were a feature of the centuries-old Scandinavian ombudsman system of administrative control and were introduced in many other countries in the 1970s and 1980s (Relyea 1977; Bennett 1988; 1990; 1991; 1992; Bennett and Raab 2003; Bennett and Bayley 1999; Howe and Johnson 2000). These are sometimes accompanied by 'whistleblower' acts; that is, bills intended to protect people who speak out about problems in the government's bureaucracy. Through such legislation, bureaucrats are often offered legal protection against reprisals for reporting government wrongdoing. Both represent popular forms of procedural information tool design.

Information release prevention tools

There is also a wide range of such tools designed to protect certain kinds of information on government activities or in government files. These include protecting not only information collected by governments but that which comes into their possession (for example from a foreign government or via documents filed in court cases, and the like). These range from wartime (and peacetime, for example a film review board) censorship and bans on political parties and speech such as hate crimes legislation, to official secrets acts with various levels of confidentiality and penalties imposed for publicizing or releasing government secrets.

Censorship

This has occurred in many countries during wartime but also in peacetime, for example as media, film or theatre censorship. This latter use has been slowly whittled away in most advanced countries as individual rights in democratic states have been ruled to trump government or collective ones but wartime prohibitions remain very common (Qualter 1985).

Official secrets acts

Official secrets acts are a replacement for censorship in many areas. They are often the most important statute relating to national security in many countries and are designed to prohibit and control access to and the disclosure of sensitive government information (Pasquier and Villeneuve 2007). Offences tend to cover espionage and leakage of government information. The term 'official secret' varies dramatically in meaning from country to country but broadly, allows governments to classify documents and prohibit release of different categories for sometimes very long periods of time (e.g. 50–75 years). All countries have some form of official secrecy although the legislative and executive basis for such laws varies quite dramatically between countries.

Privacy acts

These exist in many jurisdictions as a counterpoint to access to information laws in which types of personally-specific information is excluded from such acts. Some jurisdictions have specific legislation devoted to this subject, usually with a focus on protecting personal information in areas such as health, financial or tax matters, and with respect to criminal proceedings.

These instruments are also quite varied but in general it is fair to say that restricting information is low cost to initiate but high cost to monitor and maintain, while the reverse is true of information disclosure. In terms of targeting it is true of both sets of instruments that it is very difficult to target either secrecy or disclosure on specific groups. As a result, these actions are typically more difficult to set up and take more time and effort than is often thought to be the case, making them an infrequent component of many policy designs.

Conclusion

As has been set out above, there are many different kinds of government communication and information activities, and in the past the lack of an effective taxonomy or framework for their analysis has made generalizing about their impact and patterns of use quite difficult. Describing information-based policy tools in the terms set out above helps to highlight the similarities and differences between different instruments and helps develop a relatively parsimonious taxonomy of their major types which can facilitate national and cross-national studies of their use and impact.

Information dissemination activities remain relatively low cost in terms of financial and personnel outlays, but compliance is a major issue and, as in all advertising activities, evaluating the impact of these campaigns is very uncertain (Salmon 1989a; 1989b). Adler and Pittle (1984: 161), for example, found 'many of these programs require more careful planning, larger expenditures and longer implementation periods than they usually receive'.

The assumption that greater knowledge always equals greater compliance with government aims, for example, is not always the case. Alcoholism and drug abuse, for example, are complex problems that are not 'rational' in the sense that individuals continue to consume or engage in them while knowing their destructive attributes (so-called 'demerit goods') (see Walsh 1988; Weiss and Tschirhart 1994) and greater knowledge may not affect or alter behaviour in such cases.

Thus while it may be the dream of many governments that simply monitoring and communicating with people will accomplish all of their ends, this is not usually the case. The benefits to government in using such tools may thus be much lower than anticipated if such a high visibility instrument is perceived to have failed and the blame for a continuing policy problem is focused squarely on governments (Hood 2007). Such considerations are a prominent feature in the design of policy alternatives envisioning the use of such tools.

Readings

Adcroft, Andy and Robert Willis. 2005. 'The (Un)Intended Outcome of Public Sector Performance Measurement'. *International Journal of Public Sector Management* 18, no. 5: 386–400.

Bardach, Eugene and Robert A. Kagan. 1982. ' Mandatory Disclosure'. In *Going by the Book: The Problem of Regulatory Unreasonableness* E. Bardach and R. A. Kagan (eds), Philadelphia: Temple University Press, 242–70.

Bennett, Colin and Robin Bayley. 1999. 'The New Public Administration: Canadian Approaches to Access and Privacy'. In *Public Administration and Policy: Governing in Challenging Times* M. W. Westmacott and H. P. Mellon (eds). Scarborough: Prentice Hall/Allyn and Bacon, 189–201.

Bougherara, Douadia, Gilles Grolleau and Naoufel Mzoughi. 2007. 'Is More Information Always Better? An Analysis Applied to Information-Based Policies for Environmental Protection'. *International Journal of Sustainable Development* 10, no. 3: 197–213.

Bulmer, Martin. 1981. 'Applied Social Research? The Use and Non-Use of Empirical Social Inquiry by British and American Governmental Commissions'. *Journal of Public Policy* 1: 353–80.

Cairns, Alan C. 1990. 'Reflections on Commission Research'. In *Commissions of Inquiry* A. P. Pross, I. Christie and J. A. Yogis (eds). Toronto: Carswell, 87–110.

Chapman, Richard A. 1973. 'Commissions in Policy-Making'. In *The Role of Commissions in Policy-Making* R. A. Chapman (ed.). London: George Allen and Unwin, 174–88.

Howells, Geraint. 2005. 'The Potential and Limits of Consumer Empowerment by Information'. *Journal of Law and Society* 32, no. 3: 349–70.

Jahn, Gabriele, Matthias Schramm and Achim Spiller. 2005. 'The Reliability of Certification: Quality Labels as a Consumer Policy Tool'. *Journal of Consumer Policy* 28: 53–73.

Papaioannou, G., H. Rush and J. Bassant. 2006. 'Performance Management: Benchmarking as a Policy-Making Tool: From the Private to the Public Sector'. *Science and Public Policy* 33, no. 2: 91–102.

Salmon, Charles. 1989. ' Campaigns for Social Improvement: An Overview of Values, Rationales, and Impacts'. In *Information Campaigns: Managing the Process of Social Change* C. Salmon (ed.). Newbury Park, CA: Sage, 1–32.

Sheriff, Peta E. 1983. 'State Theory, Social Science, and Governmental Commissions'. *American Behavioural Scientist* 26, no. 5: 669–80.

Vedung, Evert and Frans C. J. van der Doelen. 1998. 'The Sermon: Information Programs in the Public Policy Process – Choice, Effects and Evaluation'. In *Carrots, Sticks and Sermons: Policy Instruments and Their Evaluation* Marie-Louise Bemelmans-Videc, Ray C. Rist and Evert Vedung (eds). New Brunswick, NJ: Transaction Publishers, 103–28.

Weiss, Janet A. 2002. 'Public Information'. In *The Tools of Government: A Guide to the New Governance* L. M. Salamon (ed.) New York: Oxford University Press, 217–54.

Part IV

POLICY DESIGNS AND GOVERNANCE MODES REVISITED

Chapter 9

Understanding contemporary policy designs

As we saw in Chapter 1, in coming to terms with the challenges of globalization and the increasing networkization of society many scholars have argued that governments have developed a renewed interest in a particular set of policy tools appropriate to market or network modes of governance. Because of this purported shift in governance contexts – the presence of more flexible economic and political circumstances than have existed in the past (Lenihan and Alcock 2000) – contemporary policy designs in many advanced countries, it has been argued, have changed. Specifically, unlike in past epochs, they are argued to have become more indirect and subtle, and often much less visible than was previously the case (Rhodes 1997).

As discussed in Chapter 1, it has been argued in many circles that in response to the increased complexity of society and the international environment, governments in many countries in Western Europe, in particular, have turned away from the use of a relatively limited number of traditional, more or less command-and-control oriented, 'substantive' policy tools such as public enterprises, regulatory agencies, subsidies and exhortation, and begun to increasingly use their organizational resources to support a different set of 'procedural' tools (Klijn and Teisman 1991; Peters 1998) such as government reorganizations, reviews and inquiries, government–NGO partnerships and stakeholder consultations. These all act to guide or steer policy processes in the direction government wishes through the manipulation of policy actors and their interrelationships, and constitute a 'new governance' system (Bingham et al. 2005).

These processes and theories continue to challenge public administrators, managers and scholars (Peters 1996; Peters and Pierre 1998; Knill 1999) but have generally been found to have less grounding in actual patterns of tool use and the evolution of policy designs than their proponents allege. As the discussion in Chapters 5–8 has shown, even if some sectors have been moving in the direction of network governance, the relationship existing between governance modes and policy tool categories is far from one-to-one and, moreover, other trends exist in other sectors featuring other kinds of governance activities and preferences. And, as the discussion in Chapters 2–4 revealed, the reasons why particular instruments are selected extend beyond macro-factors such as globalization to others associated with expert discourse and historical experience in the process of policy formulation.

Students of public policy-making in many countries have thus begun to move beyond simple macro-level models and theories of policy design and have developed a renewed interest in the meso- and micro-aspects of policy formulation and the investigation of the ways in which governments actually propose and utilize the multiple different types of policy instruments available to them (Goggin et al. 1990; Dunsire 1993). Properly assessing, inventorying, categorizing and modelling procedural policy instrument use and choice has thus become a prerequisite to understanding the evolution of policy designs. And this is just as true for practitioners as it is for theorists and academics. As Evert Lindquist (1992) argued close to two decades ago, in the modern era officials need:

> new analytical tools that will help them to diagnose and map the external environments of public agencies, to recognize the inherent tensions and dynamics in these environments as they pertain to policy development and consensus-building, and to develop new strategies for 'working' these environments in the interests both of their political masters and those of the broader communities they serve. . . . If public servants are to learn from the experience of colleagues working in other sectors and levels of government, they will need a vocabulary to facilitate the dialogue.
>
> (128–29)

Modes of governance and implementation tool propensities

Summarizing the discussion in Chapters 4–8, Table 9.1 shows how each mode of governance comprises an ideal-typical mix of possible tool preferences whose use and interactions are more or less coherent and compatible. Legal governance, for example, is correlated closely with a preference for the use of direct government, laws and direct regulation, the use of excise taxes and insurance and, often, censorship and privacy laws; corporatist governance is correlated with a preference for the use of state-owned enterprises, independent and other forms of delegated regulation, the use of subsidies and grants, interest group mobilization and information campaigns; market governance is correlated with a preference for contracting out, voluntary regulation and deregulation, tax incentives, and data collection; and network governance with the use of clientele agencies, consultation mechanisms, interest group creation and access to information.

Experts in government see the links between these policy components in terms of their inter-compatibility and inner coherence and use their positions in policy advisory networks to develop policy alternatives which combine these

Table 9.1 Propensity for tool use by governance mode and resource category

| | | Governance mode | | |
		Legal	Corporatist	Market	Network
	Organization	Direct government Administrative tribunals	State-owned enterprises	Privatization Contracting out Special operating agencies Private–public partnerships	Clientele agencies Task forces Public hearings
NATO resource category	Authority	Laws Direct regulation Administrative procedures	Independent regulatory commissions Delegated regulation Advisory councils	Deregulation Voluntary and self-regulation	Stakeholder conferences
	Treasure	Excise taxes Insurance	Subsidies, grants, interest group mobilization	Tax incentives Procurement, vouchers Exhortation and suasion	Interest group creation
	Informational	Product information campaigns Censorship Official secrets	Government information campaigns Surveys	Statistics and data collection	Freedom of information

elements in more or less consistent ways, choosing particular tools based on factors such as political, social and economic feasibility, government capacity and target group structure, and calibrating specific tool components taking into account factors such as automaticity, cost, intrusiveness, visibility and precision of targeting. These factors and calculations change over time as the context of policy-making changes and shifts in governance modes and policy regime logics do occur, as globalization and network theorists rightly noted, leading to changes in overall policy design preferences.

However, these changes occur at different times and with different impacts in each policy sector and it is a mistake to think that a general macro-level societal movement such as networkization will manifest itself equally in all areas of state activity. This can be seen from even a rudimentary examination of the globalization and network literature which, in fact, argue equally vehemently that such shifts are occurring, but in two different directions: towards either the general adoption of market governance, or network governance, respectively.

In fact, as the discussion in the previous chapters has indicated, within the context of these general trends several distinct meso-level trends can be observed in the use of particular types of governing tools in contemporary public policy designs within already existing sectoral governance modes. Some of the more evident of these latter trends are set out in more detail below.

Patterns and trends in contemporary implementation tool use

Patterns of organizational tool use: direct and indirect instrument designs

Despite some moves towards the increased use of procedural tools more compatible with network modes of governance – like public hearings, task forces and the establishment of clientele agencies – most policy sectors in most governments remain firmly based in legal or corporatist modes of governance established decades ago and featuring a prominent role for direct government goods and service delivery: what Chapter 5 described as the 'forgotten fundamental' of policy instruments and policy designs (Leman 1989; Majone 1997). In recent years, direct forms of government goods and service delivery have continued to grow in most sectors, although the attention paid to this continued growth has often been overshadowed in the academic literature by that paid to continued, but much smaller scale experimentation with alternate forms of indirect government organization (Aucoin 1997). However, the pattern of change in the use of this dominant policy tool has been very uneven as governments have expanded in spurts and starts punctuated by major crises, especially in times of war or financial crises and their aftermath when more corporatist modes of governance have often flourished (Bird 1970; Hodgetts 1973).

Public enterprises, for example, grew dramatically in many countries, both in the developed world in association with war efforts and in developing countries as a function of decolonization and drives towards economic development. The spread of privatization in almost every country over the last three decades reflected a rapid and fundamental change in expert attitudes towards the use of this instrument, as governments tried to move many sectors away from corporatist modes of governance under the pressure of cost and other constraints (Le Grand 1984; Walker 1984; Savas 1987; Veljanovski 1988; Kamerman and Kahn 1989; MacAvoy et al. 1989; Salamon 1989; Starr 1989; 1990a; Ikenberry 1990; Richardson 1990; 1990b; Suleiman and Waterbury 1990; Kemp 1991; Marsh 1991).

The term 'privatization', however, carries at least two different, albeit related, meanings (Starr 1989; 1990a; 1990b). In one common usage, the term is sometimes inaccurately used as a shorthand reference for general efforts made to reduce the scale or scope of government. In this sense, the term is used to denote a basic shift in the overall relationship or governance mode existing between a government and its constituent society towards a more market mode of co-ordination. In the second sense, however, privatization refers only to those specific efforts made by the state to replace organizational instruments based on government ownership with those based on more indirect controls – like independent regulatory commissions – which does not necessarily entail a corresponding shift towards a market governance mode. In this more restricted sense, for example, a government's commitment to an existing mode remains unchanged; what changes instead is the general manner in which it meets its commitments: shifting from the use of organizational resources to more authoritative ones. Similarly, instead of regulating a company's, to provide another example, polluting activities, the government may offer it a financial incentive to modernize its equipment and curb pollution. Again this does not represent a shift in the fundamental governance mode but rather a change of regime logic within an existing one.

Patterns of authoritative tool use: indirect regulation and increased public participation

Looking at the use and promotion of authority-based substantive policy tools, the discussion in Chapter 6 showed that regulations are compatible with most modes of governance, depending on how state directed they are. Many policy designs have indeed changed over the past two decades in this tool area. Within an existing governance mode, for example, many regulatory activities have shifted from 'enforcement' to 'compliance' regimes (Hawkins and Thomas 1989; Doern and Wilks 1998). But these activities remain compatible with pre-existing modes of governance and do not necessarily infer a shift towards market or network forms of governance as proponents of phenomena such as deregulation – often linked to patterns of globalization and networkization – have alleged.

Nevertheless, it is true that many governments in recent years have made varying levels of effort, albeit often more in formulation than implementation, to deregulate important sectors of their economies; that is, to shift from earlier legal or corporatist governance modes to a more market or network mode. As the discussion in Chapter 6 showed, however, many such efforts failed to produce qualitatively superior results to the regimes they replaced, leading to a movement back towards 're-regulation' in the policy designs adopted or proposed in many jurisdictions (Jordana and Levi-Faur 2004; Ramesh and Howlett 2006).[1]

In addition to these developments in the substantive arena, with respect to procedural authoritative instruments, Chapter 6 also underscored the development of, compatible with the networkization thesis, demands for enhanced participation and consultation in government policy-making driven by domestic groups (Kernaghan et al. 2000). But this is not a new phenomenon and there has been substantial growth in the use of consultative forums and mechanisms in many sectors and countries over the past half century. This extends from the increased use of public hearings to the increased creation (and regulation) of advisory committees. As David Brown noted as early as 1955 in the USA, for example, while in 1938 there were perhaps 100 advisory boards in the US federal government, by 1955 there were fifty in the US Department of Agriculture alone (versus four in 1938). Smith (1977) also noted that this phenomenon varied by jurisdiction and that while by 1962–63 the US federal government had over 900 advisory committees and the UK in 1960 about 500, Australia only about 200 by 1975.[2]

Institutionalized forms of citizen involvement in policy-making attempt to replace agenda-setting and policy influence by only those actors intimately involved in project or policy proposals with a process in which 'outsiders' as well as 'insiders' can promote new and alternative perspectives on these issues, and can be viewed as generally attempting to move legal, corporatist and market modes of governance towards more 'network' types (Marchildon 2007). But advisory committees, commissions, task forces, and round tables already exist in many sectors and are compatible with other governance modes, not just network ones.[3]

Patterns of financial tool use: from visible to invisible instruments

There have been some interesting developments in the patterns of use found in this very old set of instruments and some interesting tool dynamics well worth additional study. While most economic theories push for visible taxes and incentives in order to promote virtues and discourage vice, the reality in most countries is a trend towards more and more hidden financial tools – especially tax-based ones which are difficult to trace and quantify.

Howard (1993; 1995; 1997; 2002), for example, has estimated that the US welfare system in the mid-1990s included $896 million in direct expenditures but also $437.9 million in tax expenditures (1995: 26).[4] He estimated tax expenditures in the USA grew by an average 4.8 per cent over the period 1967–95 versus 5.9 per cent for direct expenditure on income security, health, and housing, but over the period 1980–90 grew at a faster rate than direct expenditures (3.9 versus 3.1 per cent annual growth) with a similar pattern over the period 1975–95 (the 'Republican era' in US politics) in what was ostensibly a deficit cutting/free trade era of market-based governance.

This expansion has been fuelled by shifts in implementation preferences owing a great deal to the assessment criteria of visibility, intrusiveness, automaticity and cost. The tax system is already in place, along with a collections and enforcement apparatus, so changes to create new incentives or disincentives are largely matters of administration. There is some risk involved in their use, though, as it is often difficult to control whether or not a recipient will actually do what a government wants them to with the transferred funds. Besides problems with black and grey markets, market distortions and international prohibitions associated with this tool, agents can also often simply take the money offered with few results in terms of achievement of a principle's intentions. Avoiding such principle–agent problems can involve costly and visible enforcement agencies, which negates some of the advantages of the use of these instruments in contemporary policy designs.

With respect to procedural financial tools, a pattern in many countries and sectors has been for their increased use over the past thirty years in the effort to enhance and control the operation of interest articulation and aggregation systems in many sectors. This is compatible in many jurisdictions with pre-existing corporatist modes of governance but many groups in other governance modes now receive direct funding from governments while others are funded indirectly through tax systems which allow for transfers of funds to non-profit and charitable groups either directly or through foundations (Pross and Stewart 1993; Phillips 2001; Sharpe 2001; Carmichael 2010; Wood and Hagerman 2010).[5]

In terms of Linder and Peters' criteria, it should be noted that the use of such procedural financial tools is generally very inexpensive and can be precisely targeted, making them a preferred tool for government managers eager to control their policy environments. There are some risks involved in such activities though, since outside funding promotes oligarchy/formalization in voluntary associations and can lead to discontent both among 'co-opted' group memberships as well as from groups which do not receive funding (Saward 1990 and 1992; Lowndes and Skelcher 1998; Smith 2005a; 2005b). Ideological predispositions towards 'free association' in deliberative democratic practices, too, are jeopardized by government manipulation of interest articulation systems, which can lead to further difficulties for governments who engage in this practice in a substantial way, although the lack of visibility and accountability of such practices reduces this concern (Beetham 1991; Phillips 1991; Stanbury 1993; Webb 2000; Maddison 2005; Carmichael 2010).

Patterns of informational tool use: the growth of exhortation and public information campaigns

It is now very much a matter of course for information campaigns to accompany many government initiatives, and Chapter 8 showed how expenditures, laws and programmes in this area have grown as they have been included in more and more policy designs. This is explicable given the non-coercive nature of this tool, which accords well with the ideology and imperatives of liberal-democratic governments and their preferred legal and corporatist-based governance modes.

Information dissemination remains relatively low cost in terms of financial and personnel outlays as well, but compliance with government urgings is a major issue – and as in all advertising (Pepsi, Coke, etc.) evaluating the impact of these campaigns is very uncertain (Salmon 1989a; 1989b). Consumers may not pay attention to information provided by, for example nutritional or eco-labels, or may become inured to messages repeated too often (Howells 2005). Effective campaigns can also take some time to get started and evoke any behavioural response and behaviour can revert back to old habits and patterns once a campaign stops. Or, where too much information is provided ('information overload') intended targets may stop listening, also leading to diminishing returns over time (Bougherara et al. 2007). The political risks to government in using this tool may be high if such a high visibility instrument is perceived to have failed to alter behaviour in the desired direction, leading to demands for greater government efforts. Moreover, as the discussion of privacy and official secrets legislation in Chapter 8 showed these moves in a more network governance direction are often offset by similar moves towards a legal governance mode involving knowledge suppression, either for state or individual privacy purposes.[6]

Overall patterns and trends in contemporary policy designs

As this discussion has shown, the patterns of tool use in contemporary policy designs are much more varied than simply involving a cross-sectoral, government-wide shift towards policy mixes associated with enhanced market and network governance.

In the case of organizational tools there has been noticeable movement in many sectors away from the use of direct government instruments and public enterprises and towards the use of more indirect means of goods and service delivery such as partnerships, special operating agencies and quangos. However, this movement should not lead us to underestimate the resilience and continued presence of traditional direct government tools, especially line departments, which remain the backbone of most policy sectors. In the case of organization-based procedural tools, there has been a simultaneous movement towards the use of government organizational resources to involve larger components of the public or affected 'stakeholders' in policy deliberations. These moves, again while certainly not new, do reflect a shift in some policy sectors from state-led towards more societally driven modes of organization as efforts have been made in many countries to implement some aspects of network governance.

With respect to authoritative substantive instruments, this same pattern appears once again as traditional direct and indirect regulatory mechanisms which are a feature of implementation in legal and corporatist modes of governance, and remain predominant there, have been augmented by efforts to promote more voluntary regulatory regimes in a wide variety of issue areas – from environmental protection to food safety. This deregulatory movement has been offset in many jurisdictions and sectors, however, by the return to direct or indirect regulation through re-regulation of areas such as telecommunications and energy in many countries (Majone 1997). The relative stasis in this category of tool choice is also visible in its procedural components, as traditional mechanisms such as advisory committee creation continue to be used extensively, whether the context is regulation, deregulation or re-regulation.

In the area of financial tools, however, changes in policy designs have been more unidirectional, with most countries seeing a cross-sectoral government-wide shift in recent years from an emphasis on the use of more visible subsidies to a preference in many sectors for less visible forms of tax- and royalty-based expenditures. On the procedural front, there is not a great deal of information available from which to judge, but it appears that, in many countries, more or less covert efforts to correct collective action problems through the use of tools such as interest group creation have been attempted in many sectors, but this is a policy design which is compatible with already existing corporatist modes of governance as well as the development of new network ones.

Finally, in the area of information-based tools, the propensity for governments to undertake large-scale public information campaigns has accelerated, as has their use of devices such as surveys and other techniques for monitoring their populations. On the procedural side, however, an earlier generation's efforts at enhancing information access for the public has been somewhat curtailed in the post-9/11 environment of enhanced security and state secrecy.

The general picture this provides, in terms of measures of government involvement in specific tool choices and policy designs, is of a number of shifts, but much less *between* governance modes, as suggested by the globalization and 'government to governance' thesis, than *within* them. In some cases some efforts have been made to shift designs toward more market- or network-based ones, but not with a lot of success. In others, as Hood et al. and Majone have argued in the European case, 'modern states are placing more emphasis on the use of authority, rules and standard-setting, partially displacing an earlier emphasis on public ownership, public subsidies, and directly provided services' (Hood et al. 1999; see also Majone 1997). However, even here, most sectors in Europe remain firmly entrenched in corporatist governance modes.

These trends, therefore, are much less dramatic than those suggested by the network-globalization hypothesis and suggest a much greater resilience and continued high capacity of the state in the face of these two macro-level trends than is often alleged (Aucoin 1997; Lynn 2001; Hill and Lynn 2004; Hamelin 2010). It suggests, among other things, that governance modes are more difficult to change in many sectors than is often argued and provides additional evidence for the contention that policy designs must be compatible with previously existing governance modes if they are to survive the formulation process and be implemented successfully.[7]

Readings

Agranoff, R. and M. McGuire. 2001. 'Big Questions in Public Network Management Research'. *Journal of Public Administration Research and Theory* 11, no. 3: 295–326.

Bingham, L. B., T. Nabatchi and R. O'Leary. 2005. 'The New Governance: Practices and Processes for Stakeholder and Citizen Participation in the Work of Government'. *Public Administration Review* 65, no. 5: 547–58.

Brown, D. S. 1955. 'The Public Advisory Board as an Instrument of Government'. *Public Administration Review* 15: 196–201.

Brown-John, C. L. 1979. 'Advisory Agencies in Canada: An Introduction'. *Canadian Public Administration* 22, no. 1: 72–91.

Derthick, M. and P. J. Quirk. 1985. *The Politics of Deregulation*. Washington, DC: Brookings Institution.

Dion, L. 1973. 'The Politics of Consultation'. *Government and Opposition* 8, no. 3: 332–53.

Eisner, M. A. 1994. 'Discovering Patterns in Regulatory History: Continuity, Change and Regulatory Regimes'. *Journal of Policy History* 6, no. 2: 157–87.

Hammond, T. H. and J. H. Knott. 1988. 'The Deregulatory Snowball: Explaining Deregulation in the Financial Industry'. *Journal of Politics* 50, no. 1: 3–30.

Howard, C. 1993. 'The Hidden Side of the American Welfare States'. *Political Science Quarterly* 108, no. 3: 403–36.

Howard, C. 2002. 'Tax Expenditures'. In *The Tools of Government: A Guide to the New Governance* ed. L. M. Salamon. New York: Oxford University Press, 410–44.

Jordana, J. and D. Levi-Faur. 2004. 'The Politics of Regulation in the Age of Governance'. In *The Politics of Regulation: Institutions and Regulatory Reforms for the Age of Governance*. eds. J. Jordana and D. Lovi-Faur, Cheltenham: Edward Elgar, 1–28.

Kamerman, S. B. and A. J. Kahn. 1989. *Privatization and the Welfare State*. Princeton, NJ: Princeton University Press.

Libecap, G. D. 1986. 'Deregulation as an Instrument in Industrial Policy: Comment'. *Journal of Institutional and Theoretical Economics* 142: 70–74.

Moran, M. 2002. 'Review Article: Understanding the Regulatory State'. *British Journal of Political Science* 32, no. 2: 391–413.

Peters, B. G. and J. Pierre. 2000. 'Citizens Versus the New Public Manager: The Problem of Mutual Empowerment'. *Administration and Society* 32, no. 1: 9–28.

Phillips, J., B. Chapman and D. Stevens. (eds) 2001. *Between State and Market: Essays on Charities Law and Policy in Canada*. Toronto: University of Toronto Press.

Phillips, S. D. 2001. 'From Charity to Clarity: Reinventing Federal Government-Voluntary Sector Relationships'. In *How Ottawa Spends 2001–2002: Power in Transition*. ed. L. A. Pal, Toronto: Oxford University Press, 145–76.

Rhodes, R. A. W. 1994. 'The Hollowing Out of the State: The Changing Nature of the Public Service in Britain'. *The Political Quarterly* 65, no. 2: 138–51.

Smith, T. B. 1977. 'Advisory Committees in the Public Policy Process'. *International Review of Administrative Sciences* 43, no. 2: 153–66.

Stigler, G. J. 1975. *The Citizen and the State: Essays on Regulation*. Chicago: University of Chicago Press.

Vogel, D. 2005. *The Market for Virtue: The Potential and Limits of Corporate Social Responsibility*. Washington, DC: Brookings Institution.

Chapter 10

Conclusion

Towards a new generation of policy design studies

As Stephen Linder, B. Guy Peters, Davis Bobrow, Peter May, Patricia Ingraham, Christopher Hood, Renate Mayntz and the other pioneers of policy design research in the 1980s and 1990s argued, like other kinds of design activities in manufacturing and construction, policy design involves three fundamental aspects: (1) knowledge of the basic building blocks or materials with which actors must work in constructing a (policy) object; (2) the elaboration of a set of principles regarding how these materials should be combined in that construction; and (3) understanding the process by which a design becomes translated into reality. In a policy context this means understanding the kinds of implementation tools governments have at their disposal in attempting to alter some aspect of society and societal behaviour; elaborating a set of principles concerning which instruments should be used in which circumstances; and understanding the nuances of policy formulation and implementation processes in government.

These tasks are undertaken by experts in policy advice systems, utilizing different sets of ideas they, and other policy actors, have about the normative and cognitive contents of policies. It is in this sense that one can talk about policies being designed or consciously crafted and constructed by state actors. This does not mean that design is always done well – no more than this is the case in architecture or industrial design – and it does not mean that design is not the only activity important to studying or making public policy. Other equally important activities include 'understanding' policy-making or researching its nature and processes (Howlett, Ramesh and Perl 2009); 'managing' public policy, or ensuring that planned objectives are actually met in practice (Wu et al. 2010); and 'analyzing' public policy, that is, evaluating the experiences of past or existing policies in order to better inform future policies and developing methodologies for policy alternative appraisal and evaluation (Weimer and Vining 2004; Dunn 2008). Like all these other tasks, design can be done well or poorly, depending on the skills and knowledge of the designer and the amount of time, information and other resources at his or her disposal in the design task. Designers must not always be simply reacting to circumstances or engaging in a process of incremental policy-making, but require some autonomy and capability to systematically evaluate their circumstances and the range of instrument choices they might make if design is to occur in any meaningful sense.

Design is nevertheless a crucial activity in policy-making and considerations of policy success or failure (Marsh and McConnell 2010; McConnell 2010) since it embodies the lessons learned from other policy activities at the moment in time when a new policy is being developed or an old one reformed. Like architecture or engineering, it is critical to policy-making that the lessons of past efforts – both successes and failures – are encapsulated into principles of sound design which can offer the best chance of the attainment of government goals and objectives in prevalent circumstances (May 1981; Schneider and Ingram 1988; Weimer 1992; Rose 1993; 2005; Grabosky 1995; Gunningham and Sinclair 1999).

Revisiting the contextual orientation in design studies

As we have seen, theories of policy design and instrument choice have gone through several 'generations' (Goggin et al. 1990; O'Toole 2000) as theorists have moved from the analysis of individual substantive instruments (Salamon 1981; 2002) to comparative studies of procedural instrument selection (Howlett 1991; Bemelmans-Videc 1998; Peters and Van Nispen, 1998; Varone 2000) to the study of policy mixes (Evers and Wintersberger 1990; Braathen 2005; Bode 2006; Howlett et al. 2006). While each generation has increased the complexity of the analysis, the central assumption of all these generations of theory is that the policy design process and its outcomes are ultimately shaped by contextual factors related to state capacity in the face of different levels of social complexity (Atkinson and Nigol 1989).

Studies have noted how, for example, financial instruments should be used – indeed, can only be used effectively – when there is a high level of state fiscal capacity or 'treasure' resources and target groups are willing to respond to financial cues and change their behaviour accordingly. Similarly, when a state faces a large target it will be forced to utilize greater organizational, financial and/or treasure resources than would otherwise be the case (Tupper 1979; Laux and Molot 1988; Eisner 1994; Vogel 1996; Hall and Banting 2000).

However, more recent studies of policy design have attempted to move beyond these kinds of contextual statements to integrate instrument studies into studies of policy regime logics and especially governance modes. Among the insights gained from this most recent set of studies is that, because arrangements like governance modes typically change only very slowly over time, patterns of government instrument choices tend to exhibit a surprising amount of similarity within policy sectors and over time (de Vries 1999; 2002; 2005).

A focus on relatively long-standing structural or institutional factors in the policy formulation process which affect state capacity and network complexity helps to explain why long-lasting patterns of instrument choice such as those discussed in Chapter 9 exist at both the sectoral and national levels.

These studies have also underlined the key role played by policy experts at the policy formulation stage of the policy-making process who ensure policy alternatives are developed which accord with their conceptions of feasibility, focussing on their congruence with existing governance norms and contextual dynamics.

Policy experts, as guardians of knowledge and ideas about the appropriate relationships existing between policy tools and governance modes, occupy key positions in policy advice systems and play a key role in influencing policy formulation in such a way as, normally, outside of periods of turbulence in governance ideas and policy regimes, ensures continuity in favoured policy designs.

Lessons for students of policy design

The chapters in this book have highlighted many significant aspects of the policy formulation and design processes, describing both how these processes work, who is involved with them, and their impact on policy outcomes. What are the lessons of this analysis for students of policy design and practitioners as they go about their work? In what follows below, two central points in the book concerning the nature of policy design and the preconditions for its success are set out. These are: (1) the need for designers to thoroughly analyze and understand the 'policy space' in which they are working; and (2) the need for them to be aware of and deal with the temporal dimensions of this space.

Understanding the design space

Designing successful policies requires thinking about policy-making in such a way as to fully take into account the dual purposes – substantive and procedural – which polices can serve and the nature of the multiple levels of policy elements or components which make up a typical policy. As we have seen, policy formulation typically occurs within the confines of an existing governance mode and policy logic which simplifies the task of policy design. It does this by restricting the number of alternatives which are considered feasible in any given planning situation, reducing to manageable proportions the otherwise almost infinite range of possible specific micro-level instrument choices (Meuleman 2010); but only if these contextual constraints are diagnosed accurately.

The process of design and instrument selection is made simpler once the fact that some of the elements of public policies remain more amenable to careful thought and deliberate government manipulation than others is recognized. Understanding exactly how instrument choices are constrained by higher-order sets of variables is thus crucial to making correct policy design decisions in specific policy-making contexts.

As Linder and Peters (1991) argued, policy design can be thought of as a spatial activity. That is, as:

> a systematic activity composed of a series of choices . . . design solutions, then, will correspond to a set of possible locations in a design space . . . this construction emphasizes not only the potential for generating new mixtures of conventional solutions, but also the importance of giving careful attention to tradeoffs among design criteria when considering instrument choices.
>
> (130)

Establishing the nature of the policy design 'space' is therefore a crucial activity for policy designers. Designers must avoid simply advocating 'stock' solutions unless this is called for by the limited nature of the space available for new designs (May 1981). Rather they should 'consider the range of feasible' options possible in a given circumstance and package these into sets of 'competing strategies' to achieve policy goals (May 1981: 236, 238). As David Weimer (1992) has argued, 'Instruments, alone or in combination, must be crafted to fit particular substantive, organizational and political contexts' (373).

Adopting a multi-level, nested model of policy context helps clarify what 'room' exists at what level of policy for new or alternative policy design elements (Hamdouch and Depret 2010). High-level abstract 'macro' level policy goals typically vary in accordance with the nature of the governance mode found in a particular sector at a specific time which itself encompasses the set of political actors, ideas and institutional rules which are prevalent in that jurisdiction at the moment at which policy deliberations and decision-making takes place (Moore 1988; Braun 1999; Howlett and Ramesh 2003). The existence of these fairly long-term and stable governance arrangements helps maintain relatively constant general implementation preferences, since these derive from and are constrained by the same set of factors which influence and inform the development and articulation of abstract policy aims (Howlett 1991; May 1991; Dunsire 1993; Kooiman 2000 and 2008).

These different modes thus involve different overall preferences for general kinds of substantive and procedural policy instruments expected to attain the general aims of government. As the discussion in Chapters 5–8 has shown, the existence of a dominant governance mode in a particular sector or issue area generates certain propensities for the use of specific kinds of tools within and across Hood's resource categories. Different countries and sectors share these styles and they are the first important overall determinant of the policy design space found in specific policy and issue areas (Meuleman 2010; Hardiman and Scott 2010). An example of the logic of this design schema using a single, legal mode, is set out in Figure 10.1 below but can be easily expanded to other modes as well.

As we have seen, in many countries, the preferred instruments for policy implementation in many sectors have been configured as largely legal and corporatist rather than market or network based, but the context, style, and substance of both the marketplace and the network has infiltrated the policy formulation process in recent years (Majone 1989). However, as the discussion in the book has shown, the policy design space in most sectors in

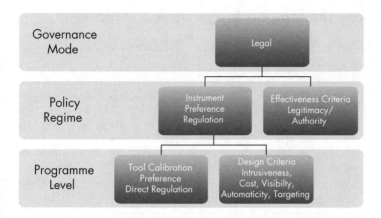

Figure 10.1 Policy design spaces and modes of governance

recent decades remains firmly fixed within earlier modes, especially, in many countries in Europe, Asia and Latin America, for example, within corporatist modes (Heritier et al. 1996; Knill 2001; Pollitt 2001). Although compliance with government intentions has been approached in some sectors in these countries in terms of market-based factors: profit margins and the economic viability of industry, employment patterns, and international competitiveness, this new emphasis on market-based policy tools – or what is sometimes referred to as 'the new governance' – has had little effect on implemented policy designs in many sectors (Rhodes 1996; Salamon 2001; O'Toole and Meier 2010). This underlines the linkages which exist in governance modes between patterns of policy instrument choices and general governance preferences and the need for policy designers to be thoroughly aware of the nature of the design space within which they are working.

Promoting 'integrated' policy designs congruent with existing design spaces multiplies the problems designers face in making choices and selection of instruments (Meijers and Stead 2004; Stead et al. 2004; Briassoulis 2005b; 2005c) and assumes a great deal of administrative and analytical capacity on the part of state actors that may or may not exist in different sectors and countries (Howlett 2009; Howlett and Newman 2010). That is, in order for 'design' to meaningfully occur at all, policy designers need a great deal of knowledge and insight into the workings of their polity and specific policy sectors, raising to the forefront questions about the capacity of policy experts involved in the policy formulation process (Bye and Bruvoll 2008; Schön 1992). In order to be able to make an appropriate decision about when to introduce new instruments and when to renew old ones, they must be familiar not only with the technical aspects of the menu of instruments before them, but also with the nature of the governance and policy contexts in which they are working, and thus require training and experience in both these aspects of the policy design process if design is to occur at all (Braathen 2005; 2007; Grant 2010 ; Skodvin, Gullberg and Aakre 2010).

CONCLUSION

Understanding the temporality of design choices

As the discussion in the book has repeatedly noted, specific instrument choices are embedded decisions, existing within a nested, multi-level environment of governance modes, policy regime logics and tool calibrations, and is heavily context laden. The basic nature of possible governance regimes, however, is well known and the general implementation preferences they entail are also quite clear. That leaves the essential design challenge in many sectors as one of the identification and articulation of specific policy measures, more or less carefully calibrated, from within each resource category, within an already existing governance mode.

However, the common existence of fairly 'routine' design situations should not be taken to suggest complete stability in all areas and it is certainly the case that preferred governance modes do change as governments move away, for example, from legalistic and corporatist modes towards more flexible modes associated with market and network governance and governance styles. And such moves, as adherents of the globalization network hypothesis have noted, can have a large impact on the types of policy design choices taken by government, such as a shift away from 'direct' government activities towards an increased reliance on the indirect manipulation of market and policy network actors.

There is a temporal aspect to these policy designs contexts, therefore, which policy designers must also take into account. As Christensen et al. have argued, the leeway or degree of manoeuvrability policy designers have in developing new designs is influenced not only by existing contextual factors and polity features but also by historical-institutionalist ones. As they argue, 'these factors place constraints on and create opportunities for purposeful choice, deliberate instrumental actions and intentional efforts taken by political and administrative leaders to launch administrative reforms through administrative design' (2002: 158).

That is, except in the case of completely new policy areas, which are relatively rare, designers are typically faced with a situation in which an already existing policy mix is in place (Thelen 2003; 2004). These arrangements commonly have emerged or evolved over relatively long periods of time through previous design decisions, and even if they had a clear logic and plan at the outset they may no longer do so (Bode 2006). This is because they may have evolved through such temporal processes as *layering* in which instruments and goals are simply added to existing ones without abandoning the previous ones, a process which has been linked to both incoherence amongst the policy ends and inconsistency with respect to policy means (Howlett and Rayner 1995; Orren and Skowronek 1999; Rayner et al. 2001). Or they may have emerged through *drift*, in which policy ends change while instruments remain unchanged, a process through which means become inconsistent with respect to changed ends and most likely ineffective in achieving them (Torenvlied and Akkerman 2004; Hacker 2005). In these contexts designers are faced with the challenge of *redesign* or the *replacement* of existing regime elements in which the design space has been altered by the continued existence of the remnants of earlier policy efforts. In such situations designers often attempt to patch or restructure existing policy elements rather than propose alternatives *de novo* although the situation may require the latter if coherence and consistency is to be achieved in the reformed policy mix (Gunningham and Sinclair 1999; Thelen 2003; 2004; Eliadis et al. 2005). In such redesigns, Howlett and Rayner (2007) and Kern and Howlett (2009) have focused attention on the importance of designers aiming to achieve 'coherence, consistency and congruence' in the new design. That is, designers should ensure that any new design elements are *coherent* in the sense that they are logically related to overall policy aims and objectives; that they be *consistent* in that they work together to support a policy goal; and that both policy goals and means should be *congruent*, rather than working at cross-purposes.

Dealing with complexity: the task of policy design in contemporary government

Studies in fields such as political science, economics, law, and public administration have all underlined that translating policy aims and objectives into practice is not as simple a task as might at first appear. Understanding the nature of a policy space and its history are prerequisites of successful design (Schön 1992).

Policies are made by a variety of different actors interacting with each other over a relatively long period of time within the confines of a set of political and economic institutions and governing norms, each with different interests and resources, and all operating within a climate of uncertainty caused both by context and time-specific knowledge and information limitations (Bressers and O'Toole 1998; 2005). Understanding who these actors are and why and how they act the way they do is a critical aspect of all public policy-making activity, including policy instrument selection and in policy design (Skodvin, Gulberg and Aakre 2010).

The analysis presented in this book suggests that many traditional ways of thinking about these activities and their impact on policy instrument choices and policy designs are badly out of date. Dichotomous sets of policy alternatives – like 'market versus state' – and metaphors – like 'carrots versus sticks', for example, – lend themselves to blunt thinking about instruments and their modalities. Administrators and politicians involved in policy design need to expand the menu of government choice to include both substantive and procedural instruments and a wider range of options of each, and to understand the important context-based nature of instrument choices.

Beyond such obvious points, however, theorists and practitioners also both need to move beyond simple notions of the pervasive impact of large-scale macro developments such as globalization and networkization. Blunt choices lend themselves to blunt thinking about instruments and their modalities which is not helpful in conducting or thinking about policy design. Scholars need more empirical analysis in order to test their models and provide better advice to governments about the process of tool selection and how to better match tools to the job at hand. Innovative policy design, especially, requires that the parameters of instrument choice be well understood, both in order to reduce the risk of policy failure and to enhance the probability of policy success (Linder and Peters 1990a; Schneider and Ingram 1997).

The challenge for a new generation of design studies is to develop not only the conceptual clarity and the methodological sophistication needed to identify changes in policy contexts, but also the techniques for understanding the influences of interaction between these contexts and the other elements of policy (Eliadis et al. 2005; Yeung and Dixon-Woods 2010; del Rio, Carillo-Hermosilla and Konnola 2010; Hamelin 2010).

Given the complexity of policy making it is not surprising that many noble efforts by governments and citizens to create a better and safer world have foundered on poor policy design. However, while not an optimal outcome, this has led to a greater appreciation of the difficulties encountered in designing public policies, and the attempt to correct gaps in our understanding, a process which, albeit slowly, has improved our knowledge of the principles and elements of the nature of policy instruments and their governance contexts of policy design.

As the basis for the design and implementation of carefully calibrated policy measures, the templates developed by Doern, Hood, Linder and Peters, Schneider and Ingram, and Salamon in the mid-1980s are still very useful in helping to organize the literature and focus design discussions. But, in spite of this work and the centrality and importance of design to public policy-making, the subject still remains in many respects a 'missing link' in policy studies (Hargrove 1975). The design process is complex, often internally orchestrated between bureaucrats and target groups, and usually much less accessible to public scrutiny than many other kinds of policy deliberations, but this should not be allowed to stand in the way of its further elaboration and refinement (Kiviniemi 1986; Donovan 2001).

Readings

Balch, George I. 1980. 'The Stick, the Carrot, and Other Strategies: A Theoretical Analysis of Governmental Intervention'. *Law and Policy Quarterly* 2, no. 1: 35–60.

Baxter-Moore, N. 1987. 'Policy Implementation and the Role of the State: A Revised Approach to the Study of Policy Instruments'. In *Contemporary Canadian Politics: Readings and Notes*. R. J. Jackson, D. Jackson and N. Baxter-Moore (eds). Scarborough: Prentice Hall, 336–55.

Braathen, N. A. 2005. 'Environmental Agreements Used in Combination with Other Policy Instruments'. In *The Handbook of Environmental Voluntary Agreements Vol 43*. E. Croci (ed.). Dordrecht: Springer, 335–64.

Donovan, Mark C. 2001. *Taking Aim: Target Populations and the Wars on AIDS and Drugs*. Washington, DC: Georgetown University Press, 85–109.

Grabosky, Peter N. 1995a. 'Using Non-Governmental Resources to Foster Regulatory Compliance'. *Governance* 8, no. 4: 527–50.

—— 1995b. 'Counterproductive Regulation'. *International Journal of the Sociology of Law* 23: 347–69.

Gunningham, Neil, Peter Grabosky and Darren Sinclair. 1998. *Smart Regulation: Designing Environmental Policy*. Oxford: Clarendon Press, 422–53.

Hood, Christopher. 1983. 'Using Bureaucracy Sparingly'. *Public Administration* 61, no. 2: 197–208.

Howlett, Michael and Jeremy Rayner. 2004. '(Not so) "Smart Regulation"? Canadian Shellfish Aquaculture Policy and the Evolution of Instrument Choice for Industrial Development'. *Marine Policy* 28, no. 2: 171–184.

Howlett, Michael, Jonathan Kim and Paul Weaver. 2006. 'Assessing Instrument Mixes through Program- and Agency-Level Data: Methodological Issues in Contemporary Implementation Research'. *Review of Policy Research* 23, no. 1: 129–51.

Jordan, Andrew, Rudiger K. W. Wurzel and Anthony Zito. 2005 'The Rise of "New" Policy Instruments in Comparative Perspective: Has Governance Eclipsed Government?' *Political Studies* 53: 477–96.

Kagan, Robert A. 1991. 'Adversarial Legalism and American Government'. *Journal of Policy Analysis and Management* 10, no. 3: 369–406.

Lindquist, Evert A. 1992 'Public Managers and Policy Communities: Learning to Meet New Challenges'. *Canadian Public Administration* 35, no. 2: 127–59.

Salamon, Lester. 1981. 'Rethinking Public Management: Third Party Government and the Changing Forms of Government Action'. *Public Policy* 29, no. 3: 255–75.

—— 2002. 'The New Governance and the Tools of Public Action'. In *The Tools of Government: A Guide to the New Governance* L. M. Salamon (ed.). New York: Oxford University Press, 1–47.

Salamon, Lester M. and Michael S. Lund. 1989. 'The Tools Approach: Basic Analytics'. In *Beyond Privatization: The Tools of Government Action*, L. M. Salamon and Michael S. Lund (eds). Washington, DC: Urban Institute, 23–50.

Salamon, Lester M. and B. Guy Peters. 2002. 'The Politics of Tool Choice'. In *The Tools of Government: A Guide to the New Governance* L. M. Salamon (ed.). New York: Oxford University Press, 552–64.

Van Kersbergen, Kees and Frans Van Waarden. 2004. '"Governance" as a Bridge Between Disciplines: Cross-Disciplinary Inspiration Regarding Shifts in Governance and Problems of Governability, Accountability and Legitimacy'. *European Journal of Political Research* 43, no. 2: 143–72.

Vedung, Evert. 1997. 'Policy Instruments: Typologies and Theories'. In *Carrots, Sticks and Sermons: Policy Instruments and Their Evaluation* M. L. Bemelmans-Videc, R. C. Rist and E. Vedung (eds). New Brunswick, NJ: Transaction Publishers, 21–58.

Webb, Kernaghan. 2005. 'Sustainable Governance in the Twenty-First Century: Moving Beyond Instrument Choice'. In *Designing Government: From Instruments to Governance* P. Eliadis, M. Hill and M. Howlett (eds). Montreal: McGill-Queen's University Press, 242–80.

Woodside, K. 1986. 'Policy Instruments and the Study of Public Policy'. *Canadian Journal of Political Science* 19, no. 4: 775–93.

Notes

1 Understanding contemporary policy mixes

1   Globalization is understood here as the extensification and intensification – 'stretching and deepening' in the words of Held et al. (1999) – of cross-border interactions. While much of this process comprises trade and economic interactions, it also includes cultural, political, military and ideational relations among others.

2   While the direct effects of globalization on instrument choice are limited, indirect effects are more substantial despite their informal nature. These consist of 'spill-over' effects and of opportunities for interaction and increased learning and lesson drawing which occur as a side effect of globalization. One of the spill-over effects of increasing integration of international markets is manifested in governments' reluctance to resort to new taxes or establish new public enterprises lest they send the 'wrong' signals to financial markets. While governments still can, and do, employ an extensive array of command and control tools, they must now anticipate adverse reactions and prepare to deal with them. Deregulation and privatization measures are widely reported in the international media and help to build the international reputation of governments undertaking them. Hence, a side effect of globalization is that governments may resort to increased use of information provision as a means to advertise a market-friendly outlook and a favourable disposition towards foreign direct investment. If these measures succeed in attracting foreign investment, the success is cited as a reason for further deregulation and privatization, and for further use of state advertising.

Globalization also increases opportunities for cross-sectoral and cross-national interaction among policy practitioners and commentators. Policy-makers now not only have instant access to information available on the internet but routinely get together with their foreign counterparts at countless governmental and non-governmental meetings that are held on the entire gamut of policy subjects. The meetings are forums for learning from each other's experiences and to better appreciate the technical, economic and political potential and limitations of different policy tools. Other countries' experiences often form the starting point for governments embarking on national policy reforms. Thus policy learning, emulation or transfer play a critical role in efforts to reform policy instruments used to implement public policies (Huber 1991; Bennett and Howlett 1993; Hall 1993; Dolowitz and Marsh 2000; Stone 2000). Meseguer (2003) and Simmons and Elkins (2004), for instance, list learning and emulation as the key factors underlying the spread of privatization and liberalization; the former finds no evidence that international pressures played any significant role. Another example of policy diffusion through learning is the emulation of pollution trading rights in other areas after its perceived success in controlling use of CFCs (Parson and Fisher-Vanden 1999). But again we need to recognize that policy learning and emulation are constrained by political and institutional factors. Domestic political opposition to the adoption of measures that have successfully worked elsewhere is commonplace, forcing policy-makers to baulk or at least compromise. The imperatives of path dependency – the tendency for old choices to become entrenched and institutionalized – also often make it difficult to adopt any policy instrument that is substantially different from current practice (March and Olsen 1989, Pierson 2000).

3   The nature of regulatory activity, for example, focuses on the formal or informal nature of the legal instruments deployed in policy implementation. 'Hard' law is thus typically conceived as synonymous with formal, state-centric, command-and-control types of regulation that impose generally applicable obligations onto target groups of actors, articulated with a relatively high degree of precision and directly enforceable through the courts. In contrast, 'soft' law represents a weakening (or softening) along these key metrics of obligation, precision and enforceability (Tollefson 2004; Tollefson et al. 2008).

2 Key definitions and concepts in the study of policy design

1   While there is no doubt that some aspects of policy-making can be heavily symbolic and ritualized (Edelman 1964 and 1971), from a design perspective these are not the defining characteristics of policy-making, which is typically viewed as a much more pragmatic activity: that is, one intended to effectively alter practices on-the-ground in a more or less conscious or deliberate way through the efficient use of available governing resources or the creation of new ones.

2   Other terms have been developed in the field of policy studies to describe the same phenomena, such as 'governing instruments', 'policy tools', and the 'tools of government', and while these sometimes are used to refer to different mechanisms and calibrations of policy means, they are more often used synonymously.

3   This distinction is apparent in common definitions of governing instruments although its significance is sometimes overlooked. Vedung, for example, has usefully defined policy instruments used in implementation activities as 'the set of techniques by which governmental authorities wield their power in attempting to ensure support and effect social change' (Vedung 1997). This definition can be seen to include both 'substantive' tools, those Hood (1986c) defined as attempting to 'effect or detect' change in the socio-economic system, as well as those 'procedural' tools designed to 'ensure support' for government actions.

3 Policy design as policy formulation

1   As Hajer (2005) has noted, the tools and techniques used to engage input about policy options can make a considerable difference in the effects of that participation, both on the policy process and on the participants themselves. Formulation instruments such as formal consultations and public hearings, for example, tend to privilege expert input and frustrate new participants, while techniques that engage participants from less established organizations and points of view can add energy and enthusiasm to the dialogue over policy options.

2   This helps to explain why different styles of policy analysis can be found in different policy fields (Howlett and Lindquist 2004; Mayer et al. 2004) since these can be linked to larger patterns of behaviour of political actors and knowledge suppliers that condition how policy advice is generated and deployed (Aberbach and Rockman 1989; Bennett and McPhail 1992; Bevir and Rhodes 2001; Peled 2002; Bevir et al. 2003; Howlett and Lindquist 2004). That is, the personal and professional components of the policy advice supply system, along with their internal and external sourcing, can be expected to be combined in different ratios in different policy-making situations (Prince 1983; Wollmann 1989; Hawke 1993; Rochet 2004). Understanding these variations is critical in understanding how policy formulation and design activities are carried out.

3   Developed originally to describe enduring sets of cognitive ideas that are present in the natural sciences, the term 'paradigm' was later applied to long-lasting points of view on 'the way the world works' that are found in the social sciences (Kuhn 1962, Kuhn and Suppe 1974; Hall 1990; 1992; 1993). The concept is closely related to traditional philosophical notions of 'ideologies' as overarching frameworks of ideas influencing action and to more recent sociological notions of 'discourses' or 'frames' (Goffman 1974; Surel 2000), but has a larger cognitive component.

4   In the policy realm, this notion of ideas creating claims or demands on governments was taken up by Frank Fischer and John Forester (1993) and Paul Sabatier (1987; 1988), among others writing in the 1980s and 1990s (see George 1969). The concept of causal stories, in particular, was applied to agenda-setting by Deborah Stone (1988; 1989). In Stone's view, agenda-setting usually involved constructing a 'story' of what caused the policy problem in question. As she has argued:

> Causal theories, if they are successful, do more than convincingly demonstrate the possibility of human control over bad conditions. First, they can either challenge or protect an existing social order. Second, by identifying causal agents, they can assign responsibility to particular political actors so that someone will have to stop an activity, do it differently, compensate its victims, or possibly face punishment. Third, they can legitimate and empower particular actors as 'fixers' of the problem. And fourth, they can create new political alliances among people who are shown to stand in the same victim relationship to the causal agent.
>
> (Stone 1989: 295)

5   However, as Halligan also noted, 'the emphasis on elements such as the role of political operatives. . . . depends very much on whether [they] are accorded seniority within the system of government', a practice that is a feature of the US system but 'less so in other countries' (1995: 162), suggesting that the role played by advisors varies cross-nationally and, probably, cross-sectorally as well (Freeman 1985).

4 Policy design and implementation tool choices

1   Nevertheless, as late as the 1980s many critics of policy studies could still argue that much policy-making activity remained a 'black box'. Policy implementation, especially, was criticized for being thought of simply in 'functional' terms; that is, as 100 per cent determined by inputs in a simple 'input–process–output' model of politics and policy-making (Easton 1965; Stewart and Ayres 2001) while policy formulation was criticized for being under-studied and under-investigated (May 1981).

2   Most of these studies, however, focused exclusively upon what were referred to in Chapter 2 as 'substantive instruments'; that is, those which directly affect the production and delivery of goods and services in society. These early studies failed to adequately address procedural tools, and consequently until around the year 2000 developed only a partial description of policy tools and an understanding of how instrument choices related to policy design.

3   Salamon argued that this perspective had revealed that not only did, as traditional studies had maintained, 'politics determine policy', but also the reverse (Landry et al. 1998). That is, via the feedback mechanism in the policy cycle (Pierson 1992 and 1993), tool choices led to the establishment of a 'political economy' of a policy regime: a tool choice such as, for example, a decision to use tax incentives to accomplish some end, created a constituency for continuation of that incentive (and sometimes one opposed to it), affecting future policy deliberations and decisions including those related to instrument choices (Linder and Peters 1984; Bobrow and Dryzek 1987; Dryzek and Ripley 1988).

4   On this methodology, generally, see McKelvey (1978 and 1982) and Stevens (1994).

5   A government regulation requiring a licence in order to use a particular pesticide, for example, is a policy tool expected to give effect to a set of policy objectives (in this case a problem with externalities from pollution and information asymmetries between producers and consumers of sophisticated chemical products) within a set of aims (such as environmental protection and species preservation) and preferred implementation preferences (such as market-based service delivery within a market mode of governance). Such a mechanism requires an organization to implement it, some funding to pay the personnel involved in that activity, information notices to regulatees that a licence is required and that the requirement will be enforced, and some legal authority to create a licence scheme and enforce it. Such an instrument thus involves the use of many types of governing resources, but the *primary* resource it relies upon is the legal authority to enforce compliance, without which all of the other resources would be ineffective and unnecessary.

6   Salamon and Lund (1989) for example, suggested that different instruments involve varying degrees of effectiveness, efficiency, equity, legitimacy, and partisan support that affect their appropriateness for a particular situation.

7   Their work on instrument choice influenced others working on the subject at the University of Toronto, such as Michael Trebilcock, Donald Dewees, Robert Pritchard and others, who took part in a detailed discussion of instrument choice issues commissioned as part of a government 'regulation reference' in the late 1970s (Trebilcock and Hartle 1982; Trebilcock et al. 1982).

8   This formulation has many advantages. It is not unidimensional, although it might appear so on first reading, because it, like Kirschen, does take into account several political and contextual variables and it, like Cushman, assumes instrument choices are multi-level, with finer calibrations of instruments emerging after initial broad

selections have been made. That is, it assumes that both states and societal interests in liberal-democratic regimes prefer a minimal state and choose instruments accordingly after that initial decision has been made. Preferring 'self-regulation', governments would first attempt to influence overall target group performance through exhortation and then add instruments only as required in order to compel recalcitrant societal actors to abide by its wishes, eventually culminating, if necessary, in the take-over of individual firms.

This is not an unreasonable conclusion, based as it is on much observation of the practices of such governments, and hints at the 'nested' nature of instrument choices, a subject not previously as well developed in instrument studies. However, as Woodside (1986) argued:

> Experience suggest that governments do not always seek to avoid coercive solutions, but indeed, may at times seem to revel in taking a hard line from the start. While there are undoubtedly many reasons for these heavy handed responses, surely some of the most important ones include the constituency or group at which the policy is aimed, the circumstances in which the problem has appeared, and the nature of the problem involved.
>
> (786)

Further, Woodside noted:

> The idea that politicians and officials can choose, in theory from among the whole range of policy instruments is appealing, but it ignores how issues get on the agenda, the highly specified and legally determined choice of instruments available to departments and agencies, and the traditions within an area of policy that suggest certain problems should be dealt with through the use of a specific policy instrument. Furthermore the range of 'politically tenable' choices from among the possible policy instruments has varied over time in response to ideological trends, the presence of crisis conditions and concerns about their budgetary implications. . . . Quite clearly, political scientists need to be more careful in their discussions of policy instruments if an unrealistic sense of choice is to be avoided.
>
> (787)

9 Trebilcock et al. questioned the likelihood of state actors adhering to a minimalist notion of their own proper role in society, preferring public choice inspired notions about bureaucratic expansionism and political credit-mongering motivating administrative and political policy-makers; especially notions of a political cost–benefit calculus aimed at vote maximization. See Trebilcock et al. 1982: ch. 3. These authors also questioned the notion of instrument substitutability found in Doern's work, arguing that constitutional restraints, financial limitations and other technical criteria prevented certain instruments from being utilized in specific circumstances (Trebilcock and Prichard 1983). Thompson and Stanbury did much the same, focusing on visibility and its linkages to political advantage and disadvantage as a criterion of instrument choice. Democratic politicians, they argued, are not ideologically predisposed towards a small state or minimal instruments but would adopt whatever instrument generates the most political benefits for them while minimizing the political costs (Howard and Stanbury 1984; Stanbury 1986). Baxter-Moore, from a neo-Marxist perspective, similarly challenged Doern's notion

that the state is committed to a minimal role in society. He argued that 'the state will generally use less intrusive instruments when seeking the compliance of the dominant capitalist class and deploy more intrusive measures to direct or control the behaviour of subordinate classes' (Baxter-Moore 1987: 346). However, despite these criticisms, the Doern model remains one of the dominant ones in studies of public policy tools; its virtues of simplicity and parsimony apparently outweighing its empirical and conceptual difficulties.

10   It was more or less replicated, for example, though without the effector/detector distinction, in Bemelmans-Videc et al.'s influential 1998 volume on the topic which identified four basic kinds of instruments: 'carrots', 'sticks', 'sermons' and 'organizations' (Vedung 1997).

11   This also was investigated by Tinbergen and later Mundel in the economics litéraure. On the Tinbergen–Mundell theorem that 'there must be as many independent policy instruments as there are policy targets and secondly that a policy instrument should be assigned to the policy target on which it has the maximal effect', see Ergas 2010.

12   On the basis of this analysis Schneider and Ingram, following Elmore and his colleagues, identified five general types of instruments corresponding to these 'behavioural assumptions'. These they called 'authority', 'incentives', 'capacity-building', 'symbolic and hortatory' and 'learning' instruments. As was the case with Bressers and Klok, this scheme included both 'procedural' and 'substantive' tools. While their discussion, like many in the USA at the time, virtually ignored pure public provision of goods and services by government agencies and corporations (Leman 1989), the 'authority' and 'incentive' examples cited are typical substantive instruments involving mixed provision of goods and services by a combination of private and public actors. 'Capacity', 'symbolic' and 'learning' tools, however, are much more procedurally oriented, affecting the policy institutions and processes within which policy decisions take place.

13   Hence, for example, the well-known implementation style found in many US policy sectors, dubbed 'adversarial legalism' by Robert Kagan, is composed of a preferred substantive instrument – regulation – and a characteristic procedural one – judicial review – based on widespread, easily accessible, legal procedures. See Kagan 1991.

14   Assessing these interaction effects in practice can be quite difficult. For examples of sophisticated, if somewhat subjective, efforts to do so, primarily in the energy and climate change areas see Bonnekamp 2006; Oikonomou and Grajakos 2010; and del Rio 2010.

5   Organizational implementation tools

1   However, this distinction in the nomenclature is not maintained rigorously.

2   Hence, for example, in Canada the Ontario Auditor's Act defines 'public enterprise' as 'a corporation which is not an agency of the Crown and having 50 percent or more of its issued and outstanding shares vested in the government or having the appointment of a majority of its Board of directors made or approved by the Lt. Gov in Council', thus including a specified level of ownership and a means of control within the definition itself (Prichard 1983).

3   The difference between the two figures having to do with the fact that many expenditures are composed of transfers to individuals which can involve large sums but only a small administrative overhead – for example, unemployment insurance or old age security payments.

6 Authoritative implementation tools

1   For an empirical assessment of European regulatory agencies using similar criteria see Wonka and Rittberger (2010).
2   Even in banking, the most globalized sector, there is little or no evidence of an overall decline of regulation, and the market and credit crises of 2008 have led to increased moves in a re-regulatory direction in many countries, from Iceland to the USA (Busch 2002; Harris 2004).
3   The key issue with consultations is: who is involved and who is not, and who makes this determination. Many are structured as 'stakeholder' representative groups, but 'stakeholder' is a very poorly defined term. Glicken (2000: 306), for example, defines it very broadly as: 'A stakeholder is an individual or group influenced by – and with an ability to significantly impact (either directly or indirectly) – the topical areas of interest.'
4   This discussion has often led to the linking of specific instrument choices to larger issues such as levels of trust in government (Levy and Spiller 1994) and other aspects of administrative traditions and governance modes (see McAllister 2009; Kagan 2001; Klijn et al. 2010). A general tendency to shift regulatory activity from enforcement to persuasion has been noted but also with significant variations by nation and sector (Pautz 2009; McAllister et al. 2010) as governments attempt to deal with the nature of targets and their behaviour in complex coercion-avoidance games (Scholz 1984; 1991).
5   Understanding why deregulation occurs has proved to be a challenge to regulatory theorists, since many of the imperatives regarded as the source of regulation – such as industry collusion and the desire to retain market share through the erection of barriers to entry to new firms – continue to be vital in the deregulatory context (Crew and Rowley 1986). Some analysts have therefore searched for exogenous causes – such as foreign or technical pressures for regulatory harmonization (Derthick and Quirk 1985; Libecap 1986; Quirk 1988; Lazer and Mayer-Schonberger 2002; Garcia-Murillo 2005).

7 Financial implementation tools

1   Corporatism was the official fascist mode of social organization. In order to avoid this association and connotation, modern studies tend to use the term 'neo-corporatism' to distinguish modern forms of (liberal-democratic) corporatism found in states such as Austria or Sweden from older ones – though examples also exist of this form in liberal-democratic states in crises, for example during wartime or for example during the Rooseveltian New Deal
2   Other variants also exist, such as, for example, consociationalism – where corporatist systems exist but divisions are on ethnic or religious grounds (e.g. The Netherlands); or 'concertations' (France) where there is more pluralism in some areas than others (e.g. social versus economic planning); or 'parentela pluralism' (Atkinson and Coleman 1989) where divisions are partisan (e.g. Italy) (Lijphart 1969; Lehmbruch 1979). Until recently, interest group theory in North America was largely pluralist (Bentley 1908; Truman 1964) whereby it was argued that interest group formation was a quasi-automatic, 'naturalistic process' in which state activity was minimal. The empirical basis for this assessment, however, was

155

lacking (see Mancur Olson 1965; Salisbury 1969, Bachrach and Baratz 1970; and especially Jack Walker 1991 and later Anthony Nownes 2000).

3　Olson had the idea that this could be overcome by providing 'selective incentives' for membership in mass groups – a practice followed, for example, by many environmental groups who offer a variety of services and free goods, like calendars and book discounts, to attract and retain members. More recent works, however, point to the significance of a variety of factors in the process of group creation, such as the nature of a country's associational rights, the existence of 'focusing events' raising the public profile of an issue, and especially the presence of outside funds for seed money as key factors in the creation and growth of interest groups.

4　Most business groups, as well as many others, prefer 'insider action' and only revert to 'outside agitation' in order to attract new members in a competitive situation with other groups (Binderkrantz (2005)). Designing these programmes can therefore be quite complex. See Phillips, Laforest and Graham 2010 for an overview of the issues involved.

5　Over fifty organizations in Stanbury's sample were funded by a single federal agency – the Federal Secretary of State – mainly in the area of multiculturalism. Pal found a total of $80 million going from the Federal Secretary of State to minority language groups over the period 1970–82, $50 million in 1978–82 alone while multicultural groups received over $125 million from 1976–88, $94 million in 1983–88. Women's programmes received $63 from 1973–88 and $46 million over 1984–88 (Stasiulis 1988; Pal 1993; Stanbury 1993). Phillips (1991) found the Federal Secretary of State to have spent $130 million over much the same period on over 3,000 groups with five major areas accounting for about one-third of all recipients: 337 groups for official languages; 457 women's groups; 195 disabled groups; 160 aboriginal groups; and 175 multicultural groups.

8 Information-based implementation tools

1　The federal government of Canada, for example, has been the largest advertiser in the country since 1976 (Stanbury et al. 1983) with the larger provincial governments in the top ten as well. Ryan (1995) noted that federal advertising expanded from $3.4 million in 1968 to $106.5 million in 1992, a 3,000 per cent increase. Even inflation adjusted this amounted to a 665 per cent increase in 25 years. Specific national issue campaigns, in particular, can be very costly. Alasdair Roberts and Jonathan Rose (1995) for example, conducted an in-depth study of a mass media campaign conducted by the Federal Government of Canada to introduce a new goods and services tax (GST) in 1989–90. They found the federal Department of Finance to have spent $11.6 million on public education in a combined print/radio/TV campaign, $5 million on direct mail materials, $5 million on a call centre; Revenue Canada (Customs) to have spent $10.6 million on advertising, $9.2 million on instructional material; Revenue Canada (Taxation) to have spent a further $28 million advertising a GST credit; while a specially created GST Consumer Information Office spent $7.4 million on advertising and $6.9 million on production. The total for this one campaign was $85 million. This was more than the largest private sector advertisers spent in all of 1989. For example, Proctor and Gamble, with its hundreds of consumer products, had a total advertising budget of $56.7 million. This has led to some calls in some countries for greater regulation or control on government advertising, but these proposals have shown few results (Young 2007).

9 Understanding contemporary policy designs

1   While the different phases of regulatory activities are little studied, Bernstein (1955) postulated the existence of a regulatory 'life cycle' moving from birth to senescence and regulatory decline and termination or *deregulation*. In Bernstein's work the idea was that a regulatory agency or regime would gradually suffer a decline in autonomy due to the accumulation of decisions which would generate a cadre of skilled regulators who moved back and forth between regulators and regulatees, undermining the independence of the regulating body and its legitimacy as an impartial protector of the public interest. Eventually the regulator would be 'captured' by the regulatee and the regime would decline into oblivion (Bernstein 1955). However the linkages between the different phases are not well understood and recent studies suggest that rather than just decline into abolition, regulatory agencies and regimes move in cycles of regulation–deregulation–re-regulation (Jordana and Levi-Faur 2004; Ramesh and Howlett 2006). While deregulation certainly occurred in many areas in the 1980s and 1990s, studies are very limited with respect to clarifying the general historical processes through which this step took place and whether or not this was due only, or always, to regulatory capture. Some early studies of deregulation initiatives in North America and Europe do exist (Swann 1988; Rubsamen 1989; Gayle and Goodrich 1990; Richardson 1990; Beesley 1992; Collier 1998), as do some theoretical works attempting to explain the origins of that deregulatory initiative (Crew and Rowley 1986; Derthick and Quirk 1985; Hammond and Knott 1988; Daugbjerg 1997; Lazer and Mayer-Schonberger 2002) but they are far from conclusive.

These studies generally show that regulatory regimes everywhere evolved gradually, emerging in response to the turbulence caused by industrialization and the growth of unfettered market capitalism (Eisner 1993; 1994a; 1994b). Their development, in fact, is co-terminate with that of the enhancement of the bureau-cratic capacity of the modern state (Hodgetts 1964; Skowronek 1982). As an inexpensive and plentiful source of government control, it was often invoked by governments eager to reduce their direct government agency-level involvement in the provision of goods and services in society but unwilling to trust politically important functions entirely to market actors. Although regulation was often initially opposed by industry and many professional economists as promoting inefficiency, it was generally accepted in mainstream policy circles as essential for addressing market imperfections and dealing with the uncertainties of modern economic and social life. It is only recently that a broad body of opinion emerged which regards regulations as often inefficient and burdensome for the state itself (Cheung 2005). The expansion of reservations and even antipathy towards regulations led to two quite distinct movements: towards, on the one hand, 'regulatory reform' and, on the other, 'deregulation'. These two movements are quite different and represent two separate approaches to resolving 'the regulatory dilemma' highlighted in Bernstein's work (Birch 1984). However, as Eisner has pointed out, deregulatory activities and regulatory reforms, or streamlining, are often incorrectly juxtaposed (Eisner 1994). While regulatory reform has involved activities such as the mandating of cost–benefit analyses before the enactment of any new rules, deregulation involves the wholesale roll back and even abolition of existing rules (McGarity 1991).

2   Lloyd Brown-John (1979) counted 1,500 in the USA at the state and federal levels.

3   As Dion argued as early as 1973, at least part of this growth is due to the decline of political parties as a vehicle to aggregate public interests, and of legislative and

representative institutions to articulate them, and is very compatible with corporatist and other forms of governance (Dion 1973). Over the past several decades new avenues for public participation – various kinds of boards, commissions, and tribunals – have provided more institutionalized means for citizen involvement. In many countries and sectors, the 1990s in particular ushered in an era in which a number of new procedural authoritative instruments were established through which the public's participation was actively sought by the state. Environmental task forces, round tables, land-use planning commissions, and other advisory tools have been used by governments in various countries and sectors, while new legislation – embodying processes such as mandatory environmental assessment reviews – created additional instruments mandating public participation. However problems with limited community group resources and too many consultative exercises can lead to diminishing returns and ineffectiveness if they are utilized too often (Cook 2002; Ross et al. 2002) and regulations preventing participatory abuses, such as legislation controlling lobbyists through mandatory registration, have also been deployed (Chari et al. 2007).

4 This 'hidden welfare system' he argued, since it is based primarily on non-refundable tax incentives, mainly favoured the middle class, i.e. those with taxable incomes who can benefit from these programmes – like pensions plans (US$76 billion in 1995); home mortgage deductions (US$50 billion in 1995); deferral of capital gains on home sales (US$17 billion); and employer health insurance (US$77 billion).

5 This pattern of government funding typically has some negative consequences for recipient groups (De Vita and Twombly 2005; Pittel and Rubbelke 2006; Guo 2007; Knott and McCarthy 2007). As Laforest and Orsini argued

> Rather than seeing a multiplicity of innovative practices, voluntary organizations are actually using fewer tools and fewer strategies to influence the policy process, investing most of their energy in research and evidence-based advocacy . . . becoming depoliticized and professionalized as they engage more in research and develop finely honed analytical skills . . . While voluntary organizations are increasingly being consulted and engaged in policy-making, the basis of these interventions too often lies in their capacity to generate empirical evidence and data, not in their ability to articulate the interests of their constituents.
>
> (Laforest and Orsini 2005: 482; see also Cairns et al. 2005)

6 Any general diminishment of state power in this area can be easily reversed in times of war or crisis, as has been the case in many countries in the post 9/11 environment of the US-led 'war on terror'. Freedom of information versus privacy balancing, for example, is very important ideologically in many liberal-democratic countries as it pits individual rights to know what a government is doing against individual rights to privacy (De Saulles 2007). And concerns with state and collective security in times of war or terrorism can lead to a renewed emphasis on restricting information disclosure, as we have seen recently in many countries.

7 Empirical evidence of the existence of these kinds of long-term overall governance arrangements exists in the work of Theodore Lowi, for example, who noted that while the historical record in general throughout the world has been one featuring the constant expansion of the range and scope of instruments used in governance, that in the case of the United States, at least, these arrangements proceeded through

four principle periods. As he argued in 'Four Systems of Policy, Politics, and Choice' (Lowi 1972: 300): 'It is not hard to document historically that the overwhelming proportion of policies produced by the U.S. federal government during the 19th century were distributive', while regulatory policies were introduced in the late nineteenth century and redistributive ones in the twentieth (see also Orren and Skowronek 1998 and Skowronek 1982). These arrangements roughly correspond to rotating periods of Considine's legal, market and corporate modes of governance.

Bibliography

Abelson, Donald E. 2007. 'Any Ideas? Think Tanks and Policy Analysis in Canada'. In *Policy Analysis in Canada: The State of the Art*, L. Dobuzinskis, M. Howlett and D. Laycock (eds.). Toronto: University of Toronto Press, 298–310.

Abelson, J., P. G. Forest, J. Eyles, P. Smith, E. Martin and F. P. Gauvin. 2003. 'Deliberations about Deliberative Methods: Issues in the Design and Evaluation of Public Participation Processes'. *Social Science and Medicine* 57: 239–51.

Aberbach, Joel D. and Bert A. Rockman. 1989. 'On the Rise, Transformation and Decline of Analysis in the US Government'. *Governance* 2, no. 3: 293–314.

Adcroft, A. and R. Willis. 2005. 'The (Un)Intended Outcome of Public Sector Performance Measurement'. *International Journal of Public Sector Management* 18, no. 5: 386–400.

Adler, R. S. and R. D. Pittle. 1984. 'Cajolry or Command: Are Education Campaigns an Adequate Substitute for Regulation?' *Yale Journal on Regulation* 1, no. 2: 159–93.

Advani, A. and S. Borins. 2001. 'Managing Airports: A Test of the New Public Management'. *International Public Management Journal* 4: 91–2007.

Agranoff, R. 1998. 'Multinetwork Management: Collaboration and the Hollow State in Local Economic Policy'. *Journal of Public Administration Research and Theory* 8, no. 1: 67–92.

Agranoff, R. and M. McGuire. 1999. 'Managing in Network Settings'. *Policy Studies Review* 16, no. 1: 18–41.

—— 2001. 'Big Questions in Public Network Management Research'. *Journal of Public Administration Research and Theory* 11, no. 3: 295–326.

Ajzen, I. 'The Theory of Planned Behavior.' *Organizational behavior and human decision processes* 50, no. 2 (1991): 179–211.

Albrow, Martin. 1970. *Bureaucracy*. London: Pall Mall Press.

Alford, R. 1972. The Political Economy of Health Care: Dynamics Without Change. *Politics and Society* 2: 127–64

Alshuwaikhat, H. M. and D. I. Nkwenti. 2002. 'Visualizing Decisionmaking: Perspectives on Collaborative and Participative Approach to Sustainable Urban

Planning and Management'. *Environment and Planning B: Planning and Design* 29: 513–31.

Anderson, Charles W. 1971. 'Comparative Policy Analysis: The Design of Measures'. *Comparative Politics* 4, no. 1: 117–31.

—— 1977. *Statecraft: An Introduction to Political Choice and Judgement.* New York: John Wiley and Sons.

Anderson, George. 1996. 'The New Focus on the Policy Capacity of the Federal Government'. *Canadian Public Administration* 39, no. 4: 469–88.

Anderson, J. E. 1975. *Public Policymaking.* New York: Praeger.

Anderson, P. A. 1983. 'Decision Making by Objection and the Cuban Missile Crisis'. *Administrative Science Quarterly* 28: 201–22.

Andersen, Simon Calmar. 2008. 'Private Schools and the Parents that Choose Them: Empirical Evidence from the Danish School Voucher System'. *Scandinavian Political Studies* 31, no. 1: 44–68.

Andrews, Richard. 1998. 'Environmental Regulation and Business "Self-Regulation"'. *Policy Sciences.* 31: 177–97

Angus, William H. 1974. 'Judicial Review: Do We Need It?' In *The Individual and the Bureaucracy* D. J. Baum (ed.), Toronto: Carswell, 101–35.

Anheier, Helmut K., Stefan Toepler and S. Wojciech Sokolowski. 1997. 'The Implications of Government Funding for Non-Profit Organizations: Three Propositions'. *International Journal of Public Sector Management* 10, no. 3: 190–213.

Anker, Helle, Vibeke Nellemann and Sten Sverdrup-Jensen. 2004. 'Coastal Zone Management in Denmark: Ways and Means for Further Integration'. *Ocean and Coastal Management* 47: 495–513

Arellano-Gault, D. and G. Vera-Cortes. 2005. 'Institutional Design and Organisation of the Civil Protection National System in Mexico: The Case for a Decentralised and Participative Policy Network'. *Public Administration and Development* 25: 185–92.

Armstrong, David. 1998. 'Globalization and the Social State'. *Review of International Studies*, 24: 461–78.

Arrow, Kenneth J. 'Tinbergen on Economic Policy.' *Journal of the American Statistical Association* 53, no. 281 (March 1958): 89–97.

Arts, Bas, Pieter Leroy and Jan van Tatenhove. 2006. 'Political Modernisation and Policy Arrangements: A Framework for Understanding Environmental Policy Change'. *Public Organization Review* 6, no. 2: 93–106.

Ascher, Kate, 1987, *The Politics of Privatization*, London: Macmillan Educational.

Atkinson, M. and W. Coleman. 1989a. *The State, Business and Industrial Change in Canada.* Toronto; University of Toronto Press.

—— 1989b. 'Strong States and Weak States: Sectoral Policy Networks in Advanced Capitalist Economies'. *British Journal of Political Science British Journal of Political Science* 19: 47–67.

Atkinson, M. M. and R. A. Nigol. 1989. 'Selecting Policy Instruments: Neo-Institutional and Rational Choice Interpretations of Automobile Insurance in Ontario'. *Canadian Journal of Political Science* 22, no. 1: 107–35.

Aucoin, Peter. 1997. 'The Design of Public Organizations for the 21st Century: Why Bureaucracy Will Survive in Public Management' in *Canadian Public Administration* 40, no. 2: 290–30.

—— 2006. 'Accountability and Coordination with Independent Foundations: A Canadian Case of Autonomization'. In *Autonomy and Regulation: Coping with Agencies in the Modern State,* Tom Christensen and Per Laegreid (eds.), 110–33. Cheltenham: Edward Elgar.

Auer, Matthew. 1998. 'On Agency Reform as Decision Process'. *Policy Sciences* 31: 81–105.

Averch, H. 1990. *Private Markets and Public Interventions: A Primer for Policy Designers*. Pittsburgh: University of Pittsburgh Press.

Bache, Ian. 2010. 'Partnership as an EU Policy Instrument: A Political History'. *West European Politics* 33, no. 1: 58–74.

Bachrach, P. and M. S. Baratz 1970. *Power and Poverty: Theory and Practice*. New York: Oxford University Press

Baetz, M. C. and A. B. Tanguay 1998. '"Damned if You Do, Damned if You Don't": Government and the Conundrum of Consultation in the Environmental Sector'. *Canadian Public Administration* 41, no. 3: 395–418

Bajari, P. and S. Tadelis. 2001. 'Incentives Versus Transaction Costs: A Theory of Procurement Contracts'. *RAND Journal of Economics* 32, no. 3: 387–407.

Baksi, S. and P. Bose 2007. 'Credence Goods, Efficient Labeling Policies and Regulatory Enforcement'. *Environmental and Resource Economics* 37: 411–30.

Bakvis, H. 1997. 'Advising the Executive: Think Tanks, Consultants, Political Staff and Kitchen Cabinets'. In *The Hollow Crown: Countervailing Trends in Core Executives*, P. Weller, H. Bakvis and R. A. W. Rhodes (eds.). New York: St. Martin's Press.

Balch, George I. 1980. 'The Stick, the Carrot and Other Strategies: A Theoretical Analysis of Governmental Intervention'. *Law and Policy Quarterly* 2, no. 1: 35–60.

Baldwin, David A. 1985. *Economic Statecraft*. Princeton, NJ: Princeton University Press.

Baldwin, Robert and Martin Cave. 1999. *Understanding Regulation: Theory, Strategy and Practice*. Oxford: Oxford University Press.

Bang, H. P. 2003. *Governance as Social and Political Communication*. Manchester: Manchester University Press.

Banting, K. 1995. 'The Social Policy Review: Policy Making in a Semi-Sovereign Society'. *Canadian Public Administration* 38, no. 2: 283–90

Bardach, E. 1977. *The Implementation Game: What Happens after a Bill Becomes a Law*. Cambridge: MIT Press.

—— 1980. 'Implementation Studies and the Study of Implements'. *American Political Science Association*. Berkeley: Graduate School of Public Policy University of California.

—— 1989a. 'Moral Suasion and Taxpayer Compliance'. *Law and Policy* 11, no. 1: 49–69.

—— 1989b. 'Social Regulation as a Generic Policy Instrument'. In *Beyond Privatization: The Tools of Government Action*, L. M. Salamon (ed.) Washington D.C: Urban Institute, 197–229.

Barnett, Carole K. and Barry Shore. 2009. 'Reinventing Program Design: Challenges in Leading Sustainable Institutional Change'. *Leadership and Organization* 30, no. 1: 16–35.

Barnett, Pauline, Tim Tenbensel, Jacqueline Cuming, Calre Alyden, Toni Ashton, Megan Pledger and Mili Burnette. 2009. 'Implementing New Modes of Governance in the New Zealand Health System: An Empirical Study'. *Health Policy* 93: 118–27.

Barreiro-Hurlé, Jesús, Azucena Gracia, and Tiziana de-Magistris. 'Does Nutrition Information on Food Products Lead to Healthier Food Choices?.' *Food Policy* 35, no. 3 (June 2010): 221–229.

Bartle, Ian and Peter Vass. 2007. 'Self-Regulation within the Regulatory State: Towards a New Regulatory Paradigm?'. *Public Administration* 85, no. 4: 885–905.

Batlle, Carlos and Ignacio J. Perez-Arriaga. 2008. 'Design Criteria for Implementing a Capacity Mechanism in Deregulated Electricity Markets'. *Utilities Policy* 16: 184–93.

Bator, Francis M. 1958. 'The Anatomy of Market Failure'. *Quarterly Journal of Economics* 72, no. 3: 351–79.

Baumgartner, Frank R. and Bryan D. Jones. 1993. *Agendas and Instability in American Politics*. Chicago: University of Chicago Press, 26 and 239–41.

Bauer, Josephine. 2006. *International Forest Sector Institutions and Policy Instruments for Europe: A Source Book*. Geneva: FAO/UNECE.

Baxter-Moore, Nicholas. 1987. 'Policy Implementation and the Role of the State: A Revised Approach to the Study of Policy Instruments'. In *Contemporary Canadian Politics* R. J. Jackson, Doreen Jackson and Nicolas Baxter-Moore (eds.). Scarborough: Prentice Hall.

Bearce, David H. 2008. 'Not Complements but Substitutes: Fixed Exchange Rate Committments, Central Bank Independence and External Currency Stability'. *International Studies Quarterly* 52: 807–24.

Becker, G. S. 1983. 'A Theory of Competition Among Pressure Groups for Political Influence'. *Quarterly Journal of Economics* 98 (August): 371–400.

Beesley, M. E. 1992 *Privatization, Regulation and Deregulation*. New York: Routledge.

Beetham, D. 1987. *Bureaucracy*. Milton Keynes: Open University Press

—— 1991. *The Legitimation of Power*. London: Macmillan.

Bekke, H. A. G. M. and F. M. van der Meer. 2000. *Civil Service Systems in Western Europe*. Cheltenham: Edward Elgar.

Bellehumeur, Robert. 1997. 'Review: An Instrument of Change'. *Optimum*, 27, no. 1: 37–42

Bemelmans-Videc, M.-L. 1998. 'Introduction: Policy Instrument Choice and Evaluation'. In *Carrots, Sticks and Sermons: Policy Instruments and Their Evaluation*, M. L. Bemelmans-Videc, R. C. Rist and E. Vedung (eds.). New Brunswick, NJ: Transaction Publishers, 21–58.

Bemelmans-Videc, Marie-Louise, Ray C. Rist and Evert Vedung (eds.) 1998. *Carrots, Sticks and Sermons: Policy Instruments and Their Evaluation*. New Brunswick, NJ: Transaction Publishers.

Ben-Gera, Michal. 2007. *The Role of Ministries in the Policy System: Policy Development, Monitoring and Evaluation*. Paris: OECD.

Benjamin, Lehn M. 2008a. 'Bearing more Risk for Results: Performance Accountability and Nonprofit Relational Work'. *Administration and Society* 39, no. 8: 959–83.

—— 2008b. 'Bearing More Risk for Results: Performance Accountability and Nonprofit Relational Work'. *Administration and Society* 39, no. 8: 959–83.

Bennett, C. 1988. 'Different Processes, One Result: The Convergence of Data Protection Policy in Europe and the United States'. *Governance* 4, no. 1: 415–41.

Bennett, C. and R. Bayley. 1999. 'The New Public Administration: Canadian Approaches to Access and Privacy'. In *Public Administration and Policy: Governing in Challenging Times*, M. W. Westmacott and H. P. Mellon (eds.). Scarborough: Prentice Hall/Allyn and Bacon, 189–201.

Bennett, C. J. 1990. 'The Formation of a Canadian Privacy Policy: The Art and Craft of Lesson-Drawing'. *Canadian Public Administration* 33, no. 4: 551–70.

—— 1991. 'How States Utilize Foreign Evidence'. *Journal of Public Policy* 11, no. 1: 31–54

—— 1992. *Regulating Privacy: Data Protection and Public Policy in Europe and the United States*. Ithaca, NY: Cornell University Press.

Bennett, C. J. and C. D. Raab 2003. *The Governance of Privacy: Policy Instruments in Global Perspective*. Aldershot, Ashgate.

Bennett, Colin. 1991. 'Review Article: What is Policy Convergence and What Causes It?' *British Journal of Political Science* 21, no. 2: 215–33

Bennett, Colin and Michael Howlett. 1993. 'The Lessons of Learning: Reconciling Theories of Policy Learning and Policy Change'. *Policy Sciences* 25, no. 3: 275–94.

Bennett, Scott and Margaret McPhail. 1992. 'Policy Process Perceptions of Senior Canadian Federal Civil Servants: A View of the State and Its Environment'. *Canadian Public Administration* 35, no. 3: 299–316.

Bentley, A. F. 1908. *The Process of Government*. Chicago, IL: University of Chicago Press.

Berg, Sanford V. 2000. 'Sustainable Regulatory Systems: Laws, Resources and Values'. *Utilties Policy* 9: 159–70.

Berg, Sanford V., Ali Nawaz Memon and Rama Skelton. 2000. 'Designing an Independent Regulatory Commission'. IRC Research Paper.

Bernhagen, Patrick. 2003. 'Is Globalization What States Make of It? Micro-Foundations of the State-Market Condominium in the Global Political Economy'. *Contemporary Politics* 9, no. 3: 257–76.

Bernier, Luc, Keith Brownsey and Michael Howlett (eds.) 2005. *Executive Styles in Canada: Cabinet Structures and Leadership Practices in Canadian Government*. Toronto: University of Toronto Press.

Bernstein, M. H. 1955. *Regulating Business by Independent Commission*. Princeton, NJ: Princeton University Press.

Bernstein, Steven and Benjamin Cashore. 2007 'Can Non-State Global Governance Be Legitimate? An Analytical Framework'. *Regulation and Governance* 1: 347–71.

Berry, William D., Richard C. Fording and Russell L. Hanson. 2003 'Reassessing the 'Race to the Bottom' in State Welfare Policy'. *The Journal of Politics* 65, no. 2: 327–49.

Bertelli, A. 2006. 'The Role of Political Ideology in the Structural Design of New Governance Agencies'. *Public Administration Review* 66, no. 4: 583–95.

Bevir, M. and R. A. W. Rhodes. 2001. 'Decentering Tradition: Interpreting British Government'. *Administration and Society* 33, no. 2: 107–32.

Bevir, M., R. A. W. Rhodes and P. Weller. 2003 'Traditions of Governance: Interpreting the Changing Role of the Public Sector'. *Public Administration* 81, no. 1: 1–17.

Bhatta, G. 2002. 'Evidence-Based Analysis and the Work of Policy Shops'. *Australian Journal of Public Administration* 61, no. 3: 98–105.

Binderkrantz, Anne. 2005. 'Interest Group Strategies: Navigating between Privileged Access and Strategies of Pressure'. *Political Studies* 53: 694–715.

Bingham, Lisa Blomgren, Tina Nabatchi and Rosemary O'Leary. 2005. 'The New Governance: Practices and Processes for Stakeholder and Citizen Participation in the Work of Government'. *Public Administration Review* 65, no. 5: 547–58.

Birch, A. H. 1984. 'Overload, Ungovernability and Delegitimization: The Theories and the British Case'. *British Journal of Political Science* 14: 136–60.

Bird, R. M. 1970. *The Growth of Government Spending in Canada*. Toronto: Canadian Tax Foundation.

Birrell, Derek. 2008. 'Devolution and Quangos in the United Kingdom: The Implementation of Principles and Policies for Rationalisation and Democratisation'. *Policy Studies* 29, no. 1: 35–49.

Bishop, Patrick and Glyn Davis. 2002. 'Mapping Public Participation in Policy Choices'. *Australian Journal of Public Administration* 61, no. 1: 14–29.

Black, Amy E., Douglas L. Koopman and David K. Ryden. 2004. *Of Little Faith: The Politics of George W. Bush's Faith-Based Initiative*. Washington, DC: Georgetown University Press.

Blair, Robert. 2002. 'Policy Tools Theory and Implementation Networks: Understanding State Enterprise Zone Partnerships'. *Journal of Public Administration Research and Theory* 12, no. 2: 161–90.

Blankart, Charles. 1985. 'Market and Non-Market Alternatives in the Supply of Public Goods: General Issues'. In *Public Expenditure and Government Growth*, F. Forte and A. Peacock (eds.). London: Basil Blackwell, 192–201.

Blonz, Joshua A., Shalini P. Vajjhala and Elena Safirova. 2008. *Growing Complexities: A Cross-Sector Review of U.S. Biofuels Policies and Their Interactions*. Washington, DC:. Resources for the Future.

Boase, J. P. 2000. 'Beyond Government: The Appeal of Public Private Partnerships'. *Canadian Public Administration* 43, no. 1: 75–91.

Boardman, A. E., D. H. Greenberg, A. R. Vining and D. L. Weimer. 2001. *Cost-Benefit Analysis: Concepts and Practice*. Upper Saddle River, NJ: Prentice Hall.

Bobrow, D. B. 1977. 'Beyond Markets and Lawyers'. *American Journal of Political Science* 21, no. 2: 415–33.

—— 2006. 'Policy Design: Ubiquitous, Necessary and Difficult'. In *Handbook of Public Policy*, B. Guy Peters and Jon Pierre (eds.). London: Sage, 75–96.

Bobrow, D. B. and J. S. Dryzek. 1987. *Policy Analysis by Design*. Pittsburgh, PA: University of Pittsburgh Press.

Bode, I. 2006. 'Disorganized Welfare Mixes: Voluntary Agencies and New Governance Regimes in Western Europe'. *Journal of European Social Policy* 16, no. 4: 346–59.

Boehmke, Frederick J. 2005. *The Indirect Effect of Direct Legislation*. Columbus, OH: Ohio State University Press.

Bogart, W. A. 2002. *Consequences: The Impact of Law and Its Complexity*. Toronto: University of Toronto Press.

Boonekamp, Piet G. M. 2006. 'Actual Interaction Effects between Policy Measures for Energy Efficiency–A Qualitative Matrix Method and Quantitative Simulation Results for Households'. *Energy 31*, no. 14: 2848–73.

Borins, Sandford F. 1982. 'World War Two Crown Corporations: Their Wartime Role and Peacetime Privatization'. *Canadian Public Administration 25*, no. 3: 380–404.

Borraz, Olivier. 2007. 'Governing Standards: The Rise of Standardization Processes in France and in the EU'. *Governance* 20, no. 1: 57–84.

Bos, D. 1991. *Privatization: A Theoretical Treatment*. Oxford: Clarendon Press.

Boston, Jonathan. 1994. 'Purchasing Policy Advice: The Limits of Contracting Out'. *Governance* 7, no. 1: 1–30.

Bougherara, Douadia, Gilles Grolleau and Naoufel Mzoughi. 2007. 'Is More Information Always Better? An Analysis Applied to Information-Based Policies for Environmental Protection' *International Journal of Sustainable Development* 10, no. 3: 197–213.

Bovens, M. and P. Hart. 1996. *Understanding Policy Fiascoes*. New Brunswick, NJ: Transaction Press.

Braathen, N. A. 2005. 'Environmental Agreements Used in Combination with Other Policy Instruments'. In *The Handbook of Environmental Voluntary Agreements*, vol. 43, E. Croci (ed.) Dordrecht: Springer, 335–64.

—— 2007. *Instrument Mixes Addressing Non-Point Sources of Water Pollution*. Paris: OECD.

Braithwaite, John. 2008. *Regulatory Capitalism: How It Works, Ideas for Making It Work Better*. Cheltenham: Edward Elgar.

Braithwaite, J., J. Walker and P. Grabosky. 1987. 'An Enforcement Taxonomy of Regulatory Agencies'. *Law and Policy* 9, no. 3: 323–51.

Brandsen, T., M. Boogers and P. Tops. 2006. 'Soft Governance, Hard Consequences: The Ambiguous Status of Unofficial Guidelines'. *Public Administration Review* 66, no. 4: 546–53.

Braun, D. 'Interests or Ideas? An Overview of Ideational Concepts in Public Policy Research'. In *Public Policy and Political Ideas*, D. Braun and A. Busch (eds.), 11–29. Cheltenham: Edward Elgar, 1999.

Bregha, F., J. Benidickson, D. Gamble, T. Shillington and E. Weick. 1990. *The Integration of Environmental Considerations into Government Policy*. Ottawa: Canadian Environmental Assessment Research Council

Bressers, H. T. A. 1998. 'The Choice of Policy Instruments in Policy Networks'. In *Public Policy Instruments: Evaluating the Tools of Public Administration*, B. G. Peters and F. K. M. Van Nispen (eds.). New York: Edward Elgar, 85–105.

Bressers, H., D. Fuchs and S. Kuks. 2004. 'Institutional Resource Regimes and Sustainability: Theoretical Backgrounds and Hypotheses'. *Environment and Policy* 41: 23–58.

Bressers, H. and M. Honigh. 1986. 'A Comparative Approach to the Explanation of Policy Effects'. *International Social Science Journal* 108: 267–88.

Bressers, Hans and Pieter-Jan Klok. 1988a. 'Fundamentals for a Theory of Policy Instruments'. *International Journal of Social Economics*. 15, no. 3/4: 22–41.

Bressers, Hans Th. A. and Laurence J. O'Toole. 1998. 'The Selection of Policy Instruments: A Network-Based Perspective'. *Journal of Public Policy* 18, no. 3: 213–39.

—— 2005. 'Instrument Selection and Implementation in a Networked Context'. In *Designing Government: From Instruments to Governance*, P. Eliadis, M. Hill and M. Howlett (eds.). Montreal: McGill-Queen's University Press, 132–53.

Brewer, G. D. 1974. 'The Policy Sciences Emerge: To Nurture and Structure a Discipline'. *Policy Science* 5, no. 3: 239–44.

Brewer, G. and P. deLeon. 1983. *The Foundations of Policy Analysis*. Homewood, IL: Dorsey.

Breyer, S. 1979. 'Analyzing Regulatory Failure: Mismatches, Less Restrictive Alternatives and Reform'. *Harvard Law Review* 92, no. 3: 549–609.

—— 1982. *Regulation and Its Reform*. Cambridge, MA: Harvard University Press.

Briassoulis, Helen (ed.) 2005a. *Policy Integration for Complex Environmental Problems; The example of Mediterranean desertification*. London: Ashgate.

—— 2005b. 'Analysis of Policy Integration: Conceptual and Methodological Considerations'. In *Policy Integration for Complex Environmental Problems: The Example of Mediterranean Desertification*. Aldershot: Ashgate.

—— 2005c. 'Complex Environment Problems and the Quest of Policy Integration'. In *Policy Integration for Complex Environmental Problems: The Example of Mediterranean Desertification*. Aldershot: Ashgate.

Bridge, Linda and Albert Salman. 2000. *Policy Instruments for ICZM in Nine Selected European Countries*. Leiden: EUCC.

Brinkerhoff, Derick W. 2009. 'Developing Capacity in Fragile States'. *Public Administration and Development* 30, no. 1: 66–78.

Brinkerhoff, D. W. and B. L. Crosby. 2002. *Managing Policy Reform: Concepts and Tools for Decision-Makers in Developing and Transitional Countries*. Bloomfield, CT: Kumarian Press.

Brinkerhoff, Derick W. and Peter J. Morgan. 2010. 'Capacity and Capacity Development: Coping with Complexity'. *Public Administration and Development* 30, no. 1: 2–10.

Brint, Steven. 1990. 'Rethinking the Policy Influence of Experts: From General Characterizations to Analysis of Variation'. *Sociological Forum* 5, no. 3 (September): 361–85.

Brockman, Joan. 1998. '"Fortunate Enough to Obtain and Keep the Title of Profession": Self-regulating Organizations and the Enforcement of Professional Monopolies'. *Canadian Public Administration* 41, no. 4: 587–621.

Brooks, S. 1989. *Public Policy in Canada: An Introduction*. Toronto: McClelland and Stewart.

Brown, D. S. 1955. 'The Public Advisory Board as an Instrument of Government'. *Public Administration Review* 15: 196–201.

—— 1972. 'The Management of Advisory Committees; An Assignment for the '70's'. *Public Administration Review* 32: 334–42.

Brown, Douglas and Julia Eastman. 1981. *The Limits of Consultation*. Ottawa: Science Council of Canada.

Brown, M. P. 1992. 'Organizational Design as a Policy Instrument'. In *Canadian Environmental Policy: Ecosystems, Politics and Processes*, R. Boardman (ed.). Toronto: Oxford University Press, 24–42.

Brown, T. L. and M. Potoski. 2003 'Transaction Costs and Institutional Explanations for Government Service Production Decisions'. *Journal of Public Administration Research and Theory* 13, no. 4: 441–68.

Brown, T. L., M. Potoski and David M. Ven Syke. 2008. 'Changing Modes of Service Delivery: How Past Choices Structure future Choices'. *Environment and Planning C: Government and Policy* 26: 127–43.

Brown-John, C. L. 1979. 'Advisory Agencies in Canada: An Introduction'. *Canadian Public Administration* 22, no. 1: 72–91.

Brubaker, Rogers. 1984. *The Limits of Rationality: An Essay on the Social and Moral Thought of Max Weber*. London: Allen and Unwin.

Brunsson, Nils. 2006. *Mechanisms of Hope: Maintaining the Dream of the Rational Organizaton*. Copenhagen: Copenhagen Business School Press.

Buchanan, James M. 1980. 'Rent Seeking and Profit Seeking'. In *Toward A Theory of the Rent-Seeking Society*. James M. Buchanan, R. D. Tollison and. G. Tullock (eds.) College Station, TX: Texas A&M University Press.

Buchanan, James M. and Robert D. Tollison (eds.) 1984. *The Theory of Public Choice – II*, Ann Arbor, MI: University of Michigan Press.

Buckman, Greg and Mark Diesendorf. 2010. 'Design Limitations in Australian Renewable Electricity Policies'. *Energy Policy*. 38, no 10: 3365–76.

Bulmer, Martin. 1981. 'Applied Social Research? The Use and Non-Use of Empirical Social Inquiry by British and American Governmental Commissions'. *Journal of Public Policy* 1: 353–80.

Bulmer, Simon J. 1993. 'The Governance of the European Union: A New Institutionalist Approach'. *Journal of Public Policy* 13, no. 4: 351–80

Burns, J. P. and B. Bowornwathana. 1993. *Civil Service Systems in Asia*. Cheltenham: Edward Elgar.

Burris, Scott, Peter Drahos and Clifford Shearing. 2005. 'Nodal Governance'. *Australian Journal of Legal Philosophy* 30: 30–30.

Burstein, Paul. 1991. 'Policy Domains: Organization, Culture and Policy Outcomes'. *Annual Review of Sociology* 17: 327–50.

Burt, Sandra. 1990. 'Canadian Women's Groups in the 1980s: Organizational Development and Policy Influence'. *Canadian Public Policy* 16, no. 1: 17–28.

Busch, Andreas. 2002. *Divergence or Convergence? State Regulation of the Banking*

System in Western Europe and the United States, Contribution to the Workshop on Theories of Regulation, Nuffield College, Oxford, 25–26 May.

Busemeyer, Marius R. 2009. 'From Myth of Reality: Globalisation ad Public Spending in OECD Countries Revisited'. *European Journal of Political Research* 48: 455–82.

Bye, Torstein, and Annegrete Bruvoll. 'Multiple Instruments to Change Energy Behaviour: The Emperor's New Clothes?.' *Energy Efficiency* 1, no. 4 (November 1, 2008): 373–386.

Cahill, A. G. and E. S. Overman. 1990. 'The Evolution of Rationality in Policy Analysis'. In *Policy Theory and Policy Evaluation: Concepts, Knowledge, Causes and Norms*, S. S. Nagel (ed.). New York: Greenwood Press, 11–27.

Cairns, Alan C. 1990. 'Reflections on Commission Research'. In *Commissions of Inquiry*. Christie Innis, John A. Yogis and A. Paul Pross (eds.) Toronto: Carswell, 87–110.

Cairns, Ben, Margaret Harris and Patricia Young. 2005. 'Building the Capacity of the Voluntary Nonprofit Sector: Challenges of Theory and Practice'. *International Journal of Public Administration* 28: 869–85.

Cameron, David R. 1978. 'The Expansion of the Public Economy: A Comparative Analysis'. *American Political Science Review* 72, no. 4: 1243–61.

Campbell, C. and G. J. Szablowski. 1979. *The Superbureaucrats: Structure and Behaviour in Central Agencies*. Toronto: Macmillan.

Campbell, H. E., R. M. Johnson and E. H. Larson. 2004. 'Prices, Devices, People or Rules: The Relative Effectiveness of Policy Instruments in Water Conservation'. *Review of Policy Research* 21, no. 5: 637–62.

Campbell, J. L. 1998. 'Institutional Analysis and the Role of Ideas in Political Economy'. *Theory and Society* 27, no. 5: 377–409.

—— 2002. 'Ideas, Politics and Public Policy'. *Annual Review of Sociology* 28, no. 1: 21–38.

Campbell-Smith, Duncan. 2008. *Follow the Money: The Audit Commission, Public Money and the Management of Public Services, 1983–2008*. London: Allen Lane.

Cantor, R., S. Henry and S. Rayner. 1992. *Making Markets: An Interdisciplinary Perspective on Economic Exchange*. Westport, CT: Greenwood Press.

Cardozo, Andrew. 1996. 'Lion Taming: Downsizing the Opponents of Downsizing'. In *How Ottawa Spends 1996–97: Life under the Knife*, G. Swimmer, (ed.) Ottawa: Carleton University Press, 303–36.

Carlsson, L. 2000. 'Policy Networks as Collective Action'. *Policy Studies Journal* 28, no. 3: 502–22.

Carmel, Emma and Jenny Harlock. 2008. 'Instituting the 'Third Sector' as a Governable Terrain: Partnership, Procurement and Performance in the UK'. *Policy and Politics* 36, no. 2: 155–71.

Carmichael, Calum M. 2008. 'Doing Good Better? The Differential Subsidization of Charitable Contributions'. Paper presented to the *XII Annual Conference of the International Research Society for Public Management*, 25–28 March, Brisbane, Australia.

—— 'Doing Good Better? The Differential Subsidization of Charitable Contributions'. *Policy and Society* 29, no. 3: 201–17.

Carstensen, Martin B. 2010. 'The Nature of Ideas and Why Political Scientists Should Care: Analysing the Danish Jobcentre Reform from an Ideational Perspective'. *Political Studies*, 58(5): 847–865

Cashore, Benjamin. 2002. 'Legitimacy and the Privatization of Environmental Governance: How Non-State Market-Driven(NSMD) Governance Systems Gain Rule-Making Authority'. *Governance* 15, no. 4: 503–29.

Cashore, Ben and Michael Howlett. 2006. 'Behavioural Thresholds and Institutional Rigidities as Explanations of Punctuated Equilibrium Processes in Pacific Northwest Forest Policy Dynamics'. In *Policy Dynamics*. R. Repetto (ed.) New Haven, CT: Yale University Press, 137–61.

—— 2007. 'Punctuating Which Equilibrium? Understanding Thermostatic Policy Dynamics in Pacific Northwest Forestry'. *American Journal of Political Science* 51, no. 3: 532–51.

Cashore, B., Auld, G. and Newsom, D. 2003. 'Forest Certification (Eco-Labeling) Programs and their Policy-Making Authority: Explaining Divergence among North American and European Case Studies'. *Forest Policy and Economics* 5, 225–47.

—— 2004. *Governing Through Markets. Forest Certification and the Emergence of Non-State Authority.* New Haven, CT: Yale University Press.

Castree, Noel. 2008. 'Neoliberalising Nature: The Logics of Deregulation and Reregulation'. *Environment and Planning A* 40: 131–52.

Castells, M. 1996. *The Information Age: Economy, Society and Culture. Volume I – The Rise of Network Society.* Malden, MA: Blackwell.

Cerny, Philip G. 1990. *The Changing Architecture of Politics.* Beverly Hills, CA: Sage.

—— 1993. 'Plurilateralism: Structural Differentiation and Functional Conflict in the Post-Cold War World Order'. *Millenium* 22, no. 1: 27–51.

—— 1996. 'International Finance and the Erosion of State Policy Capacity'. In *Globalization and Public Policy*, Philip Gummett (ed.) Cheltenham: Edward Elgar, 83–104.

—— 2010. 'The Competition State Today: From Raison d'État to Raison du Monde'. *Policy Studies* 31, no. 1: 5–21.

Chadwick, A. 2000. 'Studying Political Ideas: A Public Political Discourse Approach'. *Political Studies* 48: 283–301.

Chapman, Colin. 1990. *Selling the Family Silver: Has Privatization Worked?* London: Hutchinson Business Books.

Chapman, Richard A. 1973. 'Commissions in Policy-Making'. In *The Role of Commissions in Policy-Making.* R. A. Chapman (ed.) London: George Allen and Unwin, 174–88.

Chapman, Tony, Judith Brown and Robert Crow. 2008. 'Entering a Brave New World? An Assessment of Third Sector Readiness to Tender for the Delivery of Public Services in the United Kingdom'. *Policy Studies* 29, no. 1: 1–17.

Chari, Raj, Gary Murphy and John Hogan. 2007. 'Regulating Lobbyists: A Comparative Analysis of the United States, Canada, Germany and the European Union'. *The Political Quarterly* 78, no. 3: 422–38.

Charih, Mohamed and Arthur Daniels (eds.) 1997. *New Public Management and Public Administration in Canada.* Toronto: IPAC, 143–63.

Chávez, Carlos A., Mauricio G. Villena and K. Stranlund. 2009. 'The Choice of Policy Instruments to Control Pollution under Costly Enforcement and Incomplete Information'. *Journal of Applied Economics* 12, (November): 207–27.

Chenier, J. A. 1985. 'Ministers of State to Assist: Weighing the Costs and the Benefits'. *Canadian Public Administration* 28, no. 3: 397–412.

Cheung, A. B. L. 2005. 'The Politics of Administrative Reforms in Asia: Paradigms and Legacies, Paths and Diversities'. *Governance* 18, no. 2: 257–82.

Christensen, Jorgen Gronnegaard and Thomas Pallesen. 2008. 'Public Employment Trends and the Organization of Public Sector Tasks'. In *The State at Work, Volume 2: Comparative Public Service Systems*, Hand-Ulrich Derlien and B. Guy Peters (eds.). Cheltenham: Edward Elgar.

Christensen, Tom and Per Laegreid. 2007. 'Regulatory Agencies – The Challenges of Balancing Agency Autonomy and Political Control'. *Governance* 20, no. 3: 499–520.

Christensen, T., P. Laegreid and L. Wise. 2002. 'Transforming Administrative Policy'. *Public Administration* 80, no. 1: 153–79.

Churchman, C. W. 1967. 'Wicked Problems'. *Management Science* 14, no. 4: B141–B2.

Cicin-Sain, Biliana and Robert Knecht. 1998. *Integrated Coastal and Ocean Management: Concepts and Practices*. Washington, DC: Island Press.

Cismaru, Magdalena and Anne M. Lavack. 2007. 'Tobacco Warning Labels and the Protection Motivation Model: Implications for Canadian Tobacco Control Policy'. *Canadian Public Policy* 33, no. 4: 477–86.

Citi, M. and Rhodes, M. 2007. 'New Modes of Governance in the EU: Common Objectives Versus National Preferences'. European Governance Papers no. N-07-01. Online at www.connex-network.org/eurogov/pdf/egp-newgov-N-07-01.pdf (accessed 29 February 2008).

Clark, C. D. and C. S. Russell. 2009. 'Ecological Conservation: The Problems of Targeting Policies and Designing Instruments'. *Journal of Natural Resources Policy Research* 1, no. 1: 21–34.

Clark, Ian 1998. 'Beyond the Great Divide: Globalization and the Theory of International Relations'. *Review of International Studies* 24, 479–98.

Clark, William C. and Giandomenico Majone. 1985. 'The Critical Appraisal of Scientific Inquiries with Policy Implications'. *Science, Technology and Human Values* 10, no. 3: 6–19.

Clemens, E. S. and J. M. Cook. 1999. 'Politics and Institutionalism: Explaining Durability and Change'. *Annual Review of Sociology* 25: 441–66.

Clokie, H. M. and J. W. Robinson. 1969. *Royal Commissions of Inquiry: The Significance of Investigations in British Politics*. New York, Octagon Books.

Cnossen, S. 2005. 'Economics and Politics of Excise Taxation'. In *Theory and Practice of Excise Taxation: Smoking, Drinking, Gambling, Polluting and Driving*, S. Cnossen (ed.). Oxford: Oxford University Press, 1–19.

Cobb, Roger W. and Charles D. Elder. 1972. *Participation in American Politics: The Dynamics of Agenda-Building*. Boston, MA: Allyn and Bacon.

Coglianese, C. 1997. 'Assessing Consensus: The Promise and Performance of Negotiated Rulemaking'. *Duke Law Journal* 46, no. 6: 1255–349.

Cohen, M., J. March and J. Olsen. 1972. 'A Garbage Can Model of Organizational Choice'. *Administrative Science Quarterly* 17, no. 1: 1–25.

—— 1979. 'People, Problems, Solutions and the Ambiguity of Relevance'. In *Ambiguity and Choice in Organizations*. Bergen: Universitetsforlaget, 24–37.

Cohen, Marjorie Griffin and Stephen McBride (eds.) 2003. *Global Turbulence: Social Activists' and State Responses to Globalization*. Aldershot: Ashgate.

Cohen, Mark A. and V. Santhakumar. 2007. 'Information Disclosure as Environmental Regulation: A Theoretical Analysis'. *Environmental and Resource Economics* 37: 599–620.

Coleman, William D. 1991. 'Monetary Policy, Accountability and Legitimacy: A Review of the Issues in Canada'. *Canadian Journal of Political Science* 24, no. 4: 711–34.

—— 1996. *Financial Services, Globalization and Domestic Policy Change: A Comparison of North America and the European Union*. Basingstoke: Macmillan.

Collier, Ute. 1998. *Deregulation in the European Union: Environmental Perspectives*. London: Routledge.

Collins, Alan and Guy Judge. 2008. 'Client Participation in Paid Sex Markets under Alternative Regulatory Regimes'. *International Journal of Law and Economics* 28: 294–301.

Conn, W. David. 2009. 'Applying Environmental Policy Instruments to Used Oil'. *Journal of Environmental Planning and Management* 52, no. 4: 457–75.

Connolly, M. E. H. and A. W. Stark. 1992. 'Policy Making and the Demonstration Effect: Privatization in a Deprived Region'. *Public Administration* 70, no. 3: 369–85.

Considine, Mark. 2001. *Enterprising States: The Public Management of Welfare-to-Work*. Cambridge: Cambridge University Press.

Considine, M. and Lewis, J. M. 2003. Bureaucracy, Network, or Enterprise? Comparing Models of Governance in Australia, Britain, the Netherlands and New Zealand. *Public Administration Review* 63, no. 2: 131–40.

Cook, Dee. 2002. 'Consultation, for a Change? Engaging Users and Communities in the Policy Process'. *Social Policy and Administration* 36, no. 5: 516–31.

Cook, P. and C. Kirpatrick. 1988. *Privatization in Less Developed Countries*. New York: St. Martin's Press.

Cooke, Pat. 2007. 'Building a Partnership Model to Manage Irish Heritage: A Policy Tools Analysis'. *Irish Journal of Management* 27, no. 2: 75–97.

Cowan, L. G. 1990. *Privatization in the Developing World*. New York: Greenwood Press.

Cox, Robert W. 1996. *Approaches to World Order*. Cambridge: Cambridge University Press, 296–313.

Crew, Michael and David Parker (eds.) 2006. *International Handbook on Economic Regulation*. Cheltenham: Edward Elgar.

Crew, Michael A. and Charles K. Rowley. 1986. 'Deregulation as an Instrument in Industrial Policy'. *Journal of Institutional and Theoretical Economics* 142: 52–70.

Croley, Steven P. 2007. *Regulation and Public Interests: The Possibility of Good Regulatory Government*. Princeton, NJ: University Press.

Cronin, Thomas E. and Norman C. Thomas. 1970. 'Educational Policy Advisors and the Great Society'. *Public Policy* 18, no. 5: 659–86.

Cross, William. 2007. 'Policy Study and Development in Canada's Political Parties'. In *Policy Analysis in Canada: The State of the Art*, L. Dobuzinskis, M. Howlett and D. Laycock (eds.). Toronto: University of Toronto Press, 233–42.

Crowley, Kate. 2009. 'Can Deliberative Democracy be Practiced? A Subnational Policy Pathway'. *Politics and Policy* 37, no. 5: 995–1021.

Cubbage, Frederick, Patrice Harou and Erin Sills. 2007. 'Policy Instruments to Enhance Multifunctional Forest Management'. *Forest Policy and Economics* 9: 833–51.

Cushman, R. E. 1941. *The Independent Regulatory Commissions*. London: Oxford University Press.

Cutler, A. Claire, Virginia Haufler and Tony Porter. 1999. 'The Contours and Significance of Private Authority in International Affairs'. In *Private Authority and International Affairs*, A. C. Cutler, V. Haufler and T. Porter (eds.). Albany, NY: SUNY Press, 333–76.

Dahl, Robert A. and Charles E. Lindblom. 1953. *Politics, Economics and Welfare: Planning and Politico-Economic Systems Resolved into Basic Social Processes*. New York: Harper and Row.

Dahlberg, Lena. 2005. 'Interaction between Voluntary and Statutory Social Service Provision in Sweden: A Matter of Welfare Pluralism, Substitution or Complementarity?'. *Social Policy and Administration* 39, no. 7: 740–63.

Dalal-Clayton, B. and B. Sadler. 2005. *Strategic Environmental Assessment: A Sourcebook and Reference Guide to International Experience.* London: Earthscan.

Daniels, R. J. and M. J. Trebilcock. 1996. 'Private Provision of Public Infrastructure: An Organizational Analysis of the Next Privatization Frontier'. *University of Toronto Law Journal* 46: 375–426.

Daugbjerg, Carsten. 1997. 'Policy Networks and Agricultural Policy Reforms: Explaining Deregulation in Sweden and Re-regulation in the European Community'. *Governance.* 10, no. 2: 123–42.

—— 1998. *Policy Networks Under Pressure: Pollution Control, Policy Reform and the Power of Farmers.* Aldershot: Ashgate.

Daugbjerg, Carsten and David Marsh. 1998. 'Explaining Policy Outcomes: Integrating the Policy Network Approach with Macro-level and Micro-level Analysis'. In *Comparing Policy Networks.* David Marsh (ed.) Buckingham: Open University Press, 52–71.

Daugbjerg, C. and G. T. Svendsen. 2003. 'Designing Green Taxes in a Political Context: From Optimal to Feasible Environmental Regulation'. *Environmental Politics* 12, no. 4: 76–95.

de Bruijn, J. A. and H. A. M. Hufen. 1998. 'The Traditional Approach to Policy Instruments'. In *Public Policy Instruments: Evaluating the Tools of Public Administration,* B. G. Peters and F. K. M. V. Nispen (eds.). New York: Edward Elgar, 11–32.

de Bruijn, H. and A. L. Porter. 2004. 'The Education of a Technology Policy Analyst – to Process Management'. *Technology Analysis and Strategic Management* 16, no. 2: 261–74.

de Bruijn, J. A. and E. F. ten Heuvelhof. 1991. 'Policy Instruments for Steering Autopoietic Actors'. In *Autopoiesis and Configuration Theory: New Approaches to Societal Steering,* T. Veld, L. Schaap, C. J. A. M. Termeer and M. J. W. Van Twist (eds.). Dordrecht: Kluwer, 161–70.

—— 1995. 'Policy Networks and Governance'. In *Institutional Design,* D. L. Weimer (ed.). Boston, MA: Kluwer Academic Publishers, 161–79.

—— 1997. 'Instruments for Network Management'. In *Managing Complex Networks: Strategies for the Public Sector,* W. J. M. Kickert, E.-H Klijn and J. F. M. Koppenjan (eds.). London: Sage, 119–36.

de la Mothe, J. 1996. 'One Small Step in an Uncertain Direction: The Science and Technology Review and Public Administration in Canada'. *Canadian Public Administration* 39, no. 3: 403–17.

de Lancer Julnes, P. and M. Holzer. 2001. 'Promoting the Utilization of Performance Measures in Public Organizations: An Empirical Study of Factors Affecting Adoption and Implementation'. *Public Administration Review* 61, no. 6: 693–708.

de Moor, A. P. G. 1997. *Perverse Incentives: Hundreds of Billions of Dollars in Subsidies now Harm the Economy, the Environment, Equity and Trade.* San Jose, CA: Earth Council.

De Saulles, Martin. 2007. 'When Public Meets Private: Conflicts in Information Policy'. *Info* 9, no. 6: 10–16.

de Smith, S. A. 1973. *Judicial Review of Administrative Action.* London: Stevens and Son.

De Vita, C. J. and E. C. Twombly. 2005. 'Who Gains from Charitable Tax Credit Programs? The Arizona Model'. *Public Administration Review* 65, no. 1: 57–63.

de Vries, Michiel S. 1999. 'Developments in Europe: The Idea of Policy Generations'. *International Review of Administrative Sciences* 65, no. 4: 491–510.

—— 2002. 'The Changing Functions of Laws and its Implication for Government and Governance'. *International Review of Administrative Sciences* 68, no. 4: 599–618.

—— 2005. 'Generations of interactive Policy-Making in the Netherlands'. *International Review of Administrative Sciences* 71, no. 4: 577–91.

Deber, Raisa, Marcus J. Hollander and Philip Jacobs. 2008. 'Models of Funding and Reimbursement in Health Care: A Conceptual Framework'. *Canadian Public Administration* 51, no. 3: 381–405.

del Río, Pablo. 2010. 'Analysing the Interactions between Renewable Energy Promotion and Energy Efficiency Support Schemes: The Impact of Different Instruments and Design Elements'. *Energy Policy* 38, no. 9: 4978–89.

del Río, Pablo, Javier Carrillo-Hermosilla and Totti Könnölä. 2010. 'Policy Strategies to Promote Eco-Innovation.' *Journal of Industrial Ecology*, forthcoming.

Delacourt, Susan and Donald G. Lenihan (eds.) 2000. *Collaborative Government: Is there a Canadian Way?* Toronto: Institute of Public Administration of Canada.

DeLeon, Peter. 1979. *Development and Diffusion of the Nuclear Power Reactor: A Comparative Analysis.* Cambridge: Ballinger Publishing.

—— 1988. 'The Contextual Burdens of Policy Design'. *Policy Studies Journal* 17, no. 2: 297–309.

—— 1999. 'The Stages Approach to the Policy Process: What Has It Done? Where Is It Going?' In *Theories of the Policy Process*, P. A. Sabatier (ed.). Boulder, CO: Westview, 19–34.

Delmas, M. A. and A. K. Terlaak. 2001. 'A Framework for Analyzing Environmental Voluntary Agreements'. *California Management Review* 43, no. 3: 44–63.

Derlien, Hans-Ulrich. 2008. 'Conclusion'. In *The State at Work, Volume 1: Public Sector Employment in 10 Countries*, Hand-Ulrich Derlien and B. Guy Peters (eds.). Cheltenham: Edward Elgar, 283–91.

Derthick, Martha and Paul J. Quirk. 1985. *The Politics of Deregulation.* Washington, DC: Brookings Institution.

Dery, David. 1984. *Problem Definition in Policy Analysis.* Lawrence: University of Kansas Press.

—— 1999. 'Policy by the Way: When Policy Is Incidental to Making Other Policies'. *Journal of Public Policy* 18, no. 2: 163–76.

Deutsch, K. W. 1963. *The Nerves of Government: Models of Political Communication and Control.* New York: Free Press.

Diamond, John. 2008. 'Capacity Building in the Voluntary and Community Sectors: Towards Relative Independence – Limits and Possibilities'. *Public Policy and Administration* 23, no. 2: 153–66.

Diani, M. 1992. 'Analysing Social Movement Networks'. In *Studying Collective Action*, M. Diani and R. Eyerman (eds.). London: Sage, 107–37.

Dietzenbacher, Erik. 2000. 'Spillovers of Innovation Effects'. *Journal of Policy Modeling* 22, no. 1: 27–42.

Dimitrov, Radoslav. 2002. 'Confronting Nonregimes: Science and International Coral Reef Policy'. *The Journal of Environment Development* 11, no. 1 (March): 53–78.

—— 2005. 'Hostage to Norms: States, Institutions and Global Forest Politics'. *Global Environmental Politics* 5, no. 4: 1–24.

Dimitrov, Radoslav S., Detlef, F Sprinz, Gerald M. DiGiusto and Alexander Kelle. 2007. 'International Nonregimes: A Research Agenda'. *The International Studies Review* 9: 230–58.

Dion, Leon. 1973. 'The Politics of Consultation'. *Government and Opposition* 8, no. 3: 332–53. P. 339

Dobbin, Frank, Beth Simmons and Geoffrey Garrett. 2007. 'The Global Diffusion of Public Policies: Social Construction, Coercion, Competition, or Learning?'. *Annual Review of Sociology* 33: 449–72.

Dobuzinskis, Laurent. 1987. *The Self-Organizing Polity: An Epistemological Analysis of Political Life*. Boulder, CO: Westview.

Dobuzinskis, Laurent, Michael Howlett and David Laycock (eds.) 2007. *Policy Analysis in Canada: The State of the Art*. Toronto: University of Toronto Press.

Doern, G. B. 1967. 'The Role of Royal Commissions in the General Policy Process and in Federal-Provincial Relations'. *Canadian Public Administration* 10, no. 4: 417–33.

—— 1971. 'The Role of Central Advisory Councils: The Science Council of Canada'. In *The Structures of Policy-Making in Canada*, G. B. Doern and P. Aucoin (eds.). Toronto, Macmillan: 246–66.

—— 1974. 'The Concept of Regulation and Regulatory Reform'. In *Issues in Canadian Public Policy*, G. B. Doern and V. S. Wilson (eds.). Toronto: Macmillan, 8–35.

—— 1981. *The Nature of Scientific and Technological Controversy in Federal Policy Formation*. Ottawa: Science Council of Canada.

—— 1983. 'The Mega-Project Episode and the Formulation of Canadian Economic Development Policy'. *Canadian Public Administration* 26, no. 2: 219–38.

Doern, G. B. and R. W. Phidd. 1988. *Canadian Public Policy: Ideas, Structure, Process*. Toronto: Nelson.

Doern, G. B. and S. Wilks. 1998. *Changing Regulatory Institutions in Britain and North America*. Toronto: University of Toronto Press.

Doern, G. B. and V. S. Wilson. 1974. 'Conclusions and Observations'. In *Issues in Canadian Public Policy*, G. B. Doern and V. S. Wilson (eds.). Toronto: Macmillan.

Doerr, Audrey D. 1981. *The Machinery of Government in Canada*. Toronto: Methuen.

—— 1982. 'The Role of Coloured Papers'. *Canadian Public Administration*. 25, no. 3: 366–79.

Dollery, B. and J. Wallis. 1999. *Market Failure, Government Failure, Leadership and Public Policy*. London: Macmillan.

—— 2003. *The Political Economy of the Voluntary Sector: A Reappraisal of the Comparative Institutional Advantage of Voluntary Organizations*. Cheltenham: Edward Elgar.

Dolowitz, David P. and David Marsh. 2000. 'Learning from Abroad: The Role of Policy Transfer in Contemporary Policy-Making'. *Governance* 13, no. 1: 5–23.

d'Ombrain, N. 1997. 'Public Inquiries in Canada'. *Canadian Public Administration* 40, no. 1: 86–107.

Donahue, J. D. 1989. *The Privatization Decision: Public Ends, Private Means*. New York: Basic Books.

Donovan, M. C. 2001. *Taking Aim: Target Populations and the Wars on Aids and Drugs*. Washington, DC: Georgetown University Press.

Doremus, H. 2003. 'A Policy Portfolio Approach to Biodiversity Protection on Private Lands'. *Environmental Science and Policy* 6: 217–32

Dowd, Kevin. 1999. 'Too Big to Fail?: Long-Term Capital Management and the Federal Reserve'. *Cato Institute Briefing Papers* no. 52, www.cato.org/pubs/briefs/bp52.pdf

Drezner, D. W. 2001a. 'Reflection and Reappraisal: Globalization and Policy Convergence'. *International Studies Review* 3, no. 1: 53–78.

—— 2001b. 'Globalization and Policy Convergence'. *International Studies Review* 3, no. 1 (Spring): 53–78.

—— 2005. 'Globalization, Harmonization and Competition: The Different Pathways to Policy Convergence'. *Journal of European Public Policy* 12, no. 5: 841–59.

Dryzek, John. 1983. 'Don't Toss Coins in Garbage Cans: A Prologue to Policy Design'. *Journal of Public Policy* 3, no. 4: 345–67.

Dryzek, J. S. and B. Ripley. 1988. 'The Ambitions of Policy Design'. *Policy Studies Review* 7, no. 4: 705–19.

Dryzek, John S. and Aviezer Tucker. 2008. 'Deliberative Innovation to Different Effect: Consensus Conferences in Denmark, France and the United States'. *Public Administration Review* 68, no. 5: 864–76.

Dunleavy, Patrick. 1986. 'Explaining the Privatization Boom: Public Choice Versus Radical Approaches'. *Public Administration* 64, no. 1: 13–34.

Dunleavy, Patrick and Christopher Hood. 1994. 'From Old Public Administration to New Public Management'. *Public Money and Management* 14, no. 3: 9–16.

Dunlop, Claire A. 2009. 'Policy Transfer as Learning: Capturing Variation in What Decision-Makers Learn from Epistemic Communities'. *Policy Studies* 30, no. 3: 289–311.

Dunn, W. 1986. *Policy Analysis: Perspectives, Concepts and Methods*. New Brunswick, NJ: JAI Press.

Dunn, William N. 2008. *Public Policy Analysis: An Introduction*. Upper Saddle River, NJ: Pearson–Prentice Hall.

Dunsire, A. 1978. *The Execution Process*. Oxford: Martin Robertson.

—— 1986. 'A Cybernetic View of Guidance, Control and Evaluation in the Public Sector'. In *Guidance, Control and Evaluation in the Public Sector*. Franz-Xavier Kaufman, Giandomenico Majone and Vincent Ostrom (eds.) Berlin: Walter de Gruyter, 327–46.

—— 1993a. *Manipulating Social Tensions: Collibration as an Alternative Mode of Government Intervention*. Cologne, Germany: Max Plank Institut fur Gesellschaftsforschung Discussion Paper 93/7.

—— 1993b. 'Modes of Governance'. In *Modern Governance*, J. Kooiman (ed.). London: Sage, 21–34.

Durant, Robert F. 2008. 'Sharpening a Knife Cleverly: Organizational Change, Policy Paradox and the 'Weaponizing' of Administrative Reform'. *Public Administration Review* 68, no. 2: 282–94.

Durr, R. H. 1993. 'What Moves Policy Sentiment?' *American Political Science Review* 87: 158–72.

Dwivedi, O. P., (ed.) 1982. *The Administrative State in Canada: Essays in Honour of J.E. Hodgetts*. Toronto: University of Toronto Press.

Dye, T. R. 1972. *Understanding Public Policy*. Englewood Cliffs, NJ: Prentice-Hall.

Dyerson, Romano and Frank Mueller. 1993. 'Intervention by Outsiders: A Strategic Perspective on Government Industrial Policy'. *Journal of Public Policy* 13, no. 1: 69–88.

Easton, D. 1965. *A Systems Analysis of Political Life*. New York: Wiley.

Economic Council of Canada. 1979. *Responsible Regulation*. Ottawa: Ministry of Supply and Services.

Edelenbos, Jurian and Erik-Hans Klijn. 2005. 'Managing Stakeholder Involvement in Decision-Making: A Comparative Analysis of Six Interactive Processes in the Netherlands'. *Journal of Public Administration Research and Theory* 16, no. 3: 2.

Edelenbos, Jurian, Nienke van Schie and Lasse Gerrits. 2010. 'Organizing Interfaces between Government Institutions and Interactive Governance'. *Policy Sciences* 43, no. 1: 73–94.

Edelman, Murray. 1964. *The Symbolic Uses of Politics*. Chicago, IL: University of Illinois Press.

—— 1971. *Politics as Symbolic Action: Mass Arousal and Quiescence*. Chicago, IL: Markham Publishing.

—— 1988. *Constructing the Political Spectacle*. Chicago, IL: University of Chicago Press.

Eden, Sally. 2009. 'The Work of Environmental Governance Networks: Traceabilty, Credibility and Certification by the Forest Stewardship Council'. *Geoforum* 40: 383–94.

Eden, Sally and Christopher Bear. 2010. 'Third-Sector Global Environmental Governance, Space and Science: Comparing Fishery and Forestry Certification'. *Journal of Environmental Policy and Planning* 12, no. 1: 83–106.

Edley, C. F. J. 1990. *Administrative Law: Rethinking Judicial Control of Bureaucracy*. New Haven, CT: Yale University Press.

Eichbaum, Chris and Richard Shaw. 2008. 'Ministerial Advisers and the Politics of Policy-Making: Bureaucratic Permanence and Popular Control'. *The Australian Journal of Public Administration* 66, no. 4: 453–67.

Eijlander, P. 2005. 'Possibilities and Constraints in the Use of Self-regulation and Co-Regulation in Legislative Policy: Experiences in the Netherlands – Lessons to be Learned for the EU'. *Electronic Journal of Comparative Law* 9, no. 1: 1–8.

Eisner, Marc Allen. 1993. *Regulatory Politics in Transition*. Baltimore, MD: Johns Hopkins University Press.

—— 1994a. 'Discovering Patterns in Regulatory History: Continuity, Change and Regulatory Regimes'. *Journal of Policy History* 6, no. 2: 157–87.

—— 1994b. 'Economic Regulatory Policies: Regulation and Deregulation in Historical Context'. In *Handbook of Regulation and Administrative Law*, D. H. Rosenbloom and R. D. Schwartz (eds.). New York: Marcel Dekker, 91–116.

Elgie, R. 2006. 'Why Do Governments Delegate Authority to Quasi-Autonomous Agencies? The Case of Independent Administrative Authorities in France'. *Governance* 19, no. 2: 207–27.

Eliadis, P., M. Hill and M. Howlett. 2005. *Designing Government: From Instruments to Governance*. Montreal: McGill-Queen's University Press.

Eliste, P. and Fredriksson, P.G. 1998. *Does Open Trade Result in a Race to the Bottom? Cross Country Evidence*, Unpublished MS, World Bank.

Elkin, Stephen L. 1986. 'Regulation and Regime: A Comparative Analysis'. *Journal of Public Policy* 6, no. 1: 49–72.

Elkins, Zachary and Beth Simmons. 2005. 'On Clusters, Waves and Diffusion: A Conceptual Framework'. *Annals of the American Association of Political and Social Science* 598: 33–51.

Elliott, Chris and Rodolphe Schlaepfer. 2001. 'The Advocacy Coalition Framework: Application to the Policy Process for the Development of Forest Certification in Sweden'. *Journal of European Public Policy* 8, no. 4: 642–61.

Elliott, Dominic and Martina McGuinness. 2001. 'Public Inquiry: Panacea or Placebo?' *Journal of Contingencies and Crisis Management* 10, no. 1: 14–25.

Elmore, Richard F. 1978. 'Organizational Models of Social Program Implementation'. *Public Policy* 26, no. 2: 185–228

—— 1987. 'Instruments and Strategy in Public Policy'. *Policy Studies Review* 7, no. 1: 174–86.

Eloi, Laurent. 2009. 'Carbon Tax: The French Connection'. *The Economists' Voice* (December): 1–4.

Elson, Anthony. 2008. 'The Sovereign Wealth Funds of Singapore'. *World Economics* 9, no. 3: 73–96.

English, Linda M. and Matthew Skellern. 2005. 'Public-Private Partnerships and Public Sector Management Reform; a Comparative Analysis'. *International Journal of Public Policy* 1, no. 1/2: 1–21.

Ergas, Henry. 2010. 'New Policies Create a New Politics: Issues of Institutional Design in Climate Change Policy'. *Australian Journal of Agricultural and Resource Economics* 54, no. 2: 143–64.

Esmark, Anders. 2009. 'The Functional Differentiation of Governance: Public Governance beyond Hierarchy, Market and Networks'. *Public Administration* 87, no. 2: 351–70.

Evans, B., T. Richmond and J. Shields. 2005. 'Structuring Neoliberal Governance: The Nonprofit Sector, Emerging New Modes of Control and the Marketisation of Service Delivery'. *Policy and Society* 24, no. 1: 73–97.

Evans, Peter. 1997. 'The Eclipse of the State? Reflections on Stateness in an Era of Globalization'. *World Politics* 50, no. 1: 62–87.

Everitt, Joanna and Brenda O'Neill (eds.) 2002. *Citizen Politics: Research and Theory in Canadian Political Behaviour.* Toronto: Oxford University Press.

Evers, Adalbert. 2005. 'Mixed Welfare Systems and Hybrid Organizations: Changes in the Governance and Provision of Social Services'. *International Journal of Public Administration* 28: 737–48.

Evers, A. and H. Wintersberger (eds.) 1990. *Shifts in the Welfare Mix: Their Impact on Work, Social Services and Welfare Policies.* Frankfurt, Germany/Boulder, CO: Campus/Westview.

Falk, Richard A. 1997. 'State of Siege: Will Globalization Win Out?'. *International Affairs* 73, no. 1: 123–36.

Falkenmark, Malin. 2004. 'Towards Integrated Catchment Management: Opening the Paradigm Locks between Hydrology, Ecology and Policy-Making'. *Water Resources Development* 20, no. 3: 275–82.

Feiock, Richard C., Antonio F. Tavares and Mark Lubell. 2008. 'Policy Instrument Choices for Growth Management and Land Use Regulation'. *Policy Studies Journal* 36, no. 3: 461–80.

Feldman, Martha S. and Anne M. Khademian. 2007. 'The Role of the Public Manager in Inclusion: Creating Communities of Participation'. *Governance* 20, no. 2: 305–24.

Ferreira, Aldonio and David Otley. 2009. 'The Design and Use of Performance Management Systems: An Extended Framework for Analysis'. *Management Accounting Research,* online.

Finer, David, P. Tillgren, K. Berensson, K. Guldbrandsson and B. Hagland. 2005. 'Implementation of a Health Impact Assessment (HIA) Tool in a Regional Health Organization in Sweden – A Feasibility Study'. *Health Promotion International* 20, no. 3: 277–84.

Finkle, Peter, K. Webb, W. Stanbury and P. Pross. 1994. *Federal Government Relations with Interest Groups: A Reconsideration.* Ottawa: Privy Council Office.

Finley, Lawrence K. (ed.) 1989. *Public Sector Privatization: Alternative Approaches to Service Delivery.* New York: Quorum Books.

Firestone, O. J. 1970. *The Public Persuader: Government Advertising.* Toronto: Methuen.

Fischer, F. and J. Forester. 1993. *The Argumentative Turn in Policy Analysis and Planning.* Durham, NC: Duke University Press.

—— 1987. *Confronting Values in Policy Analysis: The Politics of Criteria.* Beverly Hills, CA: Sage.

Fligstein, Neil. 1996. 'Markets as Politics: A Political-Cultural Approach to Market Institutions' *American Sociological Review* 61 (August): 656–73.

Flinders, Matthew V. and Hugh McConnel. 1999. 'Diversity and Complexity: The Quango-Continuum'. In *Quangos, Accountability and Reform: The Politics of Quasi-Government*, ed. Matthew V. Flinders and Martin J. Smith. Sheffield: Political Economy Research Centre, 17–39.

Flitner, David. 1986. *The Politics of Presidential Commissions*. New York: Transnational Publishers.

Flumian, Maryantonett, Amanda Coe and Kenneth Kernaghan. 2007. 'Transforming Service to Canadians: The Service Canada Model'. *International Review of Administrative Sciences* 73, no. 4: 557–68.

Ford, R. and D. Zussman. 1997. *Alternative Service Delivery: Sharing Governance in Canada*. Toronto: KPMG/IPAC.

Forester, John. 1983. 'What Analysts Do'. In *Values, Ethics and the Practice of Policy Analysis*, ed. William N. Dunn. Lexington, MA: Lexington Books, 47–62.

—— 1989. *Planning in the Face of Power*. Berkeley, CA: University of California Press.

Forsyth, Ann, Carissa Schively Slotterback and Kevin J. Krizek. 2010. 'Health Impact Assessment Review'. *Environmental Impact Assessment Review* 30: 42–51.

Foster, Christopher D. and Francis J. Plowden. 1996. *The State under Stress: Can the Hollow State Be Good Government?*. Buckingham/Philadelphia, PA: Open University Press.

Foster, Elizabeth, Marcus Haward and Scott Coffen-Smout. 2005. 'Implementing Integrated Oceans Management: Australia's South East Regional Marine Plan (SERMP) and Canada's Eastern Scotian Shelf Integrated Management (ESSIM) Initiative'. *Marine Policy* 29: 391–405.

Franchino, Fabio and Bjorn Hoyland. 2009. 'Legislative Involvement in Parliamentary Systems: Opportunities, Conflict and Institutional Constraints'. *American Political Science Review* 103, no. 4: 607–21.

Franz, Jennifer S. and Colin Kirkpatrick, 'Improving the Quality of Integrated Policy Analysis: Impact Assessment for Sustainable Development in the Euorpean Commission,' *Evidence & Policy* 4, no. 2 (2008): 171–185.

Freeman, G. P. 1985. 'National Styles and Policy Sectors: Explaining Structured Variation'. *Journal of Public Policy* 5, no. 4: 467–96.

Freeman, J. 1997. 'Collaborative Governance in the Administrative State'. *UCLA Law Review* 45, no. 1: 1–98.

Freeman, J. R. 1989. *Democracy and Markets: The Politics of Mixed Economies*. Ithaca, NY: Cornell University Press.

Friedman, Thomas L. 1999. *The Lexus and the Olive Tree*. New York: HarperCollins.

Frischtak, Claudio R. 1995. 'The Changed Role of the State: Regulatory Policies and Reform in a Comparative Perspective'. In *Regulatory Policies and Reform: A Comparative Perspective*. Frischtak, Claudio R. (ed.) New York: World Bank, 1–15.

Furlong, Scott R. and Cornelius M. Kerwin. 2004. 'Interest Group Participation in Rule Making: A Decade of Change'. *Journal of Public Administration Research and Theory* 15, no. 3: 353–70

Gage, R. W. and M. P. Mandell (eds.). 1990. *Strategies for Managing intergovernmental Policies* and *Networks*. New York, Praeger.

Gall, G. L. 1983. *The Canadian Legal System*. Toronto: Carswell.

Gandy, O. H. 1982. *Beyond Agenda Setting: Information Subsidies and Public Policy*. Norwood, NJ: Ablex.

Garcia-Murillo, M. 2005. 'Regulatory Responses to Convergence; Experience from

Four Countries'. *Info – The Journal of Policy, Regulation and Strategy for Telecommunications* 7, no. 1: 20–40.

Garson, G. David. 1986. 'From Policy Science to Policy Analysis: A Quarter Century of Progress'. In *Policy Analysis: Perspectives, Concepts and Methods*, ed. William N. Dunn. Greenwich, CT: JAI Press, 3–22.

Gayle, Dennis J. and Jonathan N. Goodrich (eds.). 1990. *Privatization and Deregulation in Global Perspective*. Westport, CT: Quorum Books.

Gelders, Dave and Oyvind Ihlen. 2010. 'Government Communication about Potential Policies: Public Relations, Propaganda or Both?' *Public Relations Review* 36, no. 1: 59–62.

—— 2009. 'Minding the Gap: Applying a Service Marketing Model into Government Policy Communications'. *Government Information Quarterly* 27, no. 1: 34–40.

George, A. L. 1969. 'The 'Operational Code': A Neglected Approach to the Study of Political Leaders and Decision-Making'. *International Studies Quarterly* 13: 190–222.

Geva-May, Iris and Allan M. Maslove. 2007. 'In between Trends: Developments of Public Policy Analysis and Policy Analysis Instruction in Canada, the United States and the European Union'. In *Policy Analysis in Canada: The State of the Art*, L. Dobuzinskis, M. Howlett and D. Laycock (eds.). Toronto: University of Toronto Press, 186–216.

Geva-May, Iris and Allan Maslove. 2006. 'Canadian Public Policy Analysis and Public Policy Programs: A Comparative Perspective'. *Journal of Public Affairs Education* 12, no. 4: 413–38.

Gibson, Robert B., (ed.) 1999. *Voluntary Initiatives: The New Politics of Corporate Greening*. Peterborough: Broadview Press.

Gilardi, Fabrizio. 2002. 'Policy Credibility and Delegation to Independent Regulatory Agencies: A Comparative Empirical Analysis'. *Journal of European Public Policy* 9, no. 6: 873–93

—— 2005a. 'The Institutional Foundations of Regulatory Capitalism: The Diffusion of Regulatory Agencies in Western Europe'. *Annals of the American Academy of Political and Social Science* 595, no. 1: 84–101

—— 2005b. 'The Formal Independence of Regulators: A Comparison of 17 Countries and 7 Sectors'. *Swiss Political Science Review* 11, no. 4: 139–67.

—— 2005c. 'Evaluating Independent Regulators'. In *Designing Independent and Accountable Regulatory Authorities for High Quality Regulation – Proceedings of an Expert Meeting in London, United Kingdom 10–11 January 2005* (ed.) OECD Working Party on Regulatory Management and Reform. Paris: OECD, 101–25.

Gill, N. N. 1940. 'Permanent Advisory Committees in the Federal Government'. *Journal of Politics* 2: 411–25.

Gilmore, T. N. and J. Krantz. 1991. 'Innovation in the Public Sector: Dilemmas in the Use of Ad Hoc Processes'. *Journal of Policy Analysis and Management* 10, no. 3: 455–68.

Gipperth, Lena. 2008. 'The Legal Design of the International and European Union Ban on Tributyltin Antifouling Paint: Direct and Indirect Effects'. *Journal of Environmental Management* 90, Supplement: S86-S95.

Gleirscher, Norbert. 2008. 'Policy Instruments in Support of Organic Farming in Austria'. *International Journal of Agricultural Resources, Governance and Ecology* 7, no. 1/2: 51–62.

Glicken, Jessica. 2000. 'Getting Stakeholder Participation 'Right': A Discussion of Participatory Processes and Possible Pitfalls'. *Environmental Science and Policy* 3: 305–10.

Goetz, Anne Marie. 2007. 'Manouevring Past Clientelism: Institutions and Incentives to Generate Constituencies in Support of Governance Reforms'. *Commonwealth and Comparative Politics* 45, no. 4: 403–24.

Goffman, E. 1974. *Frame Analysis: An Essay on the Organization of Experience.* Cambridge, MA: Harvard University Press.

Goggin, Malcolm L. 1987. *Policy Design and the Politics of Implementation: The Case of Child Health Care in the American States.* Knoxville, TN: University of Tennessee Press.

Goggin, M. L., A. O. M. Bowman, J. P. Lester and O'Toole, Larry J. 1990. *Implementation Theory and Practice: Toward A Third Generation.* Glenview, IL: Scott, Foresman/Little, Brown.

Goldmann, K. 2005. 'Appropriateness and Consequences: The Logic of Neo-Institutionalism'. *Governance* 18, no. 1: 35–52.

Goldsmith, S. and W. D. Eggers. 2004. *Governing by Network: The New Shape of the Public Sector.* Washington, DC: Brookings Institution Press.

Goldstein, J. and R. O. Keohane. 1993. *Ideas and Foreign Policy: Beliefs, Institutions and Political Change.* Ithaca, NY: Cornell University Press.

Goodin, R. E. 1980. *Manipulatory Politics.* New Haven, CT: Yale University Press.

Goodin, R. E. and M. Rein. 2001. 'Regimes on Pillars: Alternative Welfare State Logics and Dynamics'. *Public Administration* 79, no. 4: 769–801

Gormley, W. T. 1998 'Regulatory Enforcement'. *Political Research Quarterly* 51, no. 2: 363–83.

—— 1989. *Taming the Bureaucracy: Muscles, Prayers and Other Strategies.* Princeton, NJ: Princeton University Press.

Gormley, William T. 2007. 'Public Policy Analysis: Ideas and Impact'. *Annual Review of Political Science* 10: 297–313.

Gossum, Peter, Bas Arts and Kris Verheyen. 2010. 'From "Smart Regulation" to "Regulatory Arrangements"'. *Policy Sciences* 43, no. 3: 245–61.

Gourevitch, Peter 2004. 'Corporate Governance: Global Markets, National Politics'. In *Governance in a Global Economy*, Kahler, M. and D. Lake (eds.) Princeton, NJ: Princeton University Press, 305–31.

Grabosky, P. N. 1994. 'Green Markets: Environmental Regulation by the Private Sector'. *Law and Policy* 16, no. 4: 419–48.

Grabosky, Peter. 1995. 'Counterproductive Regulation'. *International Journal of the Sociology of Law* 23: 347–69.

Graham, Katherine A. and Susan D. Phillips. 1997. 'Citizen Engagement: Beyond the Customer Revolution'. *Canadian Public Administration* 40, no. 2: 225–73.

Grant, Wyn and Anne MacNamara. 1995. 'When Policy Communities Intersect: The Cases of Agriculture and Banking'. *Political Studies* 43: 509–15.

Grant, Wyn. 2010. 'Policy Instruments in the Common Agricultural Policy'. *West European Politics* 33, no. 1: 22–38.

Grantham Andrew. 2001. 'How Networks Explain Unintended Policy Implementation Outcomes: The Case of UK Rail Privatization'. *Public Administration* 79, no. 4: 851–70.

Greener, Ian. 2006 'Markets in the Public Sector: When Do They Work and What Do We Do When They Don't'. *Policy and Politics* 36, no. 1: 93–108.

—— 2002. 'Understanding NHS Reform: The Policy-Transfer, Social Learning and Path Dependency Perspectives'. *Governance* 15, no. 2: 161–83.

Greenwood, Daniel J. J. 2005. 'Democracy and Delaware: The Mysterious Race to the Bottom/Top'. *Yale Law and Policy Review* 23, no. 2: 402–25.

Grima, A. 1985. 'Participatory Rites: Integrating Public Involvement in Environmental Impact Assessment'. In *Environmental Impact Assessment: The Canadian Experience*. J. B. R. Whitney and V. W. Maclaren (eds.) Toronto: University of Toronto Institute for Environmental Studies, 33–51.

Grimsey, D. and M. K. Lewis. 2004. *Public Private Partnerships: The Worldwide Revolution in Infrastructure Provision and Project Finance*. Cheltenham: Edward Elgar.

Grimshaw, D., S. Vincent and H. Willmott. 2001. 'New Control Modes and Emergent Organizational Forms: Private-Public Contracting in Public Administration'. *Administrative Theory and Practice* 23, no. 3: 407–30.

Grin, J. and H. V. d. Graaf. 1996. 'Implementation as Communicative Action: An Interpretative Understanding of Interactions between Policy Actors and Target Groups'. *Policy Sciences* 29: 291–319.

Gunningham, N., P. Grabosky and D. Sinclair. 1998. *Smart Regulation: Designing Environmental Policy*. Oxford: Clarendon Press.

Gunningham, Neil and Darren Sinclair. 2002. *Leaders and Laggards: Next Generation Environmental Regulation*. Sheffield: Greenleaf Publishing.

Gunningham, Neil and Darren Sinclair. 1999. 'Regulatory Pluralism: Designing Policy Mixes for Environmental Protection'. *Law and Policy* 21, no. 1: 49–76

Gunningham, Neil and Joseph Rees. 1997. 'Industry Self-Regulation: An Institutional Perspective'. *Law and Policy* 19, no. 4: 363–414.

Gunningham, Neil and Mike D. Young. 1997. 'Toward Optimal Environmental Policy: The Case of Biodiversity Conservation'. *Ecology Law Quarterly* 24: 243–98.

Guo, Chao. 2007. 'When Government Becomes the Principal Philanthropist: The Effects of Public Funding on Patterns of Nonprofit Governance'. *Public Administration Review* 67, no. 3: 458–73.

Haas, Ernst B. 1958. *The Uniting of Europe: Political, Social and Economical Forces 1950–1957*. London: Stevens and Sons.

Haas, P. M. 2001. 'Policy Knowledge: Epistemic Communities'. In *International Encyclopedia of the Social and Behavioral Sciences*. Oxford: Pergamon, 11578–86.

—— 2004. When Does Power Listen to Truth? A Constructivist Approach to the Policy Process'. *Journal of European Public Policy* 11, no. 4: 569–92.

Haas, Peter M. 1992. 'Introduction: Epistemic Communities and International Policy Coordination'. *International Organisation* 46: 1–36.

Habermas, Jürgen. 1973. 'What Does a Legitimation Crisis Mean Today? Legitimation Problems in Late Capitalism'. *Social Research* 40, no. 4: 643–67.

—— 1975. *Legitimation Crisis*. Boston, MA: Beacon Press.

Hacker, Jacob S. 2004a. 'Privatizing Risk without Privatizing the Welfare State: The Hidden Politics of Social Policy Retrenchment in the United States'. *American Political Science Review* 98: 243–60.

—— 2004b. 'Reform without Change, Change without Reform: The Politics of US Health Policy Reform in Comparative Perspective'. In *Transatlantic Policymaking in an Age of Austerity: Diversity and Drift*. M. A. Levin and M. Shapiro (eds.) Washington, DC: Georgetown University Press, 13–63.

—— 2004c 'Review Article: Dismantling the Health Care State? Political Institutions, Public Policies and the Comparative Politics of Health Reform'. *British Journal of Political Science*. 34: 693–724.

—— 2005. 'Policy Drift: The Hidden Politics of US Welfare State Retrenchment'. In *Beyond Continuity: Institutional Change in Advanced Political Economies*. W. Streek and K. Thelen (eds.) Oxford: Oxford University Press, 40–82.

Hahn, Robert W. 2008. *Greenhouse Gas Auctions and Taxes: Some Practical Considerations*. Washington, DC: AEI Centre for Regulatory and Market Studies Working Paper 08–12.

Haider, D. 1989. 'Grants as a Tool of Public Policy'. In *Beyond Privatization: The Tools of Government Action* ed. L. M. Salamon. Washington, DC: Urban Institute, 93–124.

Hajer, M. A. 2005. 'Setting the Stage: A Dramaturgy of Policy Deliberation'. *Administration and Society* 36, no. 6: 624–47.

Halffman, Willem and Rob Hoppe. 2005. 'Science/Policy Boundaries: A Changing Division of Labour in Dutch Expert Policy Advice'. In *Democratization of Expertise?*, S. Maasen and P. Weingart (eds.), Dordrecht: Springer, 135–51.

Hall, Michael and Keith Banting. 2000. 'The Nonprofit Sector in Canada: An Introduction'. In *The NonProfit Sector in Canada: Roles and Relationships*, Keith Banting (ed.). Montreal: McGill Queen's University Press, 1–28.

Hall, P. A. 1986. *Governing the Economy: the Politics of State Intervention in Britain and France*. Cambridge: Polity Press.

—— 1989a. 'Conclusion: The Political Power of Economic Ideas'. In *The Political Power of Economic Ideas: Keynesianism across Nations*. Peter A. Hall (ed.) Princeton, NJ: Princeton University Press, 361–92.

—— 1989b. *The Political Power of Economic Ideas: Keynesianism across Nations*. Princeton, NJ: Princeton University Press.

—— 1990. 'Policy Paradigms, Experts, and the State: The Case of Macroeconomic Policy-Making in Britain'. In *Social Scientists, Policy and the State*, S. Brooks and A. G. Gagnon (eds.). New York: Praeger, 53–78.

—— 1992. 'The Change from Keynesianism to Monetarism: Institutional Analysis and British Economic Policy in the 1970s'. In *Structuring Politics: Historical Institutionalism in Comparative Analysis*, S. Steinmo, K. Thelen and F. Longstreth (eds.). Cambridge: Cambridge University Press, 90–114.

—— 1993. 'Policy Paradigms, Social Learning and the State: The Case of Economic Policy-Making in Britain'. *Comparative Politics* 25: 3: 275–96.

Hall, Peter A. and David Soskice. 2001. 'Varieties of Capitalism: The Institutional Foundations of Comparative Advantage'. In *An Introduction to Varieties of Capitalism*. Peter A. Hall and David Soskice (eds.). New York: Oxford University Press, 1–70.

Hall, T. E. and L. J. O'Toole. 2004. 'Shaping Formal Networks through the Regulatory Process'. *Administration and Society* 36, no. 2: 186–207.

Hall, Thad E. and Laurence J. O'Toole. 2000. 'Structures for Policy Implementation: An Analysis of National Legislation, 1965–66 and 1993–94'. *Administration and Society* 31, no. 6: 667–86.

Hall, Thad. 2008. 'Steering Agencies with Short-Term Authorizations'. *Public Administration Review* 68, no. 2: 366–79.

Halligan, John. 1995. 'Policy Advice and the Public Sector'. In *Governance in a Changing Environment*, ed. B. Guy Peters and Donald T. Savoie. Montreal: McGill-Queen's University Press, 138–72.

Halpern, Charlotte. 2010. 'Governing Despite Its Instruments? Instrumentation in EU Environmental Policy'. *West European Politics* 33, no. 1: 39–57.

Hamdouch, Abdelillah, and Marc-Hubert Depret. 'Policy Integration Strategy and the

Development of the 'GreenEconomy': Foundations and Implementation Patterns.' *Journal of Environmental Planning and Management* 53, no. 4 (2010): 473.

Hamelin, Fabrice. 2010. 'Renewal of Public Policy via Instrumental Innovation: Implementing Automated Speed Enforcement in France'. *Governance* 23, no. 3: 509–30.

Hammond, Thomas H. and Jack H. Knott. 1988. 'The Deregulatory Snowball: Explaining Deregulation in the Financial Industry'. *Journal of Politics* 50, no. 1: 3–30.

Hanke, Steve H. and Stephen J. K. Walters. 1990. 'Privatization and Public Choice: Lessons for the LDCs'. In *Privatization and Deregulation in Global Perspective*. Dennis J. Gayle and Jonathan N. Goodrich (eds.). New York: Quorum Books, 97–108.

Hardiman, Niamh and Colin Scott. 2010. 'Governance as Polity: An Institutional Approach to the Evolution of State Functions in Ireland'. *Public Administration* 88, no. 1: 170–89.

Hardin, G. 1968. 'The Tragedy of the Commons'. *Science* 162: 1243–48.

Hardin, R. 1982. *Collective Action*, Baltimore, MD: Johns Hopkins University Press.

Hargrove, Erwin C. 1975. *The Missing Link: The Study of the Implementation of Social Policy*. Washington, DC: The Urban Institute.

Harrington, Winston, Richard D. Morgenstern and Thomas Sterner. 2004. 'Comparing Instrument Choices'. In *Choosing Environmental Policy: Comparing Instruments and Outcomes in the United States and Europe*. Washington DC: RFF Press, 1–22.

Harris, Paul G. 2007. 'Collective Action on Climate Change: The Logic of Regime Failure'. *Natural Resources Journal* 47, no. 1: 195–224.

Harris, Stephen L. 2004. 'Financial Sector Reform in Canada: Interests and the Policy Process'. *Canadian Journal of Political Science* 37, no. 1: 161–84.

Harrison, Kathryn. 1999. 'Retreat from Regulation: The Evolution of the Canadian Environmental Regulatory Regime'. In *Changing the Rules: Canadian Regulatory Regimes and Institutions*. G. Bruce Doern, Richard J. Schultz and Margaret M. Hill (eds.). Toronto: University of Toronto Press, 122–42.

Harrop, M. 1992. *Power and Policy in Liberal Democracies*. Cambridge: Cambridge University Press.

Harter, P. J. and G. C. Eads. 1985. 'Policy Instruments, Institutions and Objectives: An Analytical Framework for Assessing "Alternatives" to Regulation'. *Administrative Law Review* 37: 221–58.

Hasan, Samiul and Jenny Onyx (eds.) 2008. *Comparative Third Sector Governance in Asia*. Dordrecht: Springer.

Hastak, Manoj, Michael B. Mazes and Louis A. Morris. 2001. 'The Role of Consumer Surveys in Public Policy Decision Making'. *Journal of Public Policy and Marketing* 20, no. 2: 170–85.

Haufler, Virginia. 2000. 'Private Sector International Regimes'. In *Non-State Actors and Authority in the Global System*. R. A. Higgott, G. R. D. Underhill and A. Bieler (eds.). London: Routledge, 121–37.

—— 2001. *A Public Role for the Private Sector: Industry Self-Regulation in a Global Economy*. Washington, DC: Carnegie Endowment for International Peace, 2001.

Hawke, G. R. 1993. *Improving Policy Advice*. Wellington, New Zealand: Victoria University Institute of Policy Studies.

Hawkesworth, M. 1992. 'Epistemology and Policy Analysis'. In *Advances in Policy Studies*, ed. W. Dunn and R. M. Kelly. New Brunswick, NJ: Transaction Press, 291–329.

Hawkins, K. and J. M. Thomas. 1989. 'Making Policy in Regulatory Bureaucracies'. In *Making Regulatory Policy*. Pittsburgh, PA: University of Pittsburgh Press, 3–30.

Hawkins, K. and J. M. Thomas. 1989. *Making Regulatory Policy*. Pittsburgh, PA: University of Pittsburgh Press.

Hay, Colin. 2006. 'Globalization and Public Policy'. In *The Oxford Handbook of Public Policy*, ed. Michael Moran, Martin Rein and Robert E. Goodin. Oxford: Oxford University Press, 587–604.

Heald, D. 1990. 'The Relevance of Privatization to Developing Economies'. *Public Administration and Development* 10, no. 1.

Heclo, H. 1974. *Modern Social Politics in Britain and Sweden: From Relief to Income Maintenance*. New Haven, CT: Yale University Press.

Heidbreder, Eva. 2011. 'Structuring the European Administrative Space: Policy Instruments of Multi-Level Administration'. *Journal of European Public Policy*, June.

Heilman, John G. and Roberta W. Walsh. 1992. 'Introduction: Energy Program Evaluation and Policy Design'. *Policy Studies Journal* 20, no. 1: 42–47.

Heinmiller, B. Timothy. 2007. 'The Politics of "Cap and Trade" Policies'. *Natural Resources Journal* 47, no. 2: 445–67.

Heinrichs, Harald. 2005. 'Advisory Systems in Pluralistic Knowledge Societies: A Criteria-Based Typology to Assess and Optimize Environmental Policy Advice'. In *Democratization of Expertise? Exploring Novel Forms of Scientific Advice in Political Decision-Making*. S. Maasen and P. Weingart (eds.). Dordrecht: Springer, 41–61.

Heinz, John P., Edward O. Laumann, Robert H. Salisbury and Robert L. Nelson. 1990. 'Inner Circles or Hollow Cores'. *Journal of Politics* 52, no. 2: 356–90.

Held, D., Anthony McGrew, David Goldblatt and Jonathan Perraton. 1999. *Global Transformations: Politics, Economics and Culture*. Oxford: Polity.

Helleiner, Eric. 1994. *States and the Reemergence of Global Finance*. Ithaca, NY: Cornell University Press.

Hendriks, Carolyn. 2009. 'Deliberative Governance in the Context of Power'. *Policy and Society* 28, no. 3: 173–84.

Hendriks, Carolyn and Lyn Carson. 2008. 'Can the Market Help the Forum? Negotiating the Commercialization of Deliberative Democracy'. *Policy Sciences* 41, no. 4: 293–313.

Henriques, Irene and Perry Sadorsky. 2008. 'Voluntary Environmental Programs: A Canadian Perspective'. *Policy Studies Journal* 36, no. 1: 143–66.

Heritier, A., C. Knill and S. Mingers. 1996. *Ringing the Changes in Europe: Regulatory Competition and the Transformation of the State. Britain, France, Germany*. Berlin: Walter de Gruyter.

Heritier, Adrienne and Dirk Lehmkuhl. 2008. 'Introduction: The Shadow of Hierarchy and New Modes of Governance'. *Journal of Public Policy* 28, no. 1: 1–17.

Heritier, Adrienne and Sandra Eckert. 2008. 'New Modes of Governance in the Shadow of Hierarchy: Self-Regulation by Industry in Europe'. *Journal of Public Policy* 28, no. 1: 113–38.

Hermann, Charles F. 1982. 'Instruments of Foreign Policy'. In *Describing Foreign Policy Behaviour*, P. Callahan, L. P. Brady and M. G. Hermann (eds.). Beverly Hills, CA: Sage, 153–74.

Hernes, Gudmund. 1976. 'Structural Change in Social Processes'. *American Journal of Sociology* 82, no. 3: 513–47.

Herranz, Joaquin. 2007. 'The Multisectoral Trilemma of Network Management'. *Journal of Public Administration Research and Theory* 18, no. 1: 1–31.

Herrick, C. 2004. 'Objectivity versus Narrative Coherence: Science, Environmental Policy and the U.S. Data Quality Act'. *Environmental Science and Policy* 7, no. 5 (10): 419–33.

Hessing, M., M. Howlett and T. Summerville. 2005. *Canadian Natural Resource and Environmental Policy: Political Economy and Public Policy*. Vancouver: University of British Columbia Press.

Hilgartner, S. and C. L. Bosk. 1988. 'The Rise and Fall of Social Problems: A Public Arenas Model'. *American Journal of Sociology* 94, no. 1: 53–78.

Hill, C. J., Lynn, L. E. 2004. 'Is Hierarchical Governance in Decline? Evidence from Empirical Research'. *Journal of Public Administration Research and Theory* 15, no. 2: 173–95.

Hill, M. and P. Hupe. 2006. 'Analysing Policy Processes as Multiple Governance: Accountability in Social Policy'. *Policy and Politics* 34, no. 3: 557–73.

Hippes, Gjalt. 1988. 'New Instruments for Environmental Policy: A Perspective'. *International Journal of Social Economics* 15, no. 3/4: 42–51.

Hira, Anil, David Huxtable and Alexandre Leger. 2005. 'Deregulation and Participation: An international Survey of Participation in Electricity Regulation'. *Governance* 18, no. 1: 53–88.

Hird, J. A. 2005. *Power, Knowledge and Politics: Policy Analysis in the States*. Washington, DC: Georgetown University Press.

Hoberg, G. and E. Morawaski. 1997. 'Policy Change through Sector Intersection: Forest and Aboriginal Policy in Clayoquot Sound'. *Canadian Public Administration*, 40, no. 3: 387–414.

Hobson, John and M. Ramesh. 2002. 'Globalisation Makes of States What States Make of It: Between Agency and Structure in the State/Globalisation Debate'. *New Political Economy* 7, no. 1: 5–22.

Hodge, Graeme A. and Carsten Greve. 2007. 'Public-Private Partnerships: An International Performance Review'. *Public Administration Review*, May/June: 545–58.

Hodgetts, J. E. 1955. *Pioneer Public Service: and Administrative History of the United Canadas, 1841–1867*. Toronto: University of Toronto Press.

—— 1964. 'Challenge and Response: A Retrospective View of the Public Service of Canada'. *Canadian Public Administration* 7, no. 4: 409–21.

—— 1973. *The Canadian Public Service: A Physiology of Government 1867–1970*. Toronto: University of Toronto Press.

Hodgetts, J. E., G. B. Doern, V. S. Wilson and R. Whitaker. 1972. *The Biography of an Institution: The Civil Service Commission of Canada, 1908–1967*. Kingston: McGill-Queen's Press.

Hoek, Janet and Bronwyn King. 2008. 'Food Advertising and Self-Regulation: A View from the Trenches'. *Australian and New Zealand Journal of Public Health* 32, no. 3: 261–65.

Hogwood, Brian W. and B. Guy Peters. 1982. 'The Dynamics of Policy Change: Policy Succession'. *Policy Sciences* 14, no. 3: 225–45.

Hollander, M. J. and M. J. Prince. 1993. 'Analytical Units in Federal and Provincial Governments: Origins, Functions and Suggestions for Effectiveness'. *Canadian Public Administration* 36, no. 2: 190–224.

Hood, C. 1983. 'Using Bureaucracy Sparingly'. *Public Administration* 61, no. 2: 197–208.

—— 1986a. *Administrative Analysis: An Introduction to Rules, Enforcement and Organizations*. Sussex: Wheatsheaf.

—— 1986b. 'The Hidden Public Sector: The "Quangocratization" of the World?'. In *Guidance, Control and Evaluation in the Public Sector*, F.-X. Kaufman, G. Majone and V. Ostrom (eds.). Berlin: Walter de Gruyter, 183–207.

—— 1986c. *The Tools of Government*. Chatham: Chatham House Publishers.

—— 1991. 'A Public Management for All Seasons?' *Public Administration* 69, Spring: 3–19.

—— 1995. 'Contemporary Public Management: A New Global Paradigm?' *Public Policy and Administration* 10, no. 2: 104–17.

—— 2004. 'Controlling Public Services and Government: Towards a Cross-National Perspective'. In *Controlling Modern Government; Variety, Commonality and Change*, C. Hood, O. James, B. G. Peter and C. Scott (eds.). Cheltenham: Edward Elgar, 3–21.

—— 2006. 'The Tools of Government in the Information Age'. In *The Oxford Handbook of Public Policy*. Michael Moran, Martin Rein and Robert E. Goodin (eds.). New York: Oxford University Press, 469–81.

—— (2007). 'Intellectual Obsolescence and Intellectual Makeovers: Reflections on the Tools of Government after Two Decades'. *Governance* 20, no. 1: 127–44.

Hood, C. and H. Margetts 2007. *The Tools of Government in the Digital Age*. London: Palgrave Macmillan.

Hood, Christopher , 'What Happens When Transparency Meets Blame-Avoidance?,' *Public Management Review* 9, no. 2 (2007): 191–210.

Hood, Christopher, Colin Scott, Oliver James, George Jones and Tony Travers. 1999. *Regulation inside Government: Waste-Watchers, Quality Police and Sleazebusters*. Oxford: Oxford University Press.

Hooghe, L. and Marks, G. 2003. 'Unraveling the Central State, but How? Types of Multi-Level Governance'. *American Political Science Review* 97, no. 2: 233–43.

Hoogvelt, Ankie. 1997. *Globalisation and the Postcolonial World*. Basingstoke: Macmillan, 134–39.

Hornik, R. 1989. 'The Knowledge-Behavior Gap in Public Information Campaigns'. In *Information Campaigns: Managing the Process of Social Change*, C. Salmon (ed.). Newbury Park, CA: Sage.

Hosseus, D. and L. A. Pal. 1997. 'Anatomy of a Policy Area: The Case of Shipping'. *Canadian Public Policy* 23, no. 4: 399–416.

Houle, France and Lorne Sossin. 2006. 'Tribunals and Guidelines: Exploring the Relationships between Fairness and Legitimacy in Administrative Decision-Making'. *Canadian Public Administration* 49, no. 3: 282–307

Hovik, Sissel and Knut Bjorn Stokke. 2007. 'Network Governance and Policy Integration – The Case of Regional Coastal Zone Planning in Norway'. *European Planning Studies* 15, no. 7: 927–44.

Howard, C. 1995. 'Testing the Tools Approach: Tax Expenditures Versus Direct Expenditures'. *Public Administration Review* 55, no. 5: 439–47.

—— 1993. 'The Hidden Side of the American Welfare States'. *Political Science Quarterly* 108, no. 3: 403–36.

—— 1997. *The Hidden Welfare State: Tax Expenditures and Social Policy in the United States*. Princeton, NJ: Princeton University Press.

—— 2002. 'Tax Expenditures'. In *The Tools of Government: A Guide to the New Governance*. L. M. Salamon (ed.). New York: Oxford University Press, 410–44.

Howard, J. L. and W. T. Stanbury. 1984. 'Measuring Leviathan: The Size, Scope and Growth of Governments in Canada'. In *Probing Leviathan: An Investigation of Government in the Economy*, G. Lermer (ed.). Vancouver: Fraser Institute.

Howe, R. B. and D. Johnson. 2000. *Restraining Equality: Human Rights Commissions in Canada*. Toronto: University of Toronto Press.

Howells, Geraint. 2005. 'The Potential and Limits of Consumer Empowerment by Information'. *Journal of Law and Society* 32, no. 3: 349–70.

Howlett, Michael. 1990. 'The Round Table Experience: Representation and Legitimacy in Canadian Environmental Policy Making'. *Queen's Quarterly* 97, no. 4: 580–601.

—— 1991. 'Policy Instruments, Policy Styles and Policy Implementation: National Approaches to Theories of Instrument Choice'. *Policy Studies Journal* 19, no. 2: 1–21.

—— 1996. 'Legitimacy and Governance: Re-Discovering Procedural Policy Instruments'. Vancouver. Paper presented to the Annual Meeting of the British Columbia Political Studies Association.

—— 1997. 'Issue-Attention Cycles and Punctuated Equilibrium Models Re-Considered: An Empirical Examination of Agenda-Setting in Canada'. *Canadian Journal of Political Science* 30: 5–29.

—— 1998. 'Predictable and Unpredictable Policy Windows: Issue, Institutional and Exogenous Correlates of Canadian Federal Agenda-Setting'. *Canadian Journal of Political Science* 31, no. 3: 495–524.

—— 2000a. 'Managing the "Hollow State": Procedural Policy Instruments and Modern Governance'. *Canadian Public Administration* 43, no. 4: 412–31.

—— 2000b. 'Beyond Legalism? Policy Ideas, Implementation Styles and Emulation-Based Convergence in Canadian and U.S. Environmental Policy'. *Journal of Public Policy* 20, no. 3: 305–29.

—— 2001a. 'Policy Venues, Policy Spillovers and Policy Change: The Courts, Aboriginal Rights and British Columbia Forest Policy'. In *In Search of Sustainability: British Columbia Forest Policy in the 1990s*. Cashore, B., Hoberg, G., Howlett, M., Rayner, J. and Wilson, J. (eds.). Vancouver: University of British Columbia Press, 120–40.

—— 2001b. 'Complex Network Management and the Governance of the Environment: Prospects for Policy Change and Policy Stability over the Long Term'. In *Governing the Environment: Persistent Challenges, Uncertain Innovations*, E. Parsons (ed.). Toronto: University of Toronto Press.

—— 2002. 'Policy Instruments and Implementation Styles: The Evolution of Instrument Choice in Canadian Environmental Policy'. In *Canadian Environmental Policy: Context and Cases,* D. L. VanNijnatten and R. Boardman (eds). Toronto: Oxford University Press, 25–45.

—— 2004a. 'Administrative Styles and the Limits of Administrative Reform: A Neo-Institutional Analysis of Administrative Culture'. *Canadian Public Administration* 46, no. 4: 471–94.

—— 2004b. 'Beyond Good and Evil in Policy Implementation: Instrument Mixes, Implementation Styles and Second Generation Theories of Policy Instrument Choice'. *Policy and Society* 23, no. 2: 1–17.

—— 2005. 'What Is a Policy Instrument? Policy Tools, Policy Mixes and Policy Implementation Styles'. In *Designing Government: From Instruments to Governance*, P. Eliadis, M. Hill and M. Howlett (eds). Montreal: McGill-Queen's University Press, 31–50.

—— 2007. 'Analyzing Multi-Actor, Multi-Round Public Policy Decision-Making Processes in Government: Findings from Five Canadian Cases'. *Canadian Journal of Political Science* 40, no. 3: 659–84.

—— 2009a 'Policy Analytical Capacity and Evidence-Based Policy-Making: Lessons from Canada'. *Canadian Public Administration* 52, no. 2: 153–75.

—— 2009b. 'Policy Advice in Multi-Level Governance Systems: Sub-National Policy Analysts and Analysis'. *International Review of Public Administration* 13, no. 3: 1–16.

—— 2009c. 'Governance Modes, Policy Regimes and Operational Plans: A Multi-Level Nested Model of Policy Instrument Choice and Policy Design'. *Policy Sciences* 42, no. 1: 73–89.

Howlett, Michael and Benjamin Cashore. 2009. 'The Dependent Variable Problem in the Study of Policy Change: Understanding Policy Change as a Methodological Problem'. *Journal of Comparative Policy Analysis: Research and Practice* 11, no. 1: 33–46.

Howlett, Michael, Jonathan Craft and Lindsay Zibrik. 2010. 'Government Communication and Democratic Governance: Electoral and Policy-Related Information Campaigns in Canada'. *Policy and Society* 29, no. 1 (January): 13–22.

Howlett, Michael, Jonathan Kim and Paul Weaver. 2006. 'Assessing Instrument Mixes through Program- and Agency-Level Data: Methodological Issues in Contemporary Implementation Research'. *Review of Policy Research*. 23, no. 1: 129–51.

Howlett, Michael and Evert Lindquist. 2004. 'Policy Analysis and Governance: Analytical and Policy Styles in Canada'. *Journal of Comparative Policy Analysis* 6, no. 3: 225–49.

Howlett, Michael and Joshua Newman. 2010. 'Policy Analysts and Policy Work in Federal Systems: Policy Advice and Its Contribution to Evidence-Based Policy-Making in Multi-Level Governance Systems'. *Policy and Society* 29, no. 2: 1–14.

Howlett, M. and M. Ramesh. 2002. 'The Policy Effects of Internationalization: A Subsystem Adjustment Analysis of Policy Change'. *Journal of Comparative Policy Analysis* 4, no. 1: 31–50.

—— 2003. *Studying Public Policy: Policy Cycles and Policy Subsystems*. Toronto: Oxford University Press.

—— 2006. 'Globalization and the Choice of Governing Instruments: The Direct, Indirect and Opportunity Effects of Internationalization'. *International Public Management Journal* 9, no. 2: 175–94.

Howlett, M., M. Ramesh and A. Perl. 2009. *Studying Public Policy: Policy Cycles and Policy Subsystems*. Toronto: Oxford University Press.

Howlett, M. and J. Rayner. 1995. 'Do Ideas Matter? Policy Subsystem Configurations and the Continuing Conflict Over Canadian Forest Policy'. *Canadian Public Administration* 38, no. 3: 382–410.

—— 2004. '(Not so) 'Smart Regulation'? Canadian Shellfish Aquaculture Policy and the Evolution of Instrument Choice for Industrial Development'. *Marine Policy* 28, no. 2: 171–84.

—— 2006a. 'Policy Divergence as a Response to Weak International Regimes: The Formulation and Implementation of Natural Resource New Governance Arrangements in Europe and Canada'. *Policy and Society* 24, no. 2: 16–45.

—— 2006b. 'Globalization and Governance Capacity: Explaining Divergence in National Forest Programmes as Instances of "Next-Generation" Regulation in Canada and Europe'. *Governance* 19, no. 2: 251–75.

—— 2006c. 'Convergence and Divergence in "New Governance", Arrangements: Evidence from European Integrated Natural Resource Strategies'. *Journal of Public Policy* 26, no. 2: 167–89.

—— 2007. 'Design Principles for Policy Mixes: Cohesion and Coherence in "New Governance Arrangements"'. *Policy and Society* 26, no. 4: 1–18.

Howlett, Michael, Jeremy Rayner and Chris Tollefson. 2009. 'From Government to Governance in Forest Planning? Lesson from the Case of the British Columbia Great Bear Rainforest Initiative'. *Forest Policy and Economics* 11: 383–91.

Howse, R., J. R. S. Prichard and M. J. Trebilcock. 1990. 'Smaller or Smarter Government?' *University of Toronto Law Journal* 40: 498–541.

Huber, George P. 1991. 'Organization Learning: The Contributing Processes and the Literatures'. *Organization Science* 2, no. 1: 88–115.

Hudson, John, Stuart Lowe, Natalie Oscroft and Carolyn Snell. 2007. 'Activating Policy Networks: A Case Study of Local Environmental Policy-Making in the United Kingdom'. *Policy Studies* 28, no. 1: 55–70.

Huestis, Lynne. 1993. 'Enforcement of Environmental Law in Canada'. In *Environmental Law and Business in Canada* Thompson, McConnell and Huestis (eds.). Aurora: Canada Law Book, 240–55.

Huitt, R. K. 1968. 'Political Feasibility'. In *Political Science and Public Policy*, A. Rannay (ed.). Chicago: Markham Publishing Co, 263–76.

Hula, R. C. 1988. 'Using Markets to Implement Public Policy'. In *Market-Based Public Policy*, R. C. Hula (ed.). London: Macmillan, 3–20.

Hula, Richard, Cynthia Jackson-Elmoore and Laura Reese. 2007. 'Mixing God's Work and the Public Business: A Framework for the Analysis of Faith-Based Service Delivery'. *Review of Policy Research* 24, no. 1: 67–89.

Huntington, Samuel P. 1952. 'The Marasmus of the ICC: The Commissions, the Railroads and the Public Interest'. *Yale Law Review* 61, no. 4: 467–509

Hutter, Bridget M. 1989. 'Variations in Regulatory Enforcement Styles'. *Law and Policy* 11, no. 2: 153–74.

Hutter, B. M. and P. K. Manning. 1990. 'The Contexts of Regulation: The Impact upon Health and Safety Inspectorates in Britain'. *Law and Policy* 12, no. 2: 103–36.

Hysing, Erik. 2009. 'From Government to Governance? A Comparison of Environmental Governing in Swedish Forestry and Transport'. *Governance* 22, no. 4: 647–72.

Iacobucci, E., M. Trebilcock and R. A. Winter. 2006. 'The Canadian Experience with Deregulation'. *University of Toronto Law Journal* 56, no. 1: 1–63.

Iannuzzi, Alphonse. 2001. *Industry Self-Regulation and Voluntary Environmental Compliance*. Boca Raton, FL: Lewis Publishers.

Igielska, Bogumila. 2008. 'Climate Change Mitigation: Overview of the Environmental Policy Instruments'. *International Journal of Green Economics* 2, no.2: 210–25.

Ikenberry, G. Jon. 1990. 'The International Spread of Privatization Policies: Inducements, Learning and "Policy Bandwagoning"'. In *The Political Economy of Public Sector Reform and Privatization* Ezra N. Suleiman and Jon Waterbury (eds.). Boulder: Westview Press, 88–110.

in't Veld, Roeland J. 1998. 'The Dynamics of Instruments'. In *Public Policy Instruments: Evaluating the Tools of Public Administration*, B. Guy Peters and F. K. M. Van Nispen (eds.). New York: Edward Elgar, 153–62.

Ingraham, P. 1987. 'Toward More Systematic Considerations of Policy Design'. *Policy Studies Journal* 15, no. 4: 611–28.

Ingram, Helen M. and Dean E. Mann. 1980. 'Policy Failure: An Issue Deserving Analysis'. In *Why Policies Succeed or Fail* H. M. Ingram and D. E. Mann (eds.). Beverly Hills, CA: Sage Publications, 11–32.

Ingram, H. and D. E. Mann (eds) 1980. *Why Policies Succeed or Fail*. Beverly Hills, CA: Sage Publications.

Ito, Takatoshi and Anne O. Kreuger (eds.) 2004. *Governance, Regulation and Privatization in the Asia-Pacific Region*. Chicago: University of Chicago Press.

Jacobsen, J. K. 1995. 'Much Ado about Ideas: The Cognitive Factor in Economic Policy'. *World Politics* no. 47: 283–310.

Jacobzone, Stephane. 2005. 'Independent Regulatory Authorities in OECD Countries: An Overview'. In *Designing Independent and Accountable Regulatory Authorities for High Quality Regulation – Proceedings of an Expert Meeting in London, United Kingdom 10–11 January 2005*, 72–100. Paris: OECD Working Party on Regulatory Management and Reform.

Jaffe, L. L. 1965. *Judicial Control of Administrative Action*. Boston, MA: Little, Brown.

Jahn, Gabriele, Matthias Schramm and Achim Spiller. 2005 'The Reliability of Certification: Quality Labels as a Consumer Policy Tool'. *Journal of Consumer Policy* 28: 53–73.

James, Thomas E., and Paul D. Jorgensen. 'Policy Knowledge, Policy Formulation, and Change: Revisiting a Foundational Question.' *Policy Studies Journal* 37, no. 1 (2009): 141–162.

Jann, W. and K. Wegrich. 2007. 'Theories of the Policy Cycle'. In *Handbook of Public Policy Analysis: Theory, Politics and Methods*, F. Fischer, G. J. Miller and M. S. Sidney (eds.). Boca Raton, FL: CRC Press, 43–62.

Jasanoff, Sheila. 1998. *The Fifth Branch: Science Advisers as Policymakers*. Cambridge, MA: Harvard University Press.

Jayasuriya, K. 2001. 'Globalization and the Changing Architecture of the State: The Regulatory State and the Politics of Negative Co-ordination'. *Journal of European Public Policy* 8, no. 1: 101–23.

—— 2004. 'The New Regulatory State and Relational Capacity'. *Policy and Politics* 32, no. 4: 487–501.

Jenson, Jane. 1994. 'Commissioning Ideas: Representation and Royal Commissions'. In *How Ottawa Spends, 1994–95: Making Change*, Susan D. Phillips (ed.). Ottawa: Carleton University Press, , 39–69.

Jentoft, Sven. 2000. 'Legitimacy and Disappointment in Fisheries Management'. *Marine Policy* 24: 141–48.

Jochim, Ashley E. and Peter J. May. 2010. 'Beyond Subsystems: Policy Regimes and Governance'. *Policy Studies Journal* 38, no. 2: 303–27.

Johannesen, Anne Borge. 2006. 'Designing Integrated Conservation and Development Projects (ICDPs): Illegal Hunting, Wildlife Conservation and the Welfare of the Local People'. *Environment and Development Economics* 11, no. 1: 247–67.

Johansson, Roine and Klas Borell. 1999. 'Central Steering and Local Networks: Old-Age Care in Sweden'. *Public Administration* 77, no. 3: 585–98.

Jones, C. O. 1984. *An Introduction to the Study of Public Policy*. Monterey, CA: Brooks/Cole.

Johnsen, A. 2005. 'What Does 25 Years of Experience Tell Us about the State of Performance Measurement in Public Policy and Management?' *Public Money and Management* 25, no. 1: 9–17.

Jonsson, Gun and Ingrid Zakrisson. 2005. 'Organizational Dilemmas in Voluntary Associations'. *International Journal of Public Administration* 28: 849–56.

Jordan-Zachery, Julia S. 2007. 'Policy Interaction: The Mixing of Fatherhood, Crime and Urban Policies'. *Journal of Social Policy* 27, no. 1: 81–102

Jordan, A. G. 1981. 'Iron Triangles, Woolly Corporatism and Elastic Nets: Images of the Policy Process'. *Journal of Public Policy* 1, no. 1: 95–123.

—— 2008. 'The Governance of Sustainable Development: Taking Stock and Looking Forwards'. *Environment and Planning C: Government and Policy* 26: 17–33.

Jordan, A., Wurzel R. and Zito A. 2003. 'New Instruments of Environmental Governance'. *Environmental Politics* 12, no. 3: 1–24.

—— 2005. 'The Rise of "New" Policy Instruments in Comparative Perspective: Has Governance Eclipsed Government?' *Political Studies* 53, 477–96.

Jordan, Andrew, Rudiger Wurzel and Anthony Zito (eds.) 2003. *'New' Instruments of Environmental Governance: National Experiences and Prospects*. London: Frank Cass.

Jordan, G. and J. Richardson. 1982. 'The British Policy Style or the Logic of Negotiation?' In *Policy Styles in Western Europe*, J. Richardson (ed.). London: Allen and Unwin, 80–110.

Jordana, J. and D. Levi-Faur (eds.) 2004. *The Politics of Regulation: Institutions and Regulatory Reforms for the Age of Governance*. Cheltenham: Edward Elgar.

—— 2004. 'The Politics of Regulation in the Age of Governance'. In *Politics of Regulation*. Jordana, Jacint and David Levi-Faur (eds.). Cheltenham: Edward Elgar, 1–28.

Jorgensen, Henning and Flemming Larsen. 1997. 'The Blessings of Network Steering? Theoretical and Empirical Arguments for Coordination Concepts as Alternatives to Policy Design'. Aalborg: Aalborg University Working Paper.

Kagan, R. A. 1991. 'Adversarial Legalism and American Government'. *Journal of Policy Analysis and Management* 10, no. 3: 369–406.

—— 1994. 'Regulatory Enforcement'. In *Handbook of Regulation and Administrative Law*, D. H. Rosenbloom and R. D. Schwartz (eds.). New York: Marcel Dekker, 383–422

—— 1996. 'The Political Construction of American Adversarial Legalism'. In *Courts and the Political Process*, A. Ranney (ed.). Berkeley, CA: Institute of Governmental Studies Press, 19–39.

—— 1997. 'Should Europe Worry about Adversarial Legalism?' *Oxford Journal of Legal Studies* 17, no. 2: 165–83.

—— 2001. *Adversarial Legalism: The American Way of Law*. Cambridge, MA: Harvard University Press.

Kagan, Robert A. and Lee Axelrad. 1997. 'Adversarial Legalism: An International Perspective'. In *Comparative Disadvantages? Social Regulations and the Global Economy*, P. S. Nivola (ed.). Washington, DC: Brookings Institution Press, 146–202.

Kahler, M. and D. Lake (eds.) 2004. *Governance in a Global Economy*. Princeton, NJ: Princeton University Press.

Kahler, Miles. 2004. 'Modeling Races to the Bottom'. Unpublished paper. http://irpshome.ucsd.edu/faculty/mkahler/RaceBott.pdf

Kahn, A. E. 1970. *The Economic of Regulation: Principles and Institutions – Vol 1- Economic Principles*. New York: John Wiley.

Kamerman, Sheila B. and Alfred J. Kahn, (eds.) 1989. *Privatization and the Welfare State*. Princeton, NJ: Princeton University Press.

Kapstein, Ethan B. 1994. *Governing the Global Economy*. Cambridge, MA: Harvard University Press.

Karamanos, Panagiotis. 2001. 'Voluntary Environmental Agreements: Evolution and Definition of a New Environmental Policy Approach'. *Journal of Environmental Planning and Management* 44, no. 1: 67–84.

Kash, Jeffrey P. 2008. 'Enemies to Allies: The Role of Policy-Design Adaptation in Facilitating a Farmer-Environmentalist Alliance'. *Policy Studies Journal* 36, no. 1: 39–60.

Kassim, Hussein and Patrick Le Galès. 2010. 'Exploring Governance in a Multi-Level Polity: A Policy Instruments Approach'. *West European Politics* 33, no. 1: 1–21.

Katzenstein, P. J. 1977. 'Conclusion: Domestic Structures and Strategies of Foreign Economic Policy'. *International Organization* 31, no. 4: 879–920.

—— (1985) *Small States in World Markets: Industrial Policy in Europe.* Ithaca, NY: Cornell University Press.

Katzman, M. T. 1988. 'Societal Risk Management through the Insurance Market'. In *Market-Based Public Policy,* R. C. Hula (ed.). London: Macmillan: 21–42.

Kautto, Petrus and Jukka Simila. 2005. 'Recently Introduced Policy Instruments and Intervention Theories'. *Evaluation* 11, no. 1: 55–68.

Keast, R., M. Mandell and K. Brown. 2006. 'Mixing State, Market and Network Governance Modes: The Role of Government in 'Crowded' Policy Domains'. *International Journal of Organization Theory and Behaviour* 9, no. 1: 27–50.

Kemp, R. L. 1991. *Privatization: The Provision of Public Services by the Private Sector.* Jefferson, NC: McFarland and Co.

Keohane, Nathaniel O., Richard L. Revesz and Robert N. Stavins. 1998. 'The Choice of Regulatory Instruments in Environmental Policy'. *Harvard Environmental Law Review* 22: 313–67.

Keohane, Robert O. and Stanley Hoffman. 1991. 'Institutional Change in Europe in the 1980s'. In *The New European Community: Decision-Making and Institutional Change* Robert O. Keohane and Stanley Hoffman (eds.). Boulder, CO: Westview, 1–40.

Kern, Florian, and Michael Howlett. 2009. 'Implementing Transition Management as Policy Reforms: A Case Study of the Dutch Energy Sector'. *Policy Sciences* 42, no. 4: 391–408.

Kernaghan, Kenneth. 1993. 'Partnership and Public Administration: Conceptual and Practical Considerations'. *Canadian Public Administration* 36, no. 1: 57–76.

Kernaghan, Kenneth. 1985. 'Judicial Review of Administration Action'. In *Public Administration in Canada: Selected Readings,* Kenneth Kernaghan (ed.). Toronto: Methuen, 358–73.

Kernaghan, Kenneth, Brian Marson and Sandford Borins. 2000. *The New Public Organization.* Toronto: Institute of Public Administration of Canada.

Kerwin, Cornelius M. 1994. 'The Elements of Rule-Making'. In *Handbook of Regulation and Administrative Law,* D. H. Rosenbloom and R. D. Schwartz (eds.). New York: Marcel Dekker, 345–81.

—— 1999. *Rulemaking: How Government Agencies Write Law and Make Policy.* Washington, DC: CQ Press.

Keyes, John Mark. 1996. 'Power Tools: The Form and Function of Legal Instruments for Government Action'. *Canadian Journal of Administrative Law and Practice* 10: 133–74.

Keysar, Elizabeth. 2005. 'Procedural Integration in Support of Environmental Policy Objectives: Implementing Sustainability'. *Journal of Environmental Planning and Management* 48, no. 4: 549–69.

Kickert, W. J. M. 2001. 'Public Management of Hybrid Organizations: Governance of Quasi-Autonomous Executive Agencies'. *International Public Management Journal* 4: 135–50.

Kickert, W. J. M. and J. F. M. Koppenjan. 1997. 'Public Management and Network Management: An Overview'. In *Managing Complex Networks: Strategies for the Public Sector,* W. J. M. Kickert, E.-H Klijn and J. F. M. Koppenjan (eds.). London: Sage, 35–61.

Kickert, W. J. M., E.-H. Klijn and J.F.M. Koppenjan. 1997. 'Managing Networks in the Public Sector: Findings and Reflections'. In *Managing Complex Networks: Strategies for the Public Sector*, W. J. M. Kickert, E.-H. Klijn and J. F. M. Koppenjan (eds.). London: Sage, 166–91

Kiesling, Lynne. 2001. 'Flimsy Excuse for More Regulation'. *Houston Chronicle*, December 2.

King, David C. and Jack L. Walker. 1991. 'The Origins and Maintenance of Groups'. In *Mobilizing Interest Groups in America: Patrons, Professions and Social Movements* J. L. Walker (ed.). Ann Arbor: University of Michigan Pres, 75–102.

King, Graham. 2003. 'The Role of Participation in the European Demonstration Projects in ICZM'. *Coastal Management* 31, no. 2: 137–143.

Kingdon, John W. 1984. *Agendas, Alternatives and Public Policies*. Boston, MA: Little, Brown and Company.

Kirschen, E. S., J. Benard, H. Besters, F. Blackaby, O. Eckstein, J. Faaland, F. Hartog, L. Morissens and E. Tosco (eds.) 1964. *Economic Policy in Our Time*. I – General Theory. Chicago, IL: Rand McNally.

Kissane, Rebecca Joyce. 2007. 'How Do Faith-Based Organizations Compare to Secular Providers? Nonprofit Directors' and Poor Women's Assessments of FBOs'. *Journal of Poverty* 11, no. 4: 91–115.

Kiviniemi, M. 1986. 'Public Policies and Their Targets: A Typology of the Concept of Implementation'. *International Social Science Journal* 38, no. 108: 251–66.

Kleiman, M. A. R. and S. M. Teles. 2006. 'Market and Non-Market Failures'. In *The Oxford Handbook of Public Policy*, M. Moran, M. Rein and R. E. Goodin (eds.). Oxford: Oxford University Press, 624–50.

Klijn, Erik-Hans. 1996. 'Analyzing and Managing Policy Processes in Complex Networks: A Theoretical Examination of the Concept Policy Network and Its Problems'. *Administration and Society* 28, no. 1: 90–119.

—— 2002. 'Governing Networks in the Hollow State: Contracting Out, Process Management, or a Combination of the Two?' *Public Management Review* 4, no. 2: 149–65.

Klijn, E. and Koppenjan, J. 2000a. 'Interactive Decision Making and Representative Democracy: Institutional Collisions and Solutions'. In *Governance in Modern Society: Effects, Change and Formation of Government Institutions*. van Heffen, O., Kickert, W. and Thomassen, J. (eds.) Dordrecht: Kluwer, 109–34.

—— 2000b. 'Politicians and Interactive Decision Making: Institutional Spoilsports or Playmakers'. *Public Administration* 78, no. 2: 365–87.

—— 2006. 'Institutional Design: Changing Institutional Features of Networks'. *Public Management Review* 8, no. 1: 141–60.

—— 2007. 'Governing Policy Networks'. In *Handbook of Decision Making*, G. Morcol (ed.). New York: CRC/Taylor & Francis, 169–87.

Klijn, E.-H, J. Koppenjan and K. Termeer. 1995. 'Managing Networks in the Public Sector: A Theoretical Study of Management Strategies in Policy Networks'. *Public Administration* 73: 437–54.

Klijn, Erik-Hans and Chris Skelcher. 2007. 'Democracy and Governance Networks: Compatible of Not?' *Public Administration* 85, no. 3: 587–608.

Klijn, Erik-Hans, Steijn, Bram and Jurian Edelenbos. 2010. 'The Impact of Network Management on Outcomes in Governance Network'. *Public Administration*, forthcoming.

Klijn, E. H. and G. R. Teisman. 1991. 'Effective Policymaking in a Multi-Actor Setting: Networks and Steering'. In *Autopoiesis and Configuration Theory: New*

Approaches to Societal Steering, R. T. Veld, L. Schaap, C. J. A. M. Termeer, and M J. W. Van Twist (eds.). Dodrecht: Kluwer, 99–111.

Klitgaard, Michael Baggesen. 2008. 'School Vouchers and the New Politics of the Welfare State'. *Governance* 21, no. 4: 479–98.

Knill, Christoph. 1998. 'European Policies: The Impact of National Administrative Traditions'. *Journal of Public Policy* 18, no. 1: 1–28.

—— 1999. 'Explaining Cross-National Variance in Administrative Reform: Autonomous versus Instrumental Bureaucracies'. *Journal of Public Policy* 19, no. 2: 113–39.

—— 2001a. *The Europeanization of National Administrations: Patterns of Institutional Change and Persistence*. Cambridge: Cambridge University Press.

—— 2001b. 'Private Governance across Multiple Arenas: European Interest Associations as Interface Actors'. *Journal of European Public Policy* 8, no. 2: 227–46.

Knill, Christoph and Dirk Lehmkuhl. 2002. 'Private Actors and the State: Internationalization and Changing Patterns of Governance'. *Governance* 15, no. 1: 41–63.

Knill, Christoph and Andrea Lenschow. 2005. 'Compliance, Communication and Competition: Patterns of EU Environmental Policy Making and Their Impact on Policy Convergence'. *European Environment* 15: 114–28.

Knoepfel, Peter and Ingrid Kissling-Naf. 1998. 'Social Learning in Policy Networks'. *Policy and Politics* 26, no. 3: 343–67.

Knoke, D. 1987. *Political Networks: The Structural Perspective*. Cambridge: Cambridge University Press.

—— 1993. 'Networks as Political Glue: Explaining Public Policy-Making'. In *Sociology and the Public Agenda*, W. J. Wilson (ed.). London: Sage, 164–84.

—— 2004. 'The Sociopolitical Construction of National Policy Domains'. In *Interdisziplinare Sozialforschung: Theorie und Empirische andewendungen*, C. H. C. A. Henning and C. Melbeck (eds.). Frankfurt: Campus Verlag, 81–96.

Knoke, D. and J. H. Kuklinski. 1991. 'Network Analysis: Basic Concepts'. In *Markets, Hierarchies and Networks: The Coordination of Social Life*, G. Thompson, J. Frances, R. Levacic and J. Mitchell (eds.). London: Sage, 173–82.

Knott, Jack H. and Diane McCarthy. 2007. 'Policy Venture Capital: Foundations, Government Partnerships and Child Care Programs'. *Administration and Society* 39, no. 3: 319–53.

Koen, Verhoest, Paul G. Roness, Bram Verschuere, Kristin Rubecksen and Muiris MacCarthaigh. 2010. *Autonomy and Control of State Agencies: Comparing States and Agencies*. London: Palgrave Macmillan.

Kogan, Vladimir. 2010. 'Lessons from Recent State Constitutional Conventions'. *California Journal of Politics and Policy* 2, no. 2, article 3.

Kohler-Koch, B. 1996. 'Catching up with Change: The Transformation of Governance in the European Union'. *Journal of European Public Policy* 3, no. 3: 359–80.

Kooiman, Jan, (ed.) 1993. 'Governance and Governability: Using Complexity, Dynamics and Diversity'. In *Modern Governance*. London: Sage, 35–50.

—— 2000. 'Societal Governance: Levels, Models and Orders of Social-Political Interaction'. In *Debating Governance*, J. Pierre (ed.). Oxford: Oxford University Press, 138–66.

—— 2008. 'Exploring the Concept of Governability'. *Journal of Comparative Policy Analysis* 10, no. 2: 171–90.

Koppell, Jonathan G. S. 2003. *The Politics of Quasi-Government: Hybrid Organizations and the Dynamics of Bureaucratic Control*. Cambridge: Cambridge University Press.

Koppenjan, J. and E.-H. Klijn. 2004. *Managing Uncertainties in Networks: A Network Approach to Problem Solving and Decision Making*. London: Routledge.

Kritzinger, Sylvia and Helga Pulzl. 2008. 'Governance Modes and Interests: Higher Education and Innovation Policy in Austria'. *Journal of Public Policy* 28, no. 3: 289–307.

Krysiak, Frank C., and Patrick Schweitzer. 2010. 'The Optimal Size of a Permit Market'. *Journal of Environmental Economics and Management* 60, no. 2: 133–43.

Kuhlmann, Ellen and Judith Allsop. 2008. 'Professional Self-Regulation in a Changing Architecture of Governance: Comparing Health Policy in the UK and Germany'. *Policy and Politics* 36, no. 2: 173–89.

Kuhn, T. S. 1962. *The Structure of Scientific Revolutions*. Chicago, IL: University of Chicago Press.

Kuhn, T. S. and F. Suppe. 1974. 'Second Thoughts on Paradigms'. In *The Structure of Scientific Theories*. Urbana, IL: University of Illinois Press, 459–82.

La Porte, Todd (ed.) 1975. *Organized Social Complexity Challenge to Politics and Policy*. Princeton, NJ: Princeton University Press.

Ladi, Stella. 2000. 'Globalization, Think-Tanks and Policy Transfer'. In *Banking on Knowledge: The Genesis of the GDN,* D. Stone (ed.). London: Routledge, 203–20.

Laegreid, Per, Paul G. Roness and Kristin Rubecksen. 2008. 'Controlling Regulatory Agencies'. *Scandinavian Political Studies* 31, no. 1: 1–26.

Lafferty, William M. and Eivind Hovden. 2003. 'Environmental Policy Integration: Towards an Analytical Framework'. *Environmental Politics* 12, no.3: 1–22.

Laffont, Jean Jacques and Jean Tirole. 1991. 'The Politics of Government Decision-Making: A Theory of Regulatory Capture'. *The Quarterly Journal of Economics* 106, no. 4: 1089–1127.

Laforest, Rachel and Michael Orsini. 2005. 'Evidence-Based Engagement in the Voluntary Sector: Lessons from Canada'. *Social Policy and Administration* 39, no. 5: 481–97

Landes, W. M. and Posner, R. A. 1975. 'The Independent Judiciary in an Interest Group Perspective'. *Journal of Law and Economics* 18 (December): 875–901.

Landry, R. 1991. 'Party Competition in Quebec: Direct Confrontation or Selective Emphasis?' In *Party Politics in Canada*, H. G. Thorburn (ed.). Scarborough: Prentice-Hall, 401–13.

Landry, Rejean, Frédéric Varone and Malcolm L. Goggin. 1998. *The Determinants of Policy Design: The State of the Theoretical Literature*. Chicago, IL: Midwest Political Science Association.

Larsen, T. P., P. Taylor-Gooby and J. Kananen. 2006. 'New Labour's Policy Style: A Mix of Policy Approaches'. *International Social Policy* 35, no. 4: 629–49.

Larson, James S. 1980. *Why Government Programs Fail: Improving Policy Implementations*. New York: Praeger.

Lascoumes, Pierre and Patrick Le Galès. 2007. 'Introduction: Understanding Public Policy through Its Instruments – from the Nature of Instruments to the Sociology of Public Policy Instrumentation'. *Governance* 20, no. 1: 1–21.

Lasswell, Harold. 1954. 'Key Symbols, Signs and Icons'. In *Symbols and Values: An Initial Study*. Lymon Bryson, Louis Finkelstein, R. M. MacIver and Richard McKeon (eds.) New York: Harper, 77–94.

—— 1956. *The Decision Process: Seven Categories of Functional Analysis*. College Park: University of Maryland Press.

—— 1958. *Politics: Who Gets What, When, How*. New York: Meridian.

—— 1971. *A Pre-View of Policy Sciences*. New York: Elsevier.

Laux, J. 1993. 'How Private is Privatization'. *Canadian Public Policy* 19, no. 4: 398–411.

Laux, Jeanne Kirk and Maureen Appel Molot. 1988. *State Capitalism: Public Enterprise in Canada*. Ithaca, NY: Cornell University Press.

Lawrence, D. P. 2001. 'Choices for EIA Process Design and Management'. *Journal of Environmental Assessment Policy and Management* 3, no. 4: 437–64.

Lazer, David and Viktor Mayer-Schonberger. 2002. 'Governing Networks: Telecommunication Deregulation in Europe and the United States'. *Brooklyn Journal of International Law* no. 3: 820–51.

Ledingham, J. A. 2003. 'Explicating Relationship Management as a General Theory of Public Relations'. *Journal of Public Relations Research* 15, no. 2: 181–98.

Lee, Norman. 2006. 'Bridging the Gap Between Theory and Practice in Integrated Assessment'. *Environmental Impact Assessment Review* 26: 57–78

Leech, B. L., F. R. Baumgartner, T. La Pira, and N. A. Semanko. 2005. 'Drawing Lobbyists to Washington: Government Activity and the Demand for Advocacy'. *Political Research Quarterly* 58, no. 1: 19–30.

Leeuw, F. L. 1998. 'The Carrot: Subsidies as a Tool of Government'. In *Carrots, Sticks and Sermons: Policy Instruments and Their Evaluation*. Marie-Louise Bemelmans-Videc, Ray C. Rist and Evert Vedung (eds.). New Brunswick, NJ: Transaction Publishers, 77–102.

Le Grand, Julian (ed.) 1984. *Privatization and the Welfare State*. London: Allen and Unwin.

—— 1991. 'The Theory of Government Failure'. *British Journal of Political Science* 21, no. 4: 423–42.

—— 2007. *The Other Invisible Hand: Delivering Public Services through Choice and Competition*. Princeton, NJ: Princeton University Press,

—— 2009. 'Choice and Competition in Publicly Funded Health Care'. *Health Economics, Policy and Law* 4: 479–88.

Lehmbruch, G. 1979. 'Consociational Democracy, Class Conflict and the New Corporatism'. In *Trends Towards Corporatist Intermediation*, P. C. Schmitter and G. Lehmbruch (eds.). Beverley Hills, CA: Sage, 53–61.

—— 1991. 'The Organization of Society, Administrative Strategies and Policy Networks'. In *Political Choice: Institutions, Rules and the Limits of Rationality*. Roland M. Czada and Adrienne Windhoff-Heritier (eds.). Boulder, CO: Westview, 121–55.

Lehmkuhl, Dirk. 2008. 'On Government, Governance and Judicial Review: The Case of European Competition Policy'. *Journal of Public Policy* 28, no. 1: 139–59.

Lehoux, P., J.-L. Denis, S. Tailliez and M. Hivon. 2005. 'Dissemination of Health Technology Assessments: Identifying the Visions Guiding and evolving Policy Innovation in Canada'. *Journal of Health Politics, Policy and Law* 30, no. 4: 603–41.

Leik, Robert K. 1992. 'New Directions for Network Exchange Theory: Strategic Manipulation of Network Linkages'. *Social Networks* 14 309–23.

Lejano, Raul P. and Helen Ingram. 2009. 'Collaborative Networks and New Ways of Knowing'. *Environmental Science and Policy* 12, no. 6: 653–62.

Leland, Suzanne and Olga Smirnova. 2009. 'Reassessing Privatization Strategies 25 Years Later: Revisting Perry and Babitsky's Comparative Performance Study of Urban Bus Transit Services'. *Public Administration Review* 69, no. 5: 855–67.

Leman, C. K. 1989. 'The Forgotten Fundamental: Successes and Excesses of Direct Government'. In *Beyond Privatization: The Tools of Government Action*, L. M. Salamon (ed.). Washington, DC: Urban Institute, 51–92.

—— 2002. 'Direct Government'. In *The Tools of Government: A Guide to the New Governance*, L. M. Salamon (ed.). New York: Oxford University Press, 48–79.

Lenihan, D. G. and R. Alcock. 2000. *Collaborative Government in the Post-Industrial Age: Five Discussion Pieces – Changing Government Volume I*. Ottawa: Centre for Collaborative Government.

Leroux, Thérèse, Marie Hirtle and Louis-Nicolas Fortin. 1998. 'An Overview of Public Consultation Mechanisms Developed to Address the Ethical and Social Issues Raised by Biotechnology'. *Journal of Consumer Policy* 21, no. 4: 445–81.

Lester, J. P. and M. L. Goggin. 1998. 'Back to the Future: The Rediscovery of Implementation Studies'. *Policy Currents* 8, no. 3: 1–9.

Levi-Faur, D. and S. Gilad. 2005. 'The Rise of the British Regulatory State – Transcending the Privatization Debate'. *Comparative Politics* 37, no. 1: 105–24.

Levi-Faur, David. 2003. 'The Politics of Liberalisation: Privatisation and Regulation-for-Competition in Europe's and Latin America's Telecoms and Electricity Industries'. *European Journal of Political Research* 42, no. 5: 705–23.

—— 2009. 'Regulatory Capitalism and the Reassertion of the Public Interest'. *Policy and Society* 27, no. 3: 181–91.

Levy, Brian and Pablo T. Spiller. 1994. 'The Institutional Foundations of Regulatory Commitment: A Comparative Analysis of Telecommunications Regulation'. *Journal of Law, Economics and Organization* 10, no. 2: 201–46.

Libecap, Gary D. 1986. 'Deregulation as an Instrument in Industrial Policy: Comment'. *Journal of Institutional and Theoretical Economics* 142: 70–74.

Liefferink, D. 2006. 'The Dynamics of Policy Arrangements: Turning Round the Tetrahedron'. In *Institutional Dynamics in Environmental Governance* Arts, B. and Leroy, P. (eds.). Dordrecht: Springer, 45–68.

Lierse, Hanna. 2010. 'European Economic Governance: The OMC as a Road to Integration?' *International Journal of Public Policy* 6, no. 1/2: 35–49.

Lijphart, A. 1969. 'Consociational Democracy'. *World Politics* 21, no. 2: 207–25.

Lindblom, Charles E. 1958. 'Policy Analysis'. *American Economic Review* 48, no. 3: 298–312.

Lindblom, Charles E. 'Tinbergen on Policy-Making.' *The Journal of Political Economy* 66, no. 6 (December 1958): 531–538.

Linder, S. H. 1999. 'Coming to Terms with Public-Private Partnership'. *American Behavioural Scientist* 43, no. 1: 35–51.

Linder, S. H. and B. G. Peters. 1984. 'From Social Theory to Policy Design'. *Journal of Public Policy* 4, no. 3: 237–59.

—— 1988. 'The Analysis of Design or the Design of Analysis?' *Policy Studies Review* 7: 738–50.

—— 1989. 'Instruments of Government: Perception and Contexts". *Journal of Public Policy* 9, no. 1: 35–58.

—— 1990a. 'Policy Formulation and the Challenge of Conscious Design'. *Evaluation and Program Planning* 13: 303–11.

—— 1990b. 'The Design of Instruments for Public Policy'. In *Policy Theory and Policy Evaluation: Concepts, Knowledge, Causes and Norms*, S. S. Nagel (ed.). New York: Greenwood Press, 103–19.

—— 1990c. 'Research Perspectives on the Design of Public Policy: Implementation, Formulation and Design'. In *Implementation and the Policy Process: Opening up the Black Box*, D. J. Palumbo and D. J. Calista (eds.). New York: Greenwood Press.

—— 1990d. 'An Institutional Approach to the Theory of Policy-Making: The Role of

Guidance Mechanisms in Policy Formulation'. *Journal of Theoretical Politics* 2, no. 1 (January 1): 59–83.

—— 1991. 'The Logic of Public Policy Design: Linking Policy Actors and Plausible Instruments'. *Knowledge in Society* 4: 125–51.

—— 1992. 'A Metatheoretic Analysis of Policy Design'. In *Advances in Policy Studies since 1950*, W. N. Dunn and R. M. Kelly (eds.). New Brunswick, NJ: Transaction Publishers, 201–38.

Lindquist, Evert A. 1992. 'Public Managers and Policy Communities: Learning to Meet New Challenges'. *Canadian Public Administration* 35, no. 2: 127–59, at 128–29.

—— 1998. 'A Quarter Century of Canadian Think Tanks: Evolving Institutions, Conditions and Strategies'. In *Think Tanks Across Nations: A Comparative Approach*, D. Stone, A. Denham and M. Garnett (eds.). Manchester: Manchester University Press, 127–44.

—— 2006. 'Organizing for Policy Implementation: The Emergence and Role of Implementation Units in Policy Design and Oversight'. *Journal of Comparative Policy Analysis: Research and Practice* 8, no. 4: 311–24.

Lindvall, Johannes. 2009. 'The Real but Limited Influence of Expert Ideas'. *World Politics* 61, no. 4: 703–30.

Lodge, Martin. 2003. 'Institutional Choice and Policy Transfer: Reforming British and German Railway Regulation'. *Governance* 16, no. 2: 159–78.

—— 2008. 'Regulation, the Regulatory State and European Politics'. *West European Politics* 31, no. 1–2: 280–301.

Lombardo, E. 2005. 'Integrating or Setting the Agenda? Gender Mainstreaming in the European Constitution-Making Process'. *Social Politics* 12, no. 3: 412–32.

Lombe, Margaret and Michael Sherraden. 2008. 'Inclusion in the Policy Process: An Agenda for Participation of the Marginalized'. *Journal of Policy Practice* 7, no. 2–3: 199–213.

Lovan, W. Robert, Michael Murray and Ron Shaffer. 2004. 'Participatory Governance in a Changing World'. In *Participatory Governance: Planning, Conflict Mediation and Public Decision-Making in Civil Society*, W. R. Lovan, M. Murray and R. Shaffer (eds.). Aldershot: Ashgate, 1–20.

Lovink, J. A. A. 1999. 'Choosing the Right Autonomy for Operators of Privatized Government Services: The Case of NavCanada'. *Canadian Public Administration* 42, no. 3: 371–86.

Lowi, Theodore J. 1966. 'Distribution, Regulation, Redistribution: The Functions of Government'. In *Public Policies and Their Politics: Techniques of Government Control*, Randall B. Ripley (ed.). New York: W.W. Norton, 27–40.

—— 1969. *The End of Liberalism: Ideology, Policy and the Crisis of Public Authority*. New York: Norton.

—— 1972. 'Four Systems of Policy, Politics and Choice'. *Public Administration Review* 32, no. 4: 298–310.

Lowndes, Vivien and Chris Skelcher. 1998. 'The Dynamics of Multi-Organizational Partnerships: An Analysis of Changing Modes of Governance'. *Public Administration* 76 (Summer): 313–33.

Lowry, R. C. 1999. 'Foundation Patronage toward Citizen Groups and Think Tank: Who Gets Grants?'. *The Journal of Politics* 81, no. 3: 758–76.

Lutz, Susanne. 2003. *Convergence within National Diversity: A Comparative Perspective on the Regulatory State in Finance*. Max Planck Institut fur Gesellsschaftsforschung Discussion Paper 03/7. Cologne.

Lybecker, Kristina M. and Robert A. Freeman. 2007. 'Funding Pharmaceutical Innovation through Direct Tax Credits'. *Health Economics, Politics and Law* 2, no. 3: 267–84.

Lyden, F. J., G. A. Shipman and R. W. Wilkinson. 1968. 'Decision-Flow Analysis: A Methodology for Studying the Public Policy-Making Process'. In *Comparative Administrative Theory*, P. P. Le Breton (ed.). Seattle, WA: University of Washington Press, 155–68.

Lynn, Laurence E. 1980. *Designing Public Policy: A Casebook on the Role of Policy Analysis*. Tucson, AZ: Goodyear Publishing Company.

Lynn Jr, L. E. 2001. 'Globalization and Administrative Reform: What is Happening in Theory?' *Public Management Review* 3, no. 2: 191–208.

MacAvoy, P., W. T. Stanbury, George Yarrow and Richard Zeckhauser. 1989. *Privatization and State-Owned Enterprises: Lessons from the United States, Great Britain and Canada*. Boston, MA: Kluwer Academic Publishers.

MacRae, D. and D. Whittington. 1997. *Expert Advice for Policy Choice: Analysis and Discourse*. Washington, DC: Georgetown University Press.

Maddison, Sarah. 2005. 'Democratic Constraint and Embrace: Implications for Progressive Non-Government Advocacy Organisations in Australia'. *Australian Journal of Political Science* 40, no. 3: 373–89.

Mahoney, Christine and Michael Joseph Beckstrand. 2009. 'Following the Money: EU Funding of Civil Society Organizations'. Paper presented to the ECPR Joint Sessions of Workshops, Potsdam, Germany.

Majone, G. 1975. 'On the Notion of Political Feasibility'. *European Journal of Political Research* 3: 259–74.

—— 1976. 'Choice among Policy Instruments for Pollution Control'. *Policy Analysis* 2, no. 4: 589–613.

—— 1989. *Evidence, Argument, Persuasion*. New Haven, CT: Yale University Press.

—— 1997. 'From the Positive to the Regulatory State: Causes and Consequences of Changes in the Mode of Governance'. *Journal of Public Policy* 17, no. 2: 139–67.

—— 2005. 'Strategy and Structure: The Political Economy of Agency Independence and Accountability'. In *Designing Independent and Accountable Regulatory Authorities for High Quality Regulation – Proceedings of an Expert Meeting in London, United Kingdom 10–11 January 2005*, 126–55. Paris: OECD Working Party on Regulatory Management and Reform.

Maley, Maria. 2000. 'Conceptualising Advisers' Policy Work: The Distinctive Policy Roles of Ministerial Advisers in the Keating Government, 1991–96'. *Australian Journal of Political Science* 35, no. 3: 449.

Malloy, J. 1999. 'What Makes a State Advocacy Structure Effective? Conflicts Between Bureaucratic and Social Movements Criteria'. *Governance* 12, no. 3: 267–88.

—— 2003. *Colliding Worlds: The Inherent Ambiguity of Government Agencies for Aboriginal and Women's Policy*. Toronto: University of Toronto Press: IPAC Series in Public Management and Governance.

Mandell, M. P. 1994. 'Managing Interdependencies through Program Structures: A Revised Paradigm'. *American Review of Public Administration* 25, no. 1: 99–121.

—— 2000. 'A Revised Look at Management in Network Structures'. *International Journal of Organizational Theory and Behavior* 3, no. 1/2: 185–210.

Mandell, Svante. 2008. 'Optimal Mix of Emissions Taxes and Cap-and-Trade'. *Journal of Environmental Economics and Management* 56: 131–40.

Mann, Stefan and Henry Wustemann. 2010. 'Public Goverance of Information Asymmetries: the Gap Between Reality and Economic Theory'. *The Journal of Socio-Economics* 39, no. 2: 278–85.

March, J. G. and J. P. Olson. 1983. 'Organizing Political Life: What Administrative Reorganization Tells Us about Government'. *American Political Science Review* 77, no. 2: 281–96.

—— 1984. 'The New Institutionalism: Organizational Factors in Political Life'. *American Political Science Review* 78: 734–49.

—— 1989. *Rediscovering Institutions.* New York: Free Press.

—— 1996. 'Institutional Perspectives on Political Institutions'. *Governance* 9, no. 3: 247–64.

—— 2004. *The Logic of Appropriateness.* Oslo. ARENA Working Paper.

Marchildon, Gregory F. 2007. 'Royal Commissions and the Policy Cycle in Canada: The Case of Health Care'. In *Political Leadership and Representation in Canada*, Hans J. Michelmann, Donald C. Story and Jeffrey S. Steeves (eds.). Toronto: University of Toronto Press.

Margerum, Richard D. 2008. 'A Typology of Collaboration Efforts in Environmental Management'. *Environmental Management* 41: 487–500.

Marier, Patrik. 2009. 'The Power of Institutionalized Learning: The Uses and Practices of Commissions to Generate Policy Change'. *Journal of European Public Policy* 16, no. 8: 1204–23.

Marin, B. and R. Mayntz (eds.) 1991. *Policy Networks: Empirical Evidence and Theoretical Considerations.* Boulder, CO: Westview Press.

Marion, Russ. 1999. *The Edge of Organization: Chaos and Complexity Theories of Formal Social Systems.* London: Sage.

Markoff, J. and V. Montecinos. 1993. 'The Ubiquitous Rise of Economists'. *Journal of Public Policy* 13, no. 1: 37–68.

Marriott, Lisa. 'Power and Ideas: The Development of Retirement Savings Taxation in Australasia.' *Critical Perspectives on Accounting* 21, no. 7 (2010): 597–610.

Marsh, D. 1991. 'Privatization under Mrs. Thatcher: A Review of the Literature'. *Public Administration* 69, no. 4: 459–80.

Marsh, David and Allan McConnell. 2010. 'Towards a Framework for Establishing Policy Success'. *Public Administration* 88, no. 2: 564–583.

Maslove, A. M. 1978. 'The Other Side of Public Spending: Tax Expenditures in Canada'. In *The Public Evaluation of Government Spending*, G. B. Doern and A. M. Maslove (eds.). Montreal: Institute for Research on Public Policy, 149–68.

—— 1983. 'Loans and Loan Guarantees: Business as Usual Versus the Politics of Risk'. In *How Ottawa Spends: The Liberals, the Opposition and Federal Priorities*, G. B. Doern (ed.). Toronto: James Lorimer, 121–32.

Mathur, Navdeep and Chris Skelcher. 2007. 'Evaluating Democratic Performance: Methodologies for Assessing the Relationship between Network Governance and Citizens'. *Public Administration Review* 67, no. 2: 228–37.

May, Peter J. 1981. 'Hints for Crafting Alternative Policies'. *Policy Analysis* 7, no. 2: 227–44.

—— 1991. 'Reconsidering Policy Design: Policies and Publics'. *Journal of Public Policy* 11, no. 2: 187–206.

—— 1992. 'Policy Learning and Failure'. *Journal of Public Policy* 12, no. 4: 331–54.

—— 1993. 'Mandate Design and Implementation: Enhancing Implementation Efforts and Shaping Regulatory Styles'. *Journal of Policy Analysis and Management* 12, no. 4: 634–63.

—— 1996. 'Coercive Versus Cooperative Policies: Comparing Intergovernmental Mandate Performance'. *Journal of Policy Analysis and Management* 15, no. 2: 171–206.

—— 2002. 'Social Regulation'. In *The Tools of Government: A Guide to the New Governance*. L. M. Salamon (ed.) New York: Oxford University Press, 156–85.

—— 2003. 'Policy Design and Implementation'. In *Handbook of Public Administration*, B. Guy Peters and Jon Pierre (eds.). Beverly Hills, CA: Sage Publications, 223–33.

—— 2007. 'Regulatory Regimes and Accountability'. *Regulation and Governance* 1, no. 1: 8–26.

May, Peter, Bryan D. Jones, Betsi E. Beem, Emily A. Neff-Sharum and Melissa K. Poague. 2005. 'Policy Coherence and Component-Driven Policymaking: Arctic Policy in Canada and the United States'. *Policy Studies Journal* 33, no. 1: 37–63.

May, Peter J. and John W. Handmer. 1992. 'Regulatory Policy Design: Co-operative versus Deterrent Mandates'. *Australian Journal of Public Administration* 51, no. 1: 45–53.

May, Peter J., Joshua Saptichne and Samuel Workman. 2005b. 'Policy Coherence and Policy Design'. Washington, DC: Annual Research meeting of the Association for Public Analysis and Management.

May, P. J. and S. Winter. 1999. 'Regulatory Enforcement and Compliance: Examining Danish Agro-Environmental Policy'. *Journal of Policy Analysis and Management* 18, no. 4: 625–51.

Mayer, I., P. Bots and E. van Daalen. 2004. 'Perspectives on Policy Analysis: A Framework for Understanding and Design'. *International Journal of Technology, Policy and Management* 4, no. 1: 169–91.

Mayntz, Renate. 1975. 'Legitimacy and the Directive Capacity of the Political System'. In *Stress and Contradiction in Modern Capitalism* Leon N. Lindberg, Robert Alford, Colin Crouch, and Claus Offe (eds.). Lexington, MA: Lexington Books, 261–74.

—— 1979. 'Public Bureaucracies and Policy Implementation'. *International Social Science Journal* 31, no. 4: 633–45.

—— 1983. 'The Conditions of Effective Public Policy: A New Challenge for Policy Analysis'. *Policy and Politics* 11, no. 2: 123–43.

—— 1993. 'Modernization and the Logic of Interorganizational Networks'. In *Societal Change between Market and Organization* J. Child, M. Crozier and R. Mayntz (eds.). Aldershot: Avebury, 3–18.

Mazmanian, Daniel M. and Paul A. Sabatier. 1983. *Implementation and Public Policy*. Glenview, IL: Scott, Foresman, 21–25.

McAllister, Lesley K. 2009. 'Dimensions of Enforcement Style: Factoring in Autonomy and Capacity'. *Law and Policy* 32, no. 1: 61–78.

McAllister, Lesley K., Benjamin Van Rooij and Robert A. Kagan. 2010. 'Reorienting Regulation: Pollution Enforcement in Industrializing Countries'. *Law and Policy* 32, no. 1: 1–13.

McConnell, Allan. 2010. *Understanding Policy Success: Rethinking Public Policy*. Basingstoke: Palgrave Macmillan.

McCourt, Willy and Martin Minogue (eds.) 2001. *The Internationalization of Public Management: Reinventing the Third World State*. Cheltenham: Edward Elgar.

McCrudden, Christopher. 2004. 'Using Public Procurement to Achieve Social Outcomes'. *Natural Resources Journal* 28: 257–67.

McCubbins, M. D. and A. Lupia. 1994. 'Learning from Oversight: Fire Alarms and Policy Patrols Reconstructed'. *Journal of Law, Economics and Organization* 10, no.1: 96–125.

McCubbins, M. D., R. G. Noll and B. R. Weingast. 1987. 'Administrative Procedures as Instruments of Political Control'. *Journal of Law, Economics and Organization* 3, no. 2: 243–77.

McCubbins, Mathew D. and Thomas Schwartz. 1984. 'Congressional Oversight Overlooked: Policy Patrols versus Fire Alarms'. *American Journal of Political Science* 28, no. 1: 165–79.

McDavid, James C. and Eric G. Clemens. 1995. 'Contracting out Local Government Services; The BC Experience'. *Canadian Public Administration* 38, no. 2: 177–93.

McDonnell, Lorraine M. and Richard F. Elmore. 1987. *Alternative Policy Instruments*. Santa Monica, CA: Center for Policy Research in Education.

McGann, J. G. and E. C. Johnson. 2005. *Comparative Think Tanks, Politics and Public Policy*. Cheltenham: Edward Elgar.

McGarity, Thomas O. 1991. *Reinventing Rationality: The Role of Regulatory Analysis in the Federal Bureaucracy*. New York: Cambridge University Press.

McGoldrick, Daniel E. and Ann V. Boonn. 2010. 'Public Policy to Maximize Tobacco Cessation'. *American Journal of Preventive Medicine* 38, no. 3, Supplement 1 (March): S327–S332.

McGuire, M. 2002. 'Managing Networks: Propositions on What Managers Do and Why They Do It'. *Public administration review* 62, no. 5: 599–609.

McKelvey, Bill. 1978. 'Organizational Systematics: Taxonomic Lessons from Biology'. *Management Science* 24, no. 13: 1428–40.

—— 1982. *Organizational Systematics: Taxonomy, Evolution, Classification*. Berkeley, CA: University of California Press.

McKenna, John and Andrew Cooper. 2006. 'Sacred Cows in Coastal Management: The Need for a "Cheap and Transitory" Model'. *Area* 38, no. 4: 421–31.

McMillin, W. Douglas and James S. Fackler. 1984. 'Monetary vs. Credit Aggregates: An Evaluation of Monetary Policy Targets'. *Southern Economic Journal* 50, no. 3: 711–23.

McWilliams, William C. 1971. 'On Political Illegitimacy'. *Public Policy* 19, no. 3: 444–54.

Mees, Paul. 2005. 'Privatization of Rail and Tram Services in Melbourne: What Went Wrong?' *Transport Reviews* 25, no. 4: 433–49.

Meijers, Evert. 2004. 'Policy Integration: A Literature Review'. In *Policy Integration in Practice: The Integration of Land Use Planning, Transport and Environmental Policy-Making in Denmark, England and Germany* D. Stead, H. Geerlings and E. Meijers (eds.). Delft, Netherlands: Delft University Press, 9–24.

Meijers, Evert and Dominic Stead. 2004. 'Policy Integration: What Does It Mean and How Can It be Achieved? A Multi-Disciplinary Review'. Berlin: 2004 Berlin Conference on the Human Dimensions of Global Environmental Change: Greening of Policies – Interlinkages and Policy Integration.

Meltsner, Arnold. 1975. 'Bureaucratic Policy Analysts'. *Policy Analysis* 1, no. 1: 115–31.

—— 1976. *Policy Analysts in the Bureaucracy*. Berkeley, CA: University of California Press.

Menard, Claude and Michel Ghertman. 2009. *Regulation, Deregulation, Reregulation: Institutional Perspectives*. Cheltenham: Edward Elgar.

Mendes, Lucas M. Z. and Georgina Santos. 2008. 'Using Economic Instruments to Address Emissions from Air Transport in the European Union'. *Environment and Planning A* 40: 189–209.

Merelman, Richard M. 1966. 'Learning and Legitimacy'. *American Political Science Review* 60, no. 3: 548–61.

Merton, Robert K. 1936. 'The Unanticipated Consequences of Purposive Social Action'. *American Sociological Review* 6, no. 1894–1904.

—— 1948. 'The Self-Fulfilling Prophecy'. *The Antioch Review* 8, no. 2: 193–210.

—— 1949. 'The Role of Applied Social Science in the Formation of Policy: A Research Memorandum'. *Philosophy of Science* 16, no. 3: 161–81.

Meseguer, Covadonga. 2003. 'The Diffusion of Privatization in OECD and Latin America Countries: What Role for Learning?'. Paper presented at the conference on 'The Internationalization of Regulatory Reforms', Berkeley, CA, 25–26 April.

—— 2005. 'Policy Learning, Policy Diffusion and the Making of a New Order'. *Annals of the American Academy of Political and Social Science* 598, no. 1: 67–82.

—— 2006. 'Rational Learning and Bounded Learning in the Diffusion of Policy Innovations'. *Rationality and Society* 18, no. 1: 35–66.

Metcalfe, L. 2000. 'Reforming the Commission: Will Organizational Efficiency Produce Effective Governance?' *Journal of Common Market Studies* 38, no. 5: 817–41.

Meuleman, Louis. 2009. 'Metagoverning Governance Styles: Increasing the Public Manager's Toolbox'. ECPR Working Paper, Potsdam, Germany.

—— 2010. 'The Cultural Dimension of Metagovernance: Why Governance Doctrines May Fail'. *Public Organization Review* 10, no. 1: 49–70.

Meyer, Alan D. 1982. 'Adapting to Environmental Jolts'. *Administrative Science Quarterly* 27: 515–37.

Mickwitz, Per. 2003. 'A Framework for Evaluating Environmental Policy Instruments: Context and Key Concepts'. *Evaluation* 9, no. 4: 415–36.

Mickwitz, Per, Heli Hyvättinen, and Paula Kivimaa. 'The Role of Policy Instruments in the Innovation and Diffusion of Environmentally Friendlier Technologies: Popular Claims versus Case Study Experiences.' *Journal of Cleaner Production* 16, no. 1 (January 2008): S162-S170.

Mikenberg, M. 2001. 'The Radical Right in Public Office: Agenda-Setting and Policy Effects'. *West European Politics* 24, no. 4: 1–21.

Milner, Helen V. and Robert O. Keohane. 1996. 'Internationalization and Domestic Politics: A Conclusion'. In *Internationalization and Domestic Politics* R. O. Keohane and H. V. Milner (eds.). Cambridge: Cambridge University Press, 243–58.

Milward, H. B. and K. G. Provan. 2000. 'Governing the Hollow State'. *Journal of Public Administration Research and Theory* 10, no. 2: 359–80.

Milward, H. Brinton, Keith G. Provan and Barbara A. Else. 1993. 'What Does the "Hollow State" Look Like?'. In *Public Management: The State of the Art* Barry Bozeman (ed.). San Francisco, CA: Jossey-Bass, 309–23.

Minogue, M. 2002. 'Governance-Based Analysis of Regulation'. *Annals of Public and Cooperative Economics* 73, no. 4: 649–66.

Mintrom, Michael. 2007. 'The Policy Analysis Movement' In *Policy Analysis in Canada: The State of the Art*, L. Dobuzinskis, M. Howlett and D. Laycock (eds.). Toronto: University of Toronto Press, 71–84.

Mitnick, Barry M. 1978. 'The Concept of Regulation'. *Bulletin of Business Research* 53, no. 5: 1–20.

—— 1980. *The Political Economy of Regulation: Creating, Designing and Removing Regulatory Forms.* New York: Columbia University Press, 401–4.

Moffet, John and François Bregha. 1999. 'Non-Regulatory Environmental Measures'. In *Voluntary Initiatives: The New Politics of Corporate Greening*, R. B. Gibson (ed.) Peterborough: Broadview Press, 15–31.

Montgomery, J. D. 2000. 'Social Capital as a Policy Resource'. *Policy Sciences* 33: 227–43.

Montpetit, E. 2003. 'Public Consultations in Policy Network Environments'. *Canadian Public Policy* 29, no. 1: 95–110.

—— 2008. 'Policy Design for Legitimacy: Expert Knowledge, Citizens, Time and Inclusion in the United Kingdom's Biotechnology Sector'. *Public Administration* 86, no. 1: 259–77.

Moore, M. H. 1988. 'What Sort of Ideas Become Public Ideas?' In *The Power of Public Ideas*, R. B. Reich (ed.). Cambridge: Ballinger, 55–83.

Moran, M. 2002. 'Review Article: Understanding the Regulatory State'. *British Journal of Political Science* 32, no. 2: 391–413.

Moseley, A. and S. Tierney. 2004. 'Evidence-Based Practice in the Real World'. *Evidence and Policy* 1, no. 1: 113–19.

Mosley, Layna 2003. *Global Capital and National Governments*. New York: Cambridge University Press.

Moss, David A. 2002. *When All Else Fails: Government as the Ultimate Risk Manager*. Cambridge, MA: Harvard University Press.

Moynihan, Donald P. 2008. 'Combining Structural Forms in the Search for Policy Tools: Incident Command Systems in U.S. Crisis Management'. *Governance* 21, no. 2: 205–29.

Mueller, Claus. 1973. *The Politics of Communication: A Study in the Political Sociology of Language, Socialization and Legitimation*. New York: Oxford University Press.

Murphy, James J., Ariel Dinar, Richard E. Howitt, Stephen J. Rassenti, Vernon L. Smith and Marca Weinberg. 2009. 'The Design of Water Markets When Instream Flows Have Value'. *Journal of Environmental Management* 90: 1089–96.

Murray, Catherine. 2007. 'The Media'. In *Policy Analysis in Canada: The State of the Art*, L. Dobuzinskis, M. Howlett and D. Laycock (eds.). Toronto: University of Toronto Press, 286–97.

Myers, Norman and Jennifer Kent. 2001. *Perverse Subsidies: How Tax Dollars Can Undercut the Environment and the Economy*. Washington, DC: Island Press.

Natural Resources Canada. 2003. *Corporate Social Responsibility: Lessons Learned*. Ottawa: Natural Resources Canada.

Nemetz, Peter. 1986. 'The Fisheries Act and Federal-Provincial Environmental Regulation: Duplication or Complementarity?' *Canadian Public Administration* 29: 401–24.

Newbery, David M. 2003. 'Network Capacity Auctions: Promise and Problems'. *Utilities Policy* 11: 27–32.

Nilsson, Mans, Andrew Jordan, John Turnpenny, Julia Hertin, Bjorn Nykvist and Duncan Russel. 2008. 'The Use and Non-Use of Policy Appraisal Tools in Public Policy Making: An Analysis of Three European Countries and the European Union'. *Policy Sciences* 41: 335–55.

Nowlan, D. M. 1994. 'Local Taxation as an Instrument of Policy'. In *The Changing Canadian Metropolis: A Public Policy Perspective*, F. Frisken (ed.). Berkeley, CA: Institute of Governmental Studies, 799–841.

Nownes, A. J. (2000). 'Policy Conflict and the Structure of Interest Communities'. *American Politics Quarterly* 28, no. 3: 309–27.

—— 2004. 'The Population Ecology of Interest Group Formation: Mobilizing for Gay and Lesbian Rights in the United States, 1950–98'. *British Journal of Political Science* 34, no. 1: 49–67.

Nownes, Anthony and Grant Neeley. 1996. 'Toward an Explanation for Public Interest Group Formation and Proliferation: 'Seed Money'. Disturbances, Entrepreneurship and Patronage'. *Policy Studies Journal* 24, no. 1: 74–92.

Nutley, Sandra M., Isabel Walter and Huw T. O. Davies. 2007. *Using Evidence: How Research Can Inform Public Services*. Bristol: Policy Press.

O'Connor, Alan, Goran Roos and Tony Vickers-Willis. 2007. 'Evaluating an Australian Public Policy Organization's Innovation Capacity'. *European Journal of Innovation Management* 10, no. 4: 532–58.

O'Faircheallaigh, Ciaran. 2010. 'Public Participation and Environmental Impact Assessment: Purposes, Implications and Lessons for Public Policy Making'. *Environmental Impact Assessment Review* 30: 19–27.

O'Toole, L. J. 2000. 'Research on Policy Implementation: Assessment and Prospects'. *Journal of Public Administration Research and Theory* 10, no. 2: 263–88.

O'Toole, Laurence J. and Kenneth J. Meier, 'In Defense of Bureaucracy – Public Managerial Capacity, Slack and the Dampening of Environmental Shocks,' *Public Management Review* 12, no. 3 (2010): 341.

OECD. 1995. *Recommendation of the Council of the OECD on Improving the Quality of Government Regulation*. Paris: Organization for Economic Co-operation and Development.

—— 1996–97. *Issues and Developments in Public Management; Survey. 1996–97*. Paris: OECD.

Offe, C. 2006. 'Political Institutions and Social Power: Conceptual Explorations'. In *Rethinking Political Institutions: The Art of the State* Shapiro, I., Skowronek, S. and Galvin, D. (eds.). New York: New York University Press, 9–31.

Ohmae, Kenichi. 1990. *The Borderless World*. London: Collins.

Oikonomou V., A. Flamos and S. Grafakos. 2010. 'Is Blending of Energy and Climate Policy Instruments always Desirable?' *Energy Policy* 38, no. 8: 4186–95.

Oliver, P. E. 1993. 'Formal Models of Collective Action'. *Annual Review of Sociology* 19: 271–300.

Olsen, J. P. 2005. 'Maybe It Is Time to Rediscover Bureaucracy'. *Journal of Public Administration Research and Theory* 16, no. 1: 1–24.

Olsen, Johan P. and B. Guy Peters (eds.) 1996. *Lessons From Experience: Experiential Learning in Administrative Reforms in Eight Democracies*. Oslo: Scandinavian University Press.

Olson, Mancur. 1965. *The Logic of Collective Action*. Cambridge, MA: Harvard University Press.

Orren, K. and S. Skowronek. 1999. 'Regimes and Regime Building in American Government: A Review of Literature on the 1940s'. *Political Science Quarterly* 113, no. 4: 689–702.

Osborne, D. and E. Gaebler. 1992. *Reinventing Government*. Reading, MA: Addison-Wesley.

Osborne, Katy, Carol Bacchi and Catherine Mackenzie. 2008. 'Gender Analysis and Community Consultation: The Role of Women's Policy Units'. *Australian Journal of Public Administration* 67, no. 2: 149–60.

Ostrom, E. 1986. 'A Method of Institutional Analysis'. In *Guidance, Control and Evaluation in the Public Sector*, F. X. Kaufman, G. Majone and V. Ostrom (eds.). Berlin: deGruyter, 459–75.

—— 2003. 'How Types of Goods and Property Rights Jointly Affect Collective Action'. *Journal of Theoretical Politics* 15, no. 3: 239–70.

Owens, S. and T. Rayner. 1999. '"When Knowledge Matters": The Role and Influence of the Royal Commission on Environmental Pollution'. *Journal of Environmental Policy and Planning* 1: 7–24.

Padberg, D. I. 1992. 'Nutritional Labeling as a Policy Instrument'. *American Journal of Agricultural Economics* 74, no. 5: 1208–13.

Paehlke, Robert. 1990. 'Regulatory and Non-Regulatory Approaches to Environmental Protection'. *Canadian Public Administration* 33, no. 1: 17–36.

Page, Christopher. 2006. *The Roles of Public Opinion Research in Canadian Government*. Toronto: University of Toronto Press.

Page, Edward C. 2001. *Governing by Numbers: Delegated Legislation and Everyday Policy-Making*. Portland, OR: Hart Publishing.

—— 2010. 'Bureaucrats and Expertise: Elucidating a Problematic Relationship in Three Tableaux and Six Jurisdictions'. *Sociologie du Travail* 52, no. 2: 255–73.

Pal, L. A. 1987. *Public Policy Analysis: An Introduction*.Toronto: Methuen.

—— 1993. *Interests of State: The Politics of Language, Multiculturalism and Feminism in Canada*. Montreal and Kingston: McGill-Queen's University Press.

Palan, Ronen and Jason Abbott. 1996. *State Strategies in the Global Political Economy*. London: Pinter.

Palumbo, Dennis J. and Donald J. Calista. 1990. 'Opening Up the Black Box: Implementation and the Policy Process'. In *Implementation and the Policy Process*, D. J. Palumbo and D. J. Calista (eds.). New York: Greenwood Press.

Papaioannou, Howard Rush and John Bassant. 2006. 'Performance Management: Benchmarking as a Policy-Making Tool: From the Private to the Public Sector'. *Science and Public Policy* 33, no. 2: 91–102.

Parson, Edward A. and Karen Fisher-Vanden. 1999. 'Joint Implementation of Greenhouse Gas Abatement under the Kyoto Protocol's "Clean Development Mechanism': Its Scope and Limits". *Policy Sciences* 3: 207–24.

Pasquier, Martial and Jean-Patrick Villeneuve. 2007. 'Organizational Barriers to Transparency: A Typology and Analysis of Organizational Behaviour Tending to Prevent of Restrict Access to Information'. *International Review of Administrative Sciences* 73, no. 1: 147–62.

Pauly, Louis W. and Simon Reich. 1997. 'National Structures and Multinational Corporate Behaviour: Enduring Differences in the Age of Globalisation'. *International Organization* 51, no. 1: 1–30.

Pautz, Michelle C. 2009. 'Perceptions of the Regulated Community in Environmental Policy: The View from Below'. *Review of Policy Research* 26, no. 5: 533–50.

Pearse, P. H. 1980. 'Property Rights and the Regulation of Commercial Fisheries'. In *Resource Policy: International Perspectives*, P. N. Nemetz (ed.). Montreal: Institute for Research on Public Policy, 185–210.

Pedersen, Lene Holm. 2007. 'Ideas Are Transformed as They Transfer: A Comparative Study of Eco-Taxation in Scandinavia'. *Journal of European Public Policy* 14, no. 1: 59–77.

Peled, A. 2002. 'Why Style Matters: A Comparison of Two Administrative Reform Initiatives in the Israeli Public Sector, 1989–98'. *Journal of Public Administration Research and Theory* 12, no. 2: 217–40.

Pellikaan, Huib and Robert J. van der Veen, *Environmental dilemmas and policy design* (Cambridge University Press, 2002).

Peltzman, S. 1976. 'Toward a More General Theory of Regulation'. *Journal of Law and Economics* 19 (August): 211–40.

Perl, Anthony and Donald J. White. 2002. 'The Changing Role of Consultants in Canadian Policy Analysis'. *Policy and Society* 21, no. 1: 49–73.

Perrow, Charles. 1984. *Normal Accidents: Living with High Risk Technologies*. New York: Basic Books.

Perry, James L. and Hal G. Rainey. 1988. 'The Public-Private Distinction in Organization Theory: A Critique and Research Strategy'. *Academy of Management Review* 13, no. 2: 182–201.

Peters, B. Guy. 1992. 'Government Reorganization: A Theoretical Analysis'. *International Political Science Review* 13, no. 2: 199–218.

—— 1996. *The Future of Governing: Four Emerging Models*. Lawrence, KS: University Press of Kansas.

—— 1998. *Managing Horizontal Government: The Politics of Coordination*. Ottawa: Canadian Centre for Management Development.

—— 2000a. 'Policy Instruments and Public Management: Bridging the Gaps'. *Journal of Public Administration Research and Theory* 10, no. 1: 35–48.

—— (2000b) 'Public-Service Reform: Comparative Perspectives'. In *Government Restructuring and Career Public Services* E. Lindquist (ed.), Toronto: Institute of Public Administration of Canada, 27–40.

—— 2002. 'Governing in a Market Era: Alternative Models of Governing'. *Public Administration and Public Policy* 99: 85–97.

Peters, B. G. and John A. Hoornbeek. 2005. 'The Problem of Policy Problems'. In *Designing Government: From Instruments to Governance*, P. Eliadis, M. Hill and M. Howlett (eds.). Montreal: McGill-Queen's University Press, 77–105.

Peters, B. Guy and Jon Pierre. 1998. 'Governance Without Government? Rethinking Public Administration'. *Journal of Public Administration Research and Theory* 8, no. 2: 223–44.

—— 2000. 'Citizens versus the New Public Manager: The Problem of Mutual Empowerment'. *Administration and Society* 32, no. 1: 9–28.

Peters, B. Guy and F. K. M. Van Nispen (eds.) 1998. *Public Policy Instruments: Evaluating the Tools of Public Administration*. New York: Edward Elgar.

Phidd, R. W. 1975. 'The Economic Council of Canada: Its Establishment, Structure and Role in the Canadian Policy-Making System 1963–74'. *Canadian Public Administration* 18, no. 3: 428–73.

Phidd, Richard and G. Bruce Doern. 1983. *Canadian Public Policy: Ideas, Structures, Process*. Toronto: Methuen.

Phillips, Susan D. 1991. 'How Ottawa Blends: Shifting Government Relationships With Interest Groups'. In *How Ottawa Spends 1991–92: The Politics of Fragmentation*, F. Abele (ed.). Ottawa: Carleton University Press, 183–228.

—— 2001. 'From Charity to Clarity: Reinventing Federal Government-Voluntary Sector Relationships'. In *How Ottawa Spends 2001–2: Power in Transition*. L. A. Pal (ed.) Toronto: Oxford University Press, 145–76.

Phillips, Susan D. and Michael Orsini. 2002. *Mapping the Links: Citizen Involvement in Policy Processes*. Ottawa: Canadian Policy Research Networks.

Phillips, Susan D., Rachel Laforest and Andrew Graham. 2010. 'From Shopping to Social Innovation: Getting Public Financing Right in Canada'. *Policy and Society* 29, no. 3: 189–99.

Pierre, Jon. 1998. 'Public Consultation and Citizen Participation: Dilemmas of Policy Advice'. In *Taking Stock: Assessing Public Sector Reforms*, B. G. Peters and D. J. Savoie (eds.). Montreal: McGill-Queen's Press, 137–63.

Pierre, Jon and B. Guy Peters. 2005. *Governing Complex Societies: Trajectories and Scenarios*. London: Palgrave Macmillan.

Pierson, Paul. 1992. '"Policy Feedbacks" and Political Change: Contrasting Reagan and Thatcher's Pension Reform Initiatives'. *Studies in American Political Development* 6: 359–90.

—— 1993. 'When Effect Becomes Cause: Policy Feedback and Political Change'. *World Politics* 45: 595–628.

—— 2000. 'Increasing Returns, Path Dependence and the Study of Politics'. *American Political Science Review* 94, no. 2: 251–67.

—— 2004. *Politics in Time: History, Institutions and Social Analysis.* Princeton, NJ: Princeton University Press.

Pigou, A. C. 1932. *The Economics of Welfare.* London: Macmillan.

Pittel, K. and D. T. G. Rubbelke. 2006. 'Private Provision of Public Goods: Incentives for Donations'. *Journal of Economic Studies* 33, no. 6: 497–519.

Pollack, M. A. 2003. 'Control Mechanism or Deliberative Democracy? Two Images of Comitology'. *Comparative Political Studies* 36, no. 1/2: 125–55.

Pollitt, C. 2001a. 'Convergence: the Useful Myth?' *Public Administration* 79, no. 4: 933–47.

—— 2001b. 'Clarifying Convergence: Striking Similarities and Durable Differences in Public Management Reform'. *Public Management Review* 4, no. 1: 471–92.

Pontusson, J. 1995. 'From Comparative Public Policy to Political Economy: Putting Institutions in their Place and Taking Interests Seriously'. *Comparative Political Studies* 28, no. 1: 117–47.

Pope, Jeannette and Jenny M. Lewis. 2008. 'Improving Partnership Governance: Using a Network Approach to Evaluate Partnerships in Victoria'. *Australian Journal of Public Administration* 67, no. 4: 443–56.

Pope, Jeff and Anthony D. Owen. 2009. 'Emission Trading Schemes: Potential Revenue Effects, Compliance Costs and Overall Tax Policy Issues'. *Energy Policy* 37: 4595–603.

Porter, Tony and Karsten Ronit. 2006. 'Self-Regulation as Policy Process: The Multiple and Crisscrossing Stages of Private Rule-Making'. *Policy Sciences* 39: 41–72.

Posner, Richard A. 1974. 'Theories of Economic Regulation'. *Bell Journal of Economics and Management Science* 5: 335–58.

Potoski, M. 2002. 'Designing Bureaucratic Responsiveness: Administrative Procedures and Agency Choice in State Environmental Policy'. *State Politics and Policy Quarterly* 2, no. 1: 1–23.

Potoski, Matthew and Aseem Prakesh (eds.) 2009. *Voluntary Programs: A Club Theory Perspective.* Cambridge, MA: MIT Press.

Power, M. and L.S. McCarty. 2002. 'Trends in the Development of Ecological Risk Assessment and Management Frameworks'. *Human and Ecological Risk Assessment* 8, no. 1: 7–18.

Prasser, Scott. 2006. 'Royal Commissions in Australia: When Should Governments Appoint Them?'. *Australian Journal of Public Administration* 65, no. 3: 28–47.

Pratt, John W. and Richard J. Zeckhauser. 1991. *Principals and Agents: The Structure of Business.* Cambridge, MA: Harvard Business School Press.

Prichard, J. R. S. 1983. *Crown Corporations in Canada: The Calculus of Instrument Choice.* Toronto: Butterworths.

Prince, M. J. 1979. 'Policy Advisory Groups in Government Departments'. In *Public Policy in Canada: Organization, Process, Management,* G. B. Doern and P. Aucoin (eds.). Toronto: Gage, 275–300.

—— 1983. *Policy Advice and Organizational Survival.* Aldershot: Gower.

—— 2008. *Reviewing the Literature on Policy Instruments.* Ottawa: Human Resources and Social Development Canada.

Prince, M. J. and J. Chenier. 1980. 'The Rise and Fall of Policy Planning and Research Units'. *Canadian Public Administration* 22, no. 4: 536–50.

Pross, A. P. 1992. *Group Politics and Public Policy.* Toronto: Oxford University Press.

Pross, A. Paul and Iain S. Stewart. 1993. 'Lobbying, the Voluntary Sector and the Public Purse'. In *How Ottawa Spends 1993–1994: A More Democratic Canada?* S. D. Phillips (ed.) Ottawa: Carleton University Press, 109–42.

Provan, K.G and Patrick Kenis, 2008. 'Modes of Network Governance: Structure, Management and Effectiveness'. *Journal of Public Administration Research and Theory* 18, no. 2: 229–52.

Przeworski, A. 1990. *The State and the Economy under Capitalism*. Chur, Switzerland: Harwood.

Qualter, T. H. 1985. *Opinion Control in the Democracies*. London: Macmillan.

Quirk, Paul J. 1988. 'In Defense of the Politics of Ideas'. *The Journal of Politics* 50: 31–45.

Raadschelders, Jos C. N. 1998. *Handbook of Administrative History*. New Brunswick, NJ: Transaction.

—— 2000. 'Administrative History of the United States: Development and State of the Art'. *Administration and Society* 32, no. 5: 499–528.

Radaelli, C. M. 2005. 'Diffusion without Convergence: How Political Context Shapes the Adoption of Regulatory Impact Assessment'. *Journal of European Public Policy* 12, no. 5: 924–43.

Radaelli, Claudio and Anne C. M. Meuwese. 2009. 'Better Regulation in Europe: Between Public Management and Regulatory Reform'. *Public Administration* 87, no. 3: 639–54.

Rajan, Sudhir Chella. 1992. 'Legitimacy in Environmental Policy: The Regulation of Automobile Pollution in California'. *International Journal of Environmental Studies* 42: 243–58.

Ramesh, M. 1995. 'Economic Globalization and Policy Choices: Singapore'. *Governance* 8, no. 2: 243–60.

Ramesh, M. and M. Howlett (eds.) 2006. *Deregulation and Its Discontents: Rewriting the Rules in Asia*. Aldershot: Edward Elgar.

Rayner, Jeremy, Ben Cashore, Michael Howlett and Jeremy Wilson. 2001. 'Privileging the Sub-Sector: Critical Sub-Sectors and Sectoral Relationships in Forest Policy-Making'. *Forest Policy and Economics* 2, no. 3–4: 319–32.

Reagan, Michael D. 1987. *Regulation: The Politics of Policy*. Boston, MA: Little, Brown.

Reich, Robert B. 1991. *The Work of Nations*. New York: Alfred Knopf.

Reinicke, Wolfgang H. 1998. *Global Public Policy: Governing Without Government?* Washington, DC: Brookings Institution.

Relyea, Harold C. 1977. 'The Provision of Government Information: The Freedom of Information Act Experience'. *Canadian Public Administration*. 20, no. 2: 317–41.

Renn, O. 'Style of Using Scientific Expertise: a Comparative Framework.' *Science and Public Policy* 22, no. 3 (1995): 147–156.

Resodihardjo, S. L. 2006. 'Wielding a Double-Edged Sword: The Use of Inquiries at Times of Crisis'. *Journal of Contingencies and Crisis Management* 14, no. 4: 199–206.

Rhodes, R. A. W. 1994. 'The Hollowing out of the State: The Changing Nature of the Public Service in Britain'. *The Political Quarterly* 65, no. 2: 138–51.

—— 1996. 'The New Governance: Governing without Government'. *Political Studies* 44: 652–67.

—— 1997. 'From Marketisation to Diplomacy: It's the Mix that Matters'. *Australian Journal of Public Administration* 56, no. 2: 40–54.

Rhodes, R. A. W. and P. Weller. 2001. *The Changing World of Top Officials*. Buckingham: Open University Press.

Riccucci, Norma M. and Marcia K. Meyers. 2008. 'Comparing Welfare Service Delivery Among Public, Nonprofit and For-Profit Work Agencies'. *International Journal of Public Administration* 31: 1441–54.

Rich, A. 2004. *Think Tanks, Public Policy, and the Politics of Expertise*. New York: Cambridge University Press.

Richardson, J. J. (ed.) 1990. *Privatisation and Deregulation in Canada and Britain.* Aldershot: Dartmouth Publishing.

Richardson, Jeremy, Gunnel Gustafsson and Grant Jordan. 1982. 'The Concept of Policy Style'. In *Policy Styles in Western Europe.* J. J. Richardson (ed.) London: George Allen and Unwin, 1–16.

Richardson, J. J. and A. G. Jordan. 1979. *Governing Under Pressure: The Policy Process in a Post-Parliamentary Democracy.* Oxford: Martin Robertson.

Riddell, Norman. 2007. *Policy Research Capacity in the Federal Government.* Ottawa: Policy Research Initiative.

Riedel, James A. 1972. 'Citizen Participation: Myths and Realities'. *Public Administration Review* (May–June): 211–20.

Riker, William H. 1983. 'Political Theory and the Art of Heresthetics'. In *Political Science: The State of the Discipline* Ada W. Finifter (ed.). Washington, DC: American Political Science Association, 47–67.

—— 1986. *The Art of Political Manipulation.* New Haven, CT: Yale University Press.

Ring, Irene, Martin Drechsler, Astrid J. A. van Teeffelen, Silvia Irawan and Oscar Venter. 2010. 'Biodiversity Conservation and Climate Mitigation: What Role Can Economic Instruments Play?' *Current Opinion in Environmental Sustainability* 2, no. 1–2: 50–8.

Ringquist, Evan J., Jeff Worsham and Marc Allen Eisner. 2003. 'Salience, Complexity and the Legislative Direction of Regulatory Bureaucracies'. *Journal of Public Administration Research and Theory* 13, no. 2: 141–65.

Rittel, H. W. J. and M. M. Webber. 1973. 'Dilemmas in a General Theory of Planning'. *Policy Sciences* 4: 155–69.

Roberts, Alisdair. 1999. 'Retrenchment and Freedom of Information: Recent Experience under Federal, Ontario and British Columbia Law'. *Canadian Public Administration* 42, no. 4: 422–51.

Roberts, Alasdair and Jonathan Rose. 1995. 'Selling the Goods and Services Tax: Government Advertising and Public Discourse in Canada'. *Canadian Journal of Political Science* 28, no. 2: 311–30.

Roberts, R. and L. E. R. Dean. 1994. 'An Inquiry into Lowi's Policy Typology: The Conservation Coalition and the 1985 and 1990 Farm Bill'. *Environment and Planning C, Government and Policy* 12, no. 1: 71–86.

Robins, Lisa. 2008. 'Perspectives on Capacity Building to Gudie Policy and Program Development and Delivery'. *Environmental Science and Policy* 11: 687–701.

Rochefort, David A. and Roger W. Cobb (eds.) 1994. *The Politics of Problem Definition: Shaping the Policy Agenda.* Lawrence, KS: University of Kansas Press.

Rochet, C. 2004. 'Rethinking the Management of Information in the Strategic Monitoring of Public Policies by Agencies'. *Industrial Management and Data Systems* 104, no. 3: 201–8.

Rodrik, Dani. 1997. *Has Globalization Gone Too Far?.* Washington, DC: Institute for International Economics.

—— 1998. 'Why Do Open Economies Have Bigger Governments?' *Journal of Political Economy* 106, no. 5: 997–1032.

Rolfstam, Max. 2009. 'Public Procurement as an Innovation Policy Tool: The Role of Institutions'. *Science and Public Policy* 36, no. 5: 349–60.

Roman, Andrew J. and Kelly Hooey. 1993. 'The Regulatory Framework'. In *Environmental Law and Business in Canada.* G. Thompson, M.L. McConnell and L.B. Huestis (eds.) Aurora, ON: Canada Law Books, 55–75.

Romans, J. T. 1966. 'Moral Suasion as an Instrument of Economic Policy'. *American Economic Review* 56, no. 5: 1220–26.

Ronal Gainza-Carmenates et al., 'Trade-offs and Performances of a Range of Alternative Global Climate Architectures for Post-2012," *Environmental Science & Policy* 13, no. 1 (February 2010): 63–71.

Ronit, Karsten. 2001. 'Institutions of Private Authority in Global Governance: Linking Territorial Forms of Self-regulation'. *Administration and Society* 33, no. 5: 555–78.

Roots, Roger I. 2004. 'When Laws Backfire: Unintended Consequences of Public Policy'. *American Behavioral Scientist* 47, no. 11: 1376–94.

Rose, J. 1993. 'Government Advertising in a Crisis: The Quebec Referendum Precedent'. *Canadian Journal of Communication* 18: 173–96.

Rose, Richard. 1988a. 'The Growth of Government Organization: Do We Count the Number or Weigh the Programs?' In *Organizing Governance/Governing Organizations* C. Campbell and B. G. Peters (eds.). Pittsburgh, PA: University of Pittsburgh Press, 99–128.

—— 1988b. 'Comparative Policy Analysis: The Program Approach'. In *Comparing Pluralist Democracies: Strains on Legitimacy* M. Dogan (ed.). Boulder, CO: Westview Press, 219–41.

—— 1991. 'What is Lesson-Drawing?'. *Journal of Public Policy* 11, no. 1: 3–30.

—— 1993. *Lesson-Drawing in Public Policy: A Guide to Learning Across Time and Space*. Chatham: Chatham House Publishing.

—— 2005. *Learning from Comparative Public Policy*. London: Routledge.

Rosenau, James N. 1980. *The Study of Global Interdependence*. London: Pinter.

Rosenau, P. V. 1999. 'The Strengths and Weaknesses of Public-Private Policy Partnerships'. *American Behavioral Scientist* 43, no. 1: 10–34.

Rosenbloom, David H. 2007. 'Administrative Law and Regulation'. In *Handbook of Public Administration*, Jack Rabin, W. Bartley Hildreth and Gerald J. Miller (eds.). London: CRC/Taylor & Francis, 635–96.

Ross, Helen, Mariene Buchy and Wendy Proctor. 2002. 'Laying Down the Ladder: A Typology of Public Participation in Australian Natural Resource Management'. *Australian Journal of Environmental Management* 9, no. 4: 205–17.

Rothmayr, C. and S. Hardmeier. 2002. 'Government and Polling: Use and Impact of Polls in the Policy-Making Process in Switzerland'. *International Journal of Public Opinion Research* 14, no. 2: 123–40.

Rourke, Francis E. 1957. 'The Politics of Administrative organization: A Case History'. *The Journal of Politics* 19, no. 1: 461–78.

Rowe, Gene, and Lynn J. Frewer. 2005. 'A Typology of Public Engagement Mechanisms'. *Science, Technology & Human Values* 30, no. 2: 251–90.

Rowe, Mike, and Laura McAllister. 2006. 'The Roles of Commissions of Inquiry in the Policy Process'. *Public Policy and Administration* 21, no. 4: 99–115.

Royer, Annie. 2008. 'The Emergence of Agricultural Marketing Boards Revisited: A Case Study in Canada'. *Canadian Journal of Agricultural Economics* 56: 509–22.

Rubsamen, Valerie. 1989. 'Deregulation and the State in Comparative Perspective: The Case of Telecommunications'. *Comparative Politics* 22, no. 1: 105–20

Ryan, Phil. 1995. 'Miniature Mila and Flying Geese: Government Advertising and Canadian Democracy'. In *How Ottawa Spends 1995–96: Mid-Life Crises*. S. D. Phillips (ed.) Ottawa: Carleton University Press, 263–86.

Sabatier, P. 1987. 'Knowledge, Policy-Oriented Learning and Policy Change'. *Knowledge: Creation, Diffusion, Utilization* 8, no. 4: 649–92.

—— 1988. 'An Advocacy Coalition Framework of Policy Change and the Role of Policy-Oriented Learning Therein'. *Policy Sciences* 21, no. 2/3: 129–68.

Sabatier, Paul and Hank Jenkins-Smith (eds.) 1993. *Policy Change and Learning. An Advocacy Coalition Approach*. Boulder, CO: Westview Press.

Sabatier, P. A. and D. A. Mazmanian. 1981. *Effective Policy Implementation*. Lexington, MA: Lexington Books.

Sabatier, Paul A. and Neil Pelkey. 1987. 'Incorporating Multiple Actors and Guidance Instruments into Models of Regulatory Policymaking: An Advocacy Coalition Framework'. *Administration and Society* 19, no. 2: 236–63.

Sadler, Barry. 2005. *Strategic Environmental Assessment at the Policy Level: Recent Progress, Current Status and Future Prospects*. Prague: Ministry of the Environment.

Salamon, Lester M. 1981. 'Rethinking Public Management: Third party Government and the Changing Forms of Government Action'. *Public Policy* 29: 255–75.

—— (ed.) 1989. *Beyond Privatization: The Tools of Government Action*. Washington, DC: Urban Institute.

—— 2001. 'The New Governance and the Tools of Public Action: An Introduction'. *Fordham Urban Law Journal* 28, no. 5: 1611–74.

—— 2002a. 'The New Governance and the Tools of Public Action'. In *The Tools of Government: A Guide to the New Governance*, ed. L. M. Salamon. New York: Oxford University Press, 1–47.

—— 2002b. 'Economic Regulation'. In L. M. Salamon (ed.) *The Tools of Government: A Guide to the New Governance*, New York: Oxford University Press, 117–55.

—— 2002c. *The Tools of Government: A Guide to the New Governance*. New York: Oxford University Press.

Salamon, Lester M. and Michael S. Lund. 1989. 'The Tools Approach: Basic Analytics'. In *Beyond Privatization: The Tools of Government Action*. Salamon (ed.) Washington, DC: Urban Institute, 23–50.

Salisbury, R. H. 1969. 'An Exchange Theory of Interest Groups'. *Midwest Journal of Political Science* 13, no. 1: 1–32.

Salmon, Charles (ed.) 1989a. *Information Campaigns: Managing the Process of Social Change*. Newbury Park, CA: Sage.

—— 1989b. 'Campaigns for Social Improvement: An Overview of Values, Rationales and Impacts'. In *Information Campaigns: Managing the Process of Social Change*, C. Salmon (ed.) Newbury Park, CA: Sage, 1–32.

Salter, Liora. 1990. 'The Two Contradictions in Public Inquiries'. In *Commissions of Inquiry*. A. P. Pross, I. Christie and J. A. Yogis (eds.) Toronto: Carswell, 175–95.

—— 2003. 'The Complex Relationship between Inquiries and Public Controversy'. In *Commissions of Inquiry: Praise or Reappraise?*, A. Manson and D. Mullan (eds.). Toronto: Irwin Law, 185–209.

Salter, Liora and Debra Slaco. 1981. *Public Inquiries in Canada*. Ottawa: Science Council of Canada.

Santos, Georgina, Hannah Behrendt, and Alexander Teytelboym. 'Part II: Policy Instruments for Sustainable Road Transport.' *Research in Transportation Economics* 28, no. 1 (2010): 46–91.

Sappington, David E. M. 1994. 'Designing Incentive Regulation'. *Review of Industrial Organization* 9, no. 3: 245–72.

Sassen, Saskia. 1998. *Globalization and Its Discontents*. New York: New Press.

Savas, E. S. 1977. *Alternatives for Delivering Public Services: Toward Improved Performance*. Boulder, CO: Westview.

BIBLIOGRAPHY

—— 1987. *Privatization: The Key to Better Government*.Chatham: Chatham House Publishers.

—— 1989. 'A Taxonomy of Privatization Strategies'. *Policy Studies Journal* 18: 343–55.

Savoie, D. J. 1999. *Governing from the Centre: The Concentration of Power in Canadian Politics*. Toronto: University of Toronto Press.

Saward, M. 1990. 'Cooption and Power: Who Gets What from Formal Incorporation'. *Political Studies* 38: 588–602.

—— 1992. *Co-Optive Politics and State Legitimacy*. Aldershot: Dartmouth.

Schaar, John H. 1981. *Legitimacy in the Modern State*. New Brunswick, NJ: Transaction Publishers.

Scharpf, F. W. 1991. Political Institutions, Decision Styles and Policy Choices. In *Political Choice: Institutions, Rules and the Limits of Rationality*. Czada, R.M. and Windhoff-Heritier, A. (eds.) Frankfurt: Campus Verlag, 53–86.

—— 1998. 'Globalization: The Limitations on State Capacity'. *Swiss Political Science Review* 4, no. 1: 2–8.

Schattschneider, E. E. 1960. *The Semisovereign People; A Realist's View of Democracy in America*. New York: Holt, Rinehart and Winston.

Scheb, John M. and John M. Scheb II. 2005. *Law and the Administrative Process*. Toronto: Thomson Wadsworth.

Scheraga, Joel D. and John Furlow. 2001. 'From Assessment to Policy: Lessons Learned from the U.S. national Assessment'. *Human and Ecological Risk Assessment* 7, no. 5: 1227–46.

Scherer, F. M. 2008. 'The Historical Foundations of Communications Regulation'. In *Kennedy School Faculty Working Papers Series RWP08–050*. Boston, MA: Harvard University.

Schlager, Edella. 1999. 'A Comparison of Frameworks, Theories and Models of Policy Processes'. In *Theories of the Policy Process*, P. A. Sabatier (ed.) Boulder, CO: Westview Press, 233–60.

Schmitter, P. C. 1977. 'Modes of Interest Intermediation and Models of Societal Change in Western Europe'. *Comparative Political Studies* 10, no. 1: 7–38.

—— 1985. *Neo-corporatism and the State*. In W. Grant (ed.) *The Political Economy of Corporatism*. London: Macmillan, 32–62.

Schneider, A. and H. Ingram. 1988. 'Systematically Pinching Ideas: A Comparative Approach to Policy Design'. *Journal of Public Policy* 8, no. 1: 61–80.

—— 1990a. 'Behavioural Assumptions of Policy Tools'. *Journal of Politics* 52, no. 2: 511–29 at 513–14.

—— 1990b. 'Policy Design: Elements, Premises and Strategies'. In *Policy Theory and Policy Evaluation: Concepts, Knowledge, Causes and Norms*. Stuart S. Nagel (ed.) New York: Greenwood Press, 77–102.

—— 1993. 'Social Construction of Target Populations: Implications for Politics and Policy'. *American Political Science Review* 87, no. 2: 334–47.

—— 1994. 'Social Constructions and Policy Design: Implications for Public Administration'. *Research in Public Administration* 3: 137–73.

—— 1997. *Policy Design for Democracy*. Lawrence: University Press of Kansas.

Schneider, Anne and Mara Sidney. 2009. 'What is Next for Policy Design and Social Construction Theory?'. *Policy Studies Journal* 37, no. 1: 103–19.

Schneider, J. W. 1985. 'Social Problems Theory: The Constructionist View'. *Annual Review of Sociology* 11: 209–29.

Scholte, Jan Aart. 1997. 'Global Capitalism and the State'. *International Affairs* 73: 440–51.

Scholz, J. T. 1984. 'Cooperation, Deterrence, and the Ecology of Regulatory Enforcement'. *Law Society Review* 18, no. 2: 179–224.

—— 1991. 'Cooperative Regulatory Enforcement and the Politics of Administrative Effectiveness'. *American Political Science Review* 85, no. 1: 115–36.

Schön, D.A. 'Designing as Reflective Conversation with the Materials of a Design Situation.' *Knowledge-Based Systems* 5, no. 1 (March 1992): 3–14.

Schout, Adriaan, Andrew Jordan and Michelle Twena. 2010. 'From "Old" to "New" Governance in the EU: Explaining a Diagnostic Deficit'. *West European Politics* 33, no. 1: 154–70.

Schwartz, Bryan. 1997. 'Public Inquiries'. *Canadian Public Administration* 40, no. 1: 72–85.

Scott, C., J. Jordana and D. Levi-Faur. 2004. 'Regulation in the Age of Governance: The Rise of the Post-Regulatory State'. In *The Politics of Regulation: Institutions and Regulatory Reforms for the Age of Governance*. J. Jordane and D. Levi-Faur (eds.). Cheltenham: Edward Elgar, 145–74.

Scott, Colin. 2001. 'Analysing Regulatory Space: Fragmented Resources and Institutional Design'. *Public Law* (Summer): 329–53.

Scrase, J. Ivan and William R. Sheate. 2002. 'Integration and Integrated Approaches to Assessment: What Do They Mean for the Environment'. *Journal of Environmental Policy and Planning* 4, no. 1: 275–94.

Shapiro, Sidney A. and Christopher H. Schroeder. 2008. 'Beyond Cost-Benefit Analysis: A Pragmatic Reorientation'. *Harvard Environmental Law Review* 32: 433–501.

Sharma, Bishnu and John Wanna. 2005. 'Performance Measures, Measurement and Reporting in Government Organisations'. *International Journal of Business Performance Management* 7, no. 3: 320–33.

Sharpe, David. 2001. 'The Canadian Charitable Sector: An Overview'. In *Between State and Market: Essays on Charities Law and Policy in Canada*. J. Phillips, B. Chapman and D. Stevens (eds.). Toronto: University of Toronto Press, 1–30.

Sheriff, Peta E. 1983. 'State Theory, Social Science and Governmental Commissions'. *American Behavioural Scientist* 26, no. 5: 669–80.

Sidney, Mara S. 2007. 'Policy Formulation: Design and Tools'. In *Handbook of Public Policy Analysis: Theory, Politics and Methods*, Frank Fischer, Gerald J. Miller and Mara S. Sidney (eds.). New Brunswick, NJ: CRC/Taylor & Francis, 79–87.

Simmons, Alan B. and Kieran Keohane. 1992. 'Canadian Immigration Policy: State Strategies and the Quest for Legitimacy'. *Canadian Review of Sociology and Anthropology* 29, no. 4: 421–52.

Simmons, Beth A. and Zachary Elkins. 2004a. 'Globalization and Policy Diffusion: Explaining Three Decades of Liberalization'. In *Governance in a Global Economy* M. Kahler and D. Lake (eds.). Princeton, NJ: Princeton University Press, 275–304.

—— 2004b. 'The Globalization of Liberalization: Policy Diffusion in the International Political Economy'. *American Political Science Review* 98: 171–89.

Simmons, R. and J. Birchall. 2005. 'A Joined-up Approach to User Participation in Public Services: Strengthening the "Participation Chain"'. *Social Policy and Administration* 39, no. 3: 260–83

Simmons, R. H., B. W. Davis, R. J. K. Chapman and D. D. Sager. 1974. 'Policy Flow Analysis: A Conceptual Model for Comparative Public Policy Research'. *Western Political Quarterly* 27, no. 3: 457–68.

Sinclair, Darren. 1997. 'Self-Regulation versus Command and Control? Beyond False Dichotomies'. *Law and Policy* 19, no. 4: 529–59.

Skodvin, Tora, Anne Therese Gullberg and Stine Aakre. 2010. 'Target-Group Influence and Political Feasibility: The Case of Climate Policy Design in Europe'. *Journal of European Public Policy* 17, no. 6: 854.

Skowronek, Stephen. 1982. *Building a New American State: The Expansion of National Administrative Capacities 1877–1920*. Cambridge: Cambridge University Press.

Smismans, Stijn. 2008. 'New Modes of Governance and the Participatory Myth'. *West European Politics* 31, no. 5: 874–95.

Smith, Adrian. 2000 'Policy Networks and Advocacy Coalitions: Explaining Policy Change and Stability in UK Industrial Pollution Policy'. *Environment and Planning C: Government and Policy* 18: 95–114.

Smith, Bruce L. R. 1977. 'The Non-Governmental Policy Analysis Organization'. *Public Administration Review* 37, no. 3: 253–58.

Smith, M. 2005a. *A Civil Society? Collective Actors in Canadian Political Life*. Peterborough: Broadview Press.

—— 2005b. 'Diversity and Identity in the Non-profit Sector: Lessons from LGBT Organizing in Toronto'. *Social Policy and Administration* 39, no. 5: 463–80.

Smith, Mitchell P. 2008. 'All Access Points Are Not Created Equal: Explaining the Fate of Diffuse Interests in the EU'. *British Journal of Politics and International Relations* 10: 64–83.

Smith, T. B. 1977. 'Advisory Committees in the Public Policy Process'. *International Review of Administrative Sciences* 43, no. 2: 153–66.

Sousa, D. and Klyza, C. 2007. 'New Directions in Environmental Policy Making: An Emerging Collaborative Regime or Reinventing Interest Group Liberalism'. *Natural Resources Journal* 47, no. 2: 377–444.

Speers, Kimberly. 2007. 'The Invisible Public Service: Consultants and Public Policy in Canada'. In *Policy Analysis in Canada: The State of the Art*, L. Dobuzinskis, M. Howlett and D. Laycock (eds.). Toronto: University of Toronto Press, 220–31.

Spicker, P. 2005. 'Targeting, Residual Welfare and Related Concepts: Modes of Operation in Public Policy'. *Public Administration* 83, no. 2: 345–65.

Sproule-Jones, M. 1983. 'Institutions, Constitutions and Public Policies: A Public-Choice Overview'. In *The Politics of Canadian Public Policy*. M. Atkinson and M. Chandler (eds.). Toronto: University of Toronto Press, 127–50.

Stanbury, W. T. 1986. *Business-Government Relations in Canada: Grappling with Leviathan*. Toronto: Methuen.

—— 1993. 'A Sceptic's Guide to the Claims of So-Called Public Interest Groups'. *Canadian Public Administration* 36, no. 4: 580–605.

Stanbury, W. T. and Jane Fulton. 1984. 'Suasion as a Governing Instrument'. In *How Ottawa Spends 1984: The New Agenda*. A. Maslove (ed.) Toronto: Lorimer, 282–324.

Stanbury, W.T., Gerald J. Gorn and Charles B. Weinberg. 1983. 'Federal Advertising Expenditures'. In *How Ottawa Spends: The Liberals, the Opposition and Federal Priorities* G. B. Doern (ed.). Toronto: James Lorimer and Company, 133–72.

Starr, P. 1989. 'The Meaning of Privatization'. In *Privatization and the Welfare State*, S. B. Kamerman and A. J. Kahn (eds.). Princeton, NJ: Princeton University Press, 15–48.

—— 1990a. 'The Limits of Privatization'. In *Privatization and Deregulation in Global Perspective*, D. J. Gayle and J. N. Goodrich (eds.). New York: Quorum Books, 109–25.

—— 1990b. 'The New Life of the Liberal State: Privatization and the Restructuring of State-Society Relations'. In *The Political Economy of Public Sector Reform and Privatization*, E. N. Suleiman and J. Waterbury (eds.). Boulder, CO: Westview Press, 22–54.

Stasiulis, Daiva K. 1988. 'The Symbolic Mosaic Reaffirmed: Multiculturalism Policy'. In *How Ottawa Spends 1988/89: The Conservatives Heading into the Stretch*. K. A. Graham (ed.) Ottawa: Carleton University Press, 81–111.

Statistics Canada. 2004. *Cornerstones of Community: Highlights of the National Survey of Nonprofit and Voluntary Organizations*. Ottawa: Ministry of Industry.

Stavins, Robert N. 2008. 'A Meaningful U.S. Cap-and-Trade System to Address Climate Change'. *Harvard Environmental Law Review* 32: 293–364.

Stavins, Robert N. *Lessons from the American Experiment with Market-Based Environmental Policies*. Washington DC: Resources for the Future, 2001.

Stead, Dominic, Harry Geerlings and Evert Meijers (eds.) 2004. *Policy Integration in Practice: The Integration of Land Use Planning, Transport and Environmental Policy-Making in Denmark, England and Germany*. Delft, Netherlands: Delft University Press.

Stead, Dominic and Evert Meijers. 2004. *Policy Integration in Practice: Some Experiences of Integrating Transport, Land-Use Planning and Environmental Politics in Local Government*. Berlin: 2004 Berlin Conference on the Human Dimensions of Global Environmental Change: Greening of Policies – Interlinkages and Policy Integration.

Stein, Janice Gross, David Cameron and Richard Simeon. 1999. 'Citizen Engagement in Conflict Resolution: Lessons for Canada in International Experience'. In *The Referendum Papers: Essays on Secession and National Unity* David Cameron (ed.). Toronto: University of Toronto Press, 144–98.

Stern, Jon. 1997. 'What Makes and Independent Regulator Independent?' *Business Strategy Review* 8, no. 2: 67–74.

Stern, Jon and Stuart Holder. 1999. 'Regulatory Governance: Criteria for Assessing the Performance of Regulatory Systems – An Application to Infrastrucrure Industries in the Developing Countries of Asia'. *Utilities Policy* 8: 33–50.

Sterner, Thomas. 2002. *Policy Instruments for Environmental and Natural Resource Management*. Washington, DC: Resources for the Future.

Steurer, Reinhard. 'The Role of Governments in Corporate Social Responsibility: Characterising Public Policies on CSR in Europe.' *Policy Sciences* 43, no. 1 (5, 2009): 49–72.

Steurle, C. E. and E. C. Twombly. 2002. 'Vouchers'. In *The Tools of Government: A Guide to the New Governance*, L. M. Salamon (ed.). New York: Oxford University Press, 445–65.

Stevens, Peter F. 1994. *The Development of Biological Systematics*. New York: Columbia University Press.

Stewart, J. and R. Ayres. 2001. 'Systems Theory and Policy Practice: An Exploration'. *Policy Sciences* 34: 79–94.

Stewart, Jennifer and A. John Sinclair. 2007. 'Meaningful Public Participation in Environmental Assessment: Perspectives from Canadian Participants, Proponents and Government'. *Journal of Environmental Assessment Policy and Management* 9, no. 2: 161–83.

Stigler, G. J. 1971. 'Theory of Economic Regulation'. *Bell Journal of Economics and Management Science* 2 (Spring): 3–21.

—— 1975. *The Citizen and the State: Essays on Regulation*. Chicago: University of Chicago Press.

—— 1975. 'The Theory of Economic Regulation'. In *The Citizen and the State* G. Stigler (ed.). Chicago: University of Chicago, IL Press, 114–41.

Stiglitz, Joseph. 1998. 'The Private Uses of Public Interests: Incentives and Institutions'. *Journal of Economic Perspectives* 12, no. 2: 3–22.

Stillman, Peter G. 1974. 'The Concept of Legitimacy'. *Polity* 7, no. 1: 32–56.

Stimson, J. A. 1991. *Public Opinion in America: Moods Cycles and Swings*. Boulder, CO: Westview Press.

Stimson, J. A., M. B. Mackuen and R. S. Erikson. 1995. 'Dynamic Representation'. *American Political Science Review* 89: 543–65.

Stokey, Edith and Richard Zeckhauser. 1978. *A Primer for Policy Analysis*. New York: W.W. Norton.

Stone, D. A. 1988. *Policy Paradox and Political Reason*. Glenview, IL: Scott, Foresman.

—— 1989. 'Causal Stories and the Formation of Policy Agendas'. *Political Science Quarterly* 104, no. 2: 281–300.

—— 2000. *Learning Lessons, Policy Transfer and the International Diffusion of Policy Ideas*. Centre for the Study of Globalisation and Regionalisation. http://poli.haifa.ac.il/~levi/res/stone-2000.pdf

—— 2001. 'Learning Lessons, Policy Transfer and the International Diffusion of Policy Ideas'. Centre for the Study of Globalization and Regionalization, University of Warwick, Working Paper 69/01.

Stone, D. and A. Denham (eds.) 2004. *Think Tank Traditions: Policy Research and the Politics of Ideas*. Manchester: Manchester University Press.

Strange, Susan 1996. *The Retreat of the State*. Cambridge: Cambridge University Press.

Stritch, Andrew. 2007. 'Business Associations and Policy Analysis in Canada'. In *Policy Analysis in Canada: The State of the Art*, L. Dobuzinskis, M. Howlett and D. Laycock (eds.). Toronto: University of Toronto Press, 242–59.

Strolovitch, D. Z. 2006. 'Do Interest Groups Represent the Disadvantaged? Advocacy at the Intersections of Race, Class and Gender'. *The Journal of Politics* 68, no. 4: 894–910

Stutz, Jeffrey R. 2008. 'What Gets Done and Why: Implementing the Recommendations of Public Inquiries'. *Canadian Public Administration* 51, no. 3: 502–21.

Suchman, Mark C. 1995. 'Managing Legitimacy: Strategic and Institutional Approaches'. *Academy of Management Review* 20, no. 3: 571–610.

Suleiman, Ezra N. and John Waterbury (eds.) 1990. *The Political Economy of Public Sector Reform and Privatization*. Boulder, CO: Westview Press.

Sulitzeanu-Kenan, R. 2007. 'Scything the Grass: Agenda-Setting Consequences of Appointing Public Inquiries in the UK, a Longitudinal Analysis'. *Policy and Politics* 35, no. 4: 629–50.

Sulitzeanu-Kenan, Raanan. 2010. 'Reflection in the Shadow of Blame: When Do Politicians Appoint Commissions of Inquiry?' *British Journal of Political Science* 40, no. 3: 613–34.

Sunnevag, K. J. 2000. 'Designing Auctions for Offshore Petroleum Lease Allocation'. *Resources Policy* 26, no. 1: 3–16.

Surel, Y. 2000. 'The Role of Cognitive and Normative Frames in Policy-Making'. *Journal of European Public Policy* 7, no. 4: 495–512.

Surrey, S. S. 1979. 'Tax Expenditure Analysis: The Concept and Its Uses'. *Canadian Taxation* 1, no. 2: 3–14.

Suzuki, M. 1992. 'Political Business Cycles in the Public Mind'. *American Political Science Review* 86: 989–96.

Swank, Duane. 2000. *Diminished Democracy? Global Capital, Political Institutions and Policy Change in Developed Welfare States*. New York: Cambridge University Press.

—— 2002. *Global Capital, Political Institutions and Policy Change in Developed Welfare States*. New York: Cambridge University Press.

Swann, Dennis. 1988. *The Retreat of the State: Deregulation and Privatisation in the U.K. and U.S.* Hemel Hempstead: Harvester Wheatsheaf.

Tallontire, Anna. 2007. 'CSR and Regulation: Towards a Framework for Understanding Private Standards Initiatives in the Agri-Food Chain'. *Third World Quarterly* 28, no. 4: 775–91.

Taylor, Margaret. 2008. 'Beyond Technology-Push and Demand-Pull: Lessons from California's Solar Policy'. *Energy Economics* 30: 2829–54.

Teghtsoonian, Katherine and Louise Chappell. 2008. 'The Rise and Decline of Women's Policy Machinery in British Columbia and New South Wales: A Cautionary Tale'. *International Political Science Review* 29, no. 1: 29–51.

Teghtsoonian, Kathy and Joan Grace. 2001. '"Something More Is Necessary": The Mixed Achievements of Women's Policy Agencies in Canada'. In *State Feminism, Women's Movements and Job Training: Making Democracies Work in a Global Economy* Amy G. Mazur (ed.). New York: Routledge, 235–69.

Teisman, G. R. 2000. 'Models for Research into Decision-Making Processes: On Phases, Streams and Decision-Making Rounds'. *Public Administration* 78, no. 4: 937–56.

Tenbensel, T. 2005. 'Multiple Modes of Governance: Disentangling the Alternatives to Hierarchies and Markets'. *Public Management Review* 7, no. 2: 267–88.

Termeer, C. J. A. M. and J. F. M. Koppenjan. 1997. 'Managing Perceptions in Networks'. In *Managing Complex Networks: Strategies for the Public Sector*, W. J. M. Kickert, E.-H. Klijn and J. F. M. Koppenjan (eds.). London: Sage, 79–97.

Thatcher, Mark and Alec Stone-Sweet (eds.) 2003. *The Politics of Delegation*. London: Frank Cass.

Thelen, K. 2003. 'How Institutions Evolve: Insights from Comparative Historical Analysis'. In *Comparative Historical Analysis in the Social Sciences*, J. Mahoney and D. Rueschemeyer (eds.). Cambridge: Cambridge University Press, 208–40.

—— 2004. *How Institutions Evolve: The Political Economy of Skills in Germany, Britain, the United States and Japan.* Cambridge: Cambridge University Press.

Tholoniat, Luc. 2010. 'The Career of the Open Method of Coordination: Lessons from a "Soft" EU-Instrument'. *West European Politics* 33, no. 1: 93.

Thomas, H. G. 2001. 'Towards a New Higher Education Law in Lithuania: Reflections on the Process of Policy Formulation'. *Higher Education Policy* 14, no. 3: 213–23.

Thomas, Emyr V. 2003. 'Sustainable Development, Market Paradigms and Policy Integration'. *Journal of Environmental Policy and Planning* 5, no. 2: 201–16.

Thompson, G. F. 2003. *Between Hierarchies and Markets: The Logic and Limits of Network Forms of Organization.* Oxford: Oxford University Press.

Thomson, Janice E. and Stephen D. Krasner. 1989. 'Global Transactions and the Consolidation of Sovereignty'. In *Global Changes and Theoretical Challenges* E. O. Czempiel and J. N. Rosenau (eds.). Lexington, CT: Lexington Books, 195–219.

Thorelli, H. B. 1986. 'Networks: Between Markets and Hierarchies'. *Strategic Management Journal* 7: 37–51.

Timmermans, A., C. Rothmayr, U. Serduelt and F. Varone. 1998. *The Design of Policy Instruments: Perspectives and Concepts.* Paper presented at the Midwest Political Science Association, Chicago.

Tinbergen, Jan. 1958. *The Design of Development.* Baltimore, MD: Johns Hopkins University Press.

—— 1967. *Economic Policy: Principles and Design.* Chicago: Rand McNally.

Toke, David. 2008. 'Trading Schemes, Risks and Costs: The Cases of the European Union Emissions Trading Scheme and the Renewables Obligation'. *Environment and Planning C: Government and Policy* 26: 938–53.

Tollefson, C. 2004. 'Indigenous Rights and Forest Certification in British Columbia'. In *Hard Choices, Soft Law: Voluntary Standards in Global Trade, Environment and Social Governance* Kirton, J. Trebilcock, M. (eds.). Aldershot: Ashgate.

Tollefson, C., Gale, F. and Haley, D. 2008. *Setting the Standard: Certification, Governance and the Forest Stewardship Council*. Vancouver: UBC Press.

Tollison, R. D. 1991. 'Regulation and Interest Groups'. In *Regulation: Economic Theory and History* Jack High (ed.). Ann Arbor: University of Michigan Press, 59–76.

Torenvlied, Rene and Agnes Akkerman. 2004. 'Theory of "Soft" Policy Implementation in Multilevel Systems with an Application to Social Partnership in the Netherlands'. *Acta Politica* 39: 31–58.

Torgerson, D. 1985. 'Contextual Orientation in Policy Analysis: The Contribution of Harold D. Lasswell'. *Policy Sciences* 18: 240–52.

—— 1986. 'Between Knowledge and Politics: Three Faces of Policy Analysis'. *Policy Sciences* 19, no. 1: 33–59.

—— 1990. 'Origins of the Policy Orientation: The Aesthetic Dimension in Lasswell's Political Vision'. *History of Political Thought* 11 (Summer): 340–44.

Torres, Lourdes. 2004. 'Trajectories in Public Administration Reforms in European Continental Countries'. *Australian Journal of Public Administration* 63, no. 3: 99–112.

Townsend, R. E., J. McColl and M. D. Young. 2006. 'Design Principles for Individual Transferable Quotas'. *Marine Policy* 30: 131–41.

Treasury Board of Canada Secretariat. 2007. *Assessing, Selecting and Implementing Instruments for Government Action*. Ottawa: Treasury Board.

Trebilcock, Michael J. 1983. 'Regulating Service Quality in Professional Markets'. In *The Regulation of Quality: Products, Services, Workplaces and the Environment* D. N. Dewees (ed.). Toronto: Butterworths, 83–108.

—— 2008. 'Regulating the Market for Legal Services'. *Alberta Law Review* 45: 215–32.

Trebilcock, M. J., D. Dewees and Douglas G. Hartle. 1982. *The Choice of Governing Instrument*. Ottawa: Economic Council of Canada.

Trebilcock, Michael J. and D. G. Hartle. 1982. 'The Choice of Governing Instrument'. *International Review of Law and Economics* 2: 29–46.

Trebilcock, M. J. and J. R. S. Prichard. 1983. 'Crown Corporations: The Calculus of Instrument Choice'. In *Crown Corporations in Canada: The Calculus of Instrument Choice*, J. R. S. Prichard (ed.). Toronto: Butterworths, 1–50.

Trebilcock, M. J., C. J. Tuohy and A. D. Wolfson. 1979. *Professional Regulation: A Staff Study of Accountancy, Architecture, Engineering and Law in Ontario Prepared for the Professional Organizations Committee*. Toronto: Ministry of the Attorney General.

Treib, Olivier, Holger Bahr and Gerda Falkner. 2007. 'Modes of Governance: Towards a Conceptual Clarification'. *Journal of European Public Policy* 14, no. 1: 1–20.

Trondal, Jarle and Leve Jeppesen. 2008. 'Images of Agency Governance in the European Union'. *West European Politics* 31, no. 3: 417–41.

True, J. and M. Mintrom. 2001. 'Transnational Networks and Policy Diffusion: The Case of Gender Mainstreaming'. *International Studies Quarterly* 45: 27–57.

Truman, D. R. 1964. *The Governmental Process: Political Interests and Public Opinion*. New York: Knopf.

Tsasis, Peter. 2008. 'The Politics of Governance: Government-Voluntary Sector Relationships'. *Canadian Public Administration* 51, no. 2: 265–90.

Tuohy, C. J. and A. D. Wolfson. 1978. 'Self-Regulation: Who Qualifies?' In *The Professions and Public Policy*. P. Slayton and M. J. Trebilcock (eds.) Toronto: University of Toronto Press, 111–22.

Tuohy, Carolyn. 1992. *Policy and Politics in Canada: Institutionalized Ambivalence*. Philadelphia, PA: Temple University Press.

—— 1999. *Accidental Logics: The Dynamics of Change in the Health Care Arena in the United States, Britain and Canada*. New York: Oxford University Press.

Tupper, Allan. 1979. 'The State in Business'. *Canadian Public Administration* 22, no. 1: 124–50.

Tupper, A. and G. B. Doern. 1981. 'Public Corporations and Public Policy in Canada'. In *Public Corporations and Public Policy in Canada* A. Tupper and G. B. Doern (eds.). Montreal: Institute for Research on Public Policy, 1–50.

Turnpenny, John, Mans Nilsson, Duncan Russel, Andrew Jordan, Julia Hertin and Bjorn Nykvist. 2008. 'Why is Integrating Policy Assessment so Hard? A Comparative Analysis of the Institutional Capacity and Constraints'. *Journal of Environmental Planning and Management* 51, no. 6: 759–75.

Turnpenny, John, Claudio M. Radaelli, Andrew Jordan and Klaus Jacob. 2009. 'The Policy and Politics of Policy Appraisal: Emerging Trends and New Directions'. *Journal of European Public Policy* 16, no. 4: 640–53.

Underdal, Arild. 1980. 'Integrated Marine Policy; What/Why/How?' *Marine Policy* 4, no. 3: 159–69.

Utton, M. A. 1986. *The Economics of Regulating Industry*. London: Basil Blackwell.

Valkama, P. and S. J. Bailey. 2001. 'Vouchers as an Alternative Public Sector Funding System'. *Public Policy and Administration* 16, no. 1: 32–58.

Van Buuren, A. and E.-H Klijn. 2006. 'Trajectories of Institutional Design in Policy Networks: European Interventions in the Dutch Fishery Network as an Example'. *International Review of Administrative Sciences* 72, no. 3: 395–415.

van Dooren, W. 2004. 'Supply and Demand of Policy Indicators: A Cross-Sectoral Comparison'. *Public Management review* 6, no. 4: 511–30.

Van Gossum, Peter, Bas Arts and Kris Verheyen. 2009. '"Smart Regulation": Can Policy Instrument Design Solve Forest Policy Aims of Expansion and Sustainability in Flanders and the Netherlands?'. *Forest Policy and Economics* 11: 616–27.

Van Heffen, O., W. J. M. Kickert and J. J. A. Thomassen. 2000. 'Introduction: Multi-Level and Multi-Actor Governance'. In *Governance in Modern Society: Effects, Change and Formation of Government Institutions*, O. Van Heffen, W. J. M. Kickert and J. J. A. Thomassen (eds.). Dordrecht: Kluwer, 3–12.

Van Heffen, O., W. J. M. Kickert and J. A. Thomassen. 2000. *Governance in Modern Society: Effects, Change and Formation of Government Institutions*. Dordrecht: Kluwer.

Van Kersbergen, K. and F. Van Waarden. 2004. '"Governance" as a Bridge between Disciplines: Cross-Disciplinary Inspiration Regarding Shifts in Governance and Problems of Governability, Accountability an Legitimacy'. *European Journal of Political Research* 43, no. 2: 143–72.

van Meter, D. and C. van Horn. 1975. 'The Policy Implementation Process: A Conceptual Framework'. *Administration and Society* 6: 445–88.

van Nispen, Frans K. M. and Arthur B. Ringeling. 1998. 'On Instruments and Instrumentality: A Critical Assessment'. In *Public Policy Instruments: Evaluating the Tools of Public Administration* B. G. Peters and F. K. M. V. Nispen (eds.). New York: Edward Elgar, 204–17.

van Thiel, Sandra. 2008. 'The "Empty Nest" Syndrome: Dutch Ministries after the Separation of Policy and Administration'. Paper presented to the IRSPM Conference, Brisbane, Australia.

Varone, Frederic. 1998. 'Policy Design: Le Choix des Instruments des Politiques Publiques'. *Evaluation* 2 (May): 5–14.

—— 2000. 'Le Choix des Instruments de l'Action Publique: Analyse Comparee des Politiques Energetiques en Europe et en Amerique du Nord'. *Revue Internationale de Politique Comparée* 7, no. 1: 167–201.

—— 2001. 'Les Instruments de la Politique Energetique: Analyse Comparee du Canada et des Etats Unis'. *Canadian Journal of Political Science* 34, no. 1: 3–28.

Varone, Frédéric and Bernard Aebischer. 2001. 'Energy Efficiency: The Challenges of Policy Design'. *Energy Policy* 29, no. 8: 615–29.

Vedung, E. 1997. 'Policy Instruments: Typologies and Theories'. In *Carrots, Sticks and Sermons: Policy Instruments and Their Evaluation*, M. L. Bemelmans-Videc, R. C. Rist and E. Vedung (eds.). New Brunswick, NJ: Transaction Publishers, 21–58.

Vedung, Evert and Frans C. J. van der Doelen. 1998. 'The Sermon: Information Programs in the Public Policy Process – Choice, Effects and Evaluation'. In *Carrots, Sticks and Sermons: Policy Instruments and Their Evaluation* M.-L. Bemelmans-Videc, R. C. Rist and E. Vedung (eds.). New Brunswick, NJ: Transaction Publishers, 103–28.

Veggeland, Noralv. 2008. 'Path Dependence and Public Sector Innovation in Regulatory Regimes'. *Scandinavian Political Studies* 31, no. 3: 268–90.

Veljanovski, Cento. 1988. *Selling the State: Privatisation in Britain*. London: Weidenfeld and Nicolson.

Verheijen, T. 1999. *Civil Service Systems in Central and Eastern Europe*. Cheltenham: Edward Elgar.

Verschuere, Bram. 2009. 'The Role of Public Agencies in the Policy Making Process'. *Public Policy and Administration* 24, no. 1: 23–46.

Verhoest, Koen, Paul G. Roness, Bram Verschuere, Kristin Rubecksen and Muiris MacCarthaigh. 2010. *Autonomy and Control of State Agencies: Comparing States and Agencies*. London: Palgrave Macmillan.

Verhoest, Koen, Bram Verschuere and Geert Bouckaert. 2007. 'Pressure, Legitimacy and Innovative Behavior by Public Organizations'. *Governance* 20, no. 3: 469–97.

Vigoda, E. 2002. 'From Responsiveness to Collaboration: Governance, Citizens and the Next Generation of Public Administration'. *Public Administration Review* 62, no. 5: 527–40.

Vigoda, E. and E. Gilboa. 2002. 'The Quest for Collaboration: Toward a Comprehensive Strategy for Public Administration'. *Public Administration and Public Policy* 99: 99–117.

Vining, A. R. and R. Botterell. 1983. 'An Overview of the Origins, Growth, Size and Functions of Provincial Crown Corporations'. In *Crown Corporations: The Calculus of Instrument Choice*, J. R. S. Pritchard (ed.). Toronto: Butterworths, 303–68.

Vogel, David 1986. *National Styles of Regulation: Environmental Policy in Great Britain and the United States*, Ithaca, NY: Cornell University Press,

Vogel, David 2001. 'Is There a Race to the Bottom? The Impact of Globalization on National Regulatory Policies'. *The Tocqueville Review/La Revue Tocqueville* 22: 1.

—— 2005. *The Market for Virtue: The Potential and Limits of Corporate Social Responsibility*. Washington, DC: Brookings Institution.

Vogel, David and Robert A. Kagan (eds.) 2002. *Dynamics of Regulatory Change: How Globalization Affects National Regulatory Policies*. Berkeley: University of California Press.

Vogel, Steven K. 1996. *Freer Markets, More Rules: Regulatory Reform in Advanced Industrial Countries*. Ithaca, NY: Cornell University Press.

Voss, Jan-Peter. 2007. 'Innovation Process in Governance: The Development of "Emissions Trading" as a New Policy Instrument'. *Science and Public Policy* 34, no. 5: 329–43.

Voss, Jan-Peter, Adrian Smith and John Grin. 2009. 'Designing Long-term Policy: Rethinking Transition Management'. *Policy Sciences* 42, no. 4: 275–302.

Wagenaar, H., S. D. N. Cook and M. Hajer. 2003. 'Understanding Policy Practices: Action, Dialectic and Deliberation in Policy Analysis'. In *Deliberative Policy Analysis: Understanding Governance in the Network Society*. London: Cambridge University Press, 139–71.

Walker, Alan. 1984, 'The Political Economy of Privatisation'. In *Privatisation and the Welfare State* Julian Le Grand and Ray Robinson (eds.). London: George Allen and Unwin, 19–44.

Walker, Jack L. 1969. 'The Diffusion of Innovations among the States'. *American Political Science Review* 63, no. 3: 880–99.

—— 1977. 'Setting the Agenda in the U.S. Senate: A Theory of Problem Selection'. *British Journal of Political Science* 7: 423–45.

—— 1983. 'The Origins and Maintenance of Interest Groups in America'. *American Political Science Review* 77, no. 2: 390–406

—— 1991. *Mobilizing Interest Groups in America: Patrons, Professions and Social Movements*. Ann Arbor, MI: University of Michigan Press.

Walker, Warren E. 'Policy Analysis: a Systematic Approach to Supporting Policymaking in the Public Sector.' *Journal of Multi-Criteria Decision Analysis* 9, no. 1 (2000): 11–27.

Walker, Warren E., S. Adnan Rahman, and Jonathan Cave. 'Adaptive Policies, Policy Analysis, and Policy-Making.' *European Journal of Operational Research* 128, no. 2 (January 16, 2001): 282–289.

Walls, C. E. S. 1969. 'Royal Commissions: Their Influence on Public Policy'. *Canadian Public Administration* 12, no. 3: 365–71.

Walsh, C. 1988. 'Individual Irrationality and Public Policy: In Search of Merit/Demerit Policies'. *Journal of Public Policy* 7, no. 2: 103–34.

—— 1990. 'Individual Irrationality and Public Policy: In Search of Merit/Demerit Policies'. In *Rationality, individualism and Public Policy*, G. Brennan and C. Walsh (eds.). Canberra: Centre for Research on Federal Financial Relations, Australian National University, 145–77.

Walsh, J. I. 1994. 'Institutional Constraints and Domestic Choices: Economic Convergence and Exchange Rate Policy in France and Italy'. *Political Studies* 42, no. 2: 243–58.

Walsh, Peter, Myles McGregor-Lowndes and Cameron J. Newton. 2008. 'Shared Services: Lessons from the Public and Private Sectors for the Nonprofit Sector'. *Australian Journal of Public Administration* 67, no. 2: 200–212.

Walters, Lawrence C., James Aydelotte and Jessica Miller. 2000. 'Putting More Public in Policy Analysis'. *Public Administration Review* 60, no. 4: 349–59.

Walters, W. 2004. 'Some Critical Notes on 'Governance''. *Studies in Political Economy* 73, 27–46.

Weatherford, M. Stephen. 1989. 'Political Economy and Political Legitimacy: The Link between Economic Policy and Political Trust'. In *Economic Decline and Political Change: Canada, Great Britain, the United States* Harold D. Clarke, Marianne C. Stewart and Gary Zuk (eds.). Pittsburgh, PA: University of Pittsburgh Press, 225–51.

Weaver, R. Kent. 1986. 'The Politics of Blame Avoidance'. *Journal of Public Policy* 6: 371–98.

Weaver, R. K. and Rockman, B.A. 1993. 'Assessing the Effects of Institutions'. In *Do Institutions Matter? Government Capabilities in the United States and Abroad* R. K. Weaver and B. A. Rockman (eds.). Washington, DC: Brookings Institution, Institution, 1–41.

Webb, K. 1987. 'Between the Rocks and Hard Places: Bureaucrats, the Law and Pollution Control'. *Alternatives* 14, no. 2: 4–13.

—— 1990. 'On the Periphery: The Limited Role for Criminal Offences in Environmental Protection'. In *Into the Future: Environmental Law and Policy for the 1990's*, D. Tingley (ed.). Edmonton: Environmental Law Centre, 58–69.

—— 2005. 'Sustainable Governance in the Twenty-First Century: Moving Beyond Instrument Choice'. In *Designing Government: From Instruments to Governance* P. Eliadis, M. Hill and M. Howlett (eds.). Montreal: McGill-Queen's University Press, 242–80.

Webb, K. and J. C. Clifford. 1988. *Pollution Control in Canada: The Regulatory Approach in the 1980s.* Ottawa: Law Reform Commission of Canada.

Webb, Kernaghan. *Cinderella's Slippers? The Role of Charitable Tax Status in Financing Canadian Interest Groups* (Vancouver: SFU-UBC Centre for the Study of Government and Business, 2000).

Webber, D. J. 1986. 'Analyzing Political Feasibility: Political Scientists' Unique Contribution to Policy Analysis'. *Policy Studies Journal* 14, no. 4: 545–54.

Weber, Edward P. and Anne M. Khademian. 2008. 'Wicked Problems, Knowledge Challenges and Collaborative Capacity Builders in Network Settings'. *Public Administration Review* 68, no. 2: 334–49.

Weber, M. 1978. *Economy and Society: An Outline of Interpretive Sociology.* Berkeley, CA: University of California Press.

Webler, Thomas and Seth Tuler. 2000. 'Fairness and Competence in Citizen Participation'. *Administration and Society* 32, no. 5: 566–95.

Weible, Christopher M. 2008. 'Expert-Based Information and Policy Subsystems: A Review and Synthesis'. *Policy Studies Journal* 36, no. 4: 615–35.

Weimer, D. L. 2007. 'Public and Private Regulation of Organ Transplantation: Liver Allocation and the Final Rule'. *Journal of Health Politics, Policy and Law* 32, no. 1: 9–49.

Weimer, David L. 1992. 'Claiming Races, Broiler Contracts, Heresthetics and Habits: Ten Concepts for Policy Design'. *Policy Sciences* 25: 135–59.

—— 1993. 'The Current State of Design Craft: Borrowing, Tinkering and Problem Solving'. *Public Administration Review* 53, no. 2 (April): 110–20.

Weimer, David L. and Aidan R. Vining. 1989. *Policy Analysis: Concepts and Practice,* Englewood Cliffs, NJ: Prentice Hall.

—— 2004. *Policy Analysis: Concepts and Practice.* Englewood Cliffs, NJ: Prentice Hall.

Weiss, Carol. 1977. 'Research for Policy's Sake: The Enlightenment Function of Social Research'. *Policy Analysis* 3: 531–45.

Weiss, J. A. and J. E. Gruber. 1984. 'Using Knowledge for Control in Fragmented Policy Arenas'. *Journal of Policy Analysis and Management* 3, no. 2: 225–47.

Weiss, Janet A. and Mary Tschirhart. 1994. 'Public Information Campaigns as Policy Instruments'. *Journal of Policy Analysis and Management* 13, no. 1: 82–119.

Weiss, Linda. 1998. *The Myth of the Powerless State: Governing the Economy in a Global Era*. Oxford: Polity Press.

—— 1999. 'Globalization and National Governance: Antinomy or Interdependence?'. *Review of International Studies* 25, no. 5: 1–30.

—— (ed.) 2003. *States in the Global Economy: Bringing Domestic Institutions Back In*. Cambridge: Cambridge University Press.

—— 2005. 'The State-Augmenting Effects of Globalisation'. *New Political Economy* 10, no. 3: 345–53.

Wenig, Michael M. and Patricia Sutherland. 2004. 'Considering the Upstream/ Downstream Effects of the Mackenzie Pipeline: Rough Paddling for the National Energy Board'. *Resources* 86: 1–8.

Wescott, Geoff. 2002. 'Integrated Natural Resource Management in Australia'. *Australian Journal of Environmental Management* 9, no. 3: 138–40.

West, William. 2005. 'Administrative Rulemaking: An Old and Emerging Literature'. *Public Administration Review* 65, no. 6: 655–68

Wheeler, D. 2001. 'Racing to the Bottom? Foreign Investment and Air Pollution in Developing Countries'. *Journal of Environment and Development* 10, no. 3: 225–45.

Whiteman, D. 1985. 'The Fate of Policy Analysis in Congressional Decision Making: Three Types of Use in Committees'. *Western Political Quarterly* 38, no. 2: 294–311.

—— 1995. *Communication in Congress: Members, Staff and the Search for Information*. Lawrence, KS: University Press of Kansas.

Wildavsky, Aaron. 1969. 'Rescuing Policy Analysis from PPBS'. *Public Administration Review* (March–April): 189–202.

—— 1979. *Speaking Truth to Power: The Art and Craft of Policy Analysis*. Boston, MA: Little, Brown.

Wilensky, H. L. 1975. *The Welfare State and Equality: Structural and Ideological Roots of Public Expenditures*. Berkeley, CA: University of California Press.

Wilks, Stephen and Ian Battle. 2003. 'The Unanticipated Consequences of Creating Independent Competition Agencies'. In *The Politics of Delegation* M. Thatcher and A. Stone Sweet (eds.). London: Frank Cass, 148–72.

Williams, Juliet A. 2000. 'The Delegation Dilemma: Negotiated Rulemaking in Perspective'. *Policy Studies Review* 17, no. 1: 125–46.

Williamson, O. E. 1975. *Markets and Hierarchies*. New York: Free Press.

—— 1996. *The Mechanisms of Governance*. Oxford: Oxford University Press.

Wilson, Graham K. 2003. 'Changing Regulatory Systems'. Paper for the Annual Convention of the American Political Science Association, Philadelphia, August. www.lafollette.wisc.edu/facultystaff/wilson/ChangingRegulatorySystems.pdf

Wilson, James Q. 1974. 'The Politics of Regulation'. In *Social Responsibility and the Business Predicament* J. W. McKie (ed.). Washington, DC: Brookings Institution, 135–68.

Wilson, V. S. 1971. 'The Role of Royal Commissions and Task Forces'. In *The Structures of Policy-Making in Canada*, G. B. Doern and P. Aucoin (eds.). Toronto: Macmillan, 113–29.

Wilson, W. 1887. 'The Study of Administration'. *Political Science Quarterly* 2, no. 2: 197–222.

Wissel, Silvia and Frank Watzold. 2010. 'A Conceptual Analysis of the Application of Tradable Permits to Biodiversity Conservation'. *Conservation Biology* 24, no. 2: 404–11.

Wolf Jr, Charles. 1979. 'A Theory of Nonmarket Failure: Framework for Implementation Analysis'. *Journal of Law and Economics* 22, no. 1: 107–39.

—— 1987. 'Markets and Non-Market Failures: Comparison and Assessment'. *Journal of Public Policy* 7: 43–70.

—— 1988. *Markets or Governments: Choosing Between Imperfect Alternatives.* Cambridge, MA: MIT Press.

Wollmann, Helmut. 1989. 'Policy Analysis in West Germany's Federal Government: A Case of Unfinished Governmental and Administrative Modernization?' *Governance* 2, no. 3: 233–66.

Wolman, Harold. 1981. 'The Determinants of Program Success and Failure'. *Journal of Public Policy* 1, no. 4: 433–64.

—— 1992. 'Understanding Cross National Policy Transfers'. *Governance* 5, no. 1: 27–45.

Wonka, Arndt, and Berthold Rittberger. 2010. 'Credibility, Complexity and Uncertainty: Explaining the Institutional Independence of 29 EU – Agencies'. *West European Politics* 33, no. 4: 730.

Wood, B. Dan and John Bohte. 2004. 'Political Transaction Costs and the Politics of Administrative Design'. *Journal of Politics* 66, no. 1: 176–202.

Wood, David, and Lisa Hagerman. 2010. "Mission Investing and the Philanthropic Toolbox'. *Policy and Society* 29, no. 3: 257–68.

Woodley, Alice. 2008. 'Legitimating Public Policy'. *University of Toronto Law Journal* 58: 153–84.

Woodside, K. 1979. 'Tax Incentives vs. Subsidies: Political Considerations in Governmental Choice'. *Canadian Public Policy* 5, no. 2: 248–56.

—— 1983. 'The Political Economy of Policy Instruments: Tax Expenditures and Subsidies in Canada'. In *The Politics of Canadian Public Policy* M. Atkinson and M. Chandler (eds.). Toronto: University of Toronto Press, 173–97.

—— 1986. 'Policy Instruments and the Study of Public Policy'. *Canadian Journal of Political Science* 19, no. 4: 775–93.

World Economic Forum (various years) *Global Competitiveness Report*. Geneva: WEF.

Wraith, R. E. and G. B. Lamb. 1971. *Public Inquiries as an Instrument of Government.* London: George Allen and Unwin.

Wu, Irene. 2008. 'Who Regulates Phones, Television and the Internet? What Makes a Communications Regulator Independent and Why It Matters'. *Perspectives on Politics* 6, no. 4: 769–83.

Wu, Xun, M. Ramesh, Michael Howlett and Scott Fritzen. 2010. *The Public Policy Primer: Managing Public Policy.* London: Routledge.

Yeung, Karen, and Mary Dixon-Woods. 2010. 'Design-Based Regulation and Patient Safety: A Regulatory Studies Perspective'. *Social Science & Medicine* 71, no. 3: 502–09.

Young, L. and J. Everitt. 2004. *Advocacy Groups.* Vancouver: UBC Press.

Young, Sally. 2007. 'The Regulation of Government Advertising in Australia: The Politicisation of a Public Policy Issue'. *Australian Journal of Public Administration* 66, no. 4: 438–52.

Zarco-Jasso, Hugo. 2005. 'Public-Private Partnerships: A Multidimensional Model for Contracting'. *International Journal of Public Policy* 1, no. 1/2: 22–40.

Zeckhauser, R. 1981. 'Preferred Policies When There Is a Concern for Probability of Adoption'. *Journal of Environmental Economics and Management* 8: 215–37.

Zeckhauser, Richard and Elmer Schaefer. 1968. 'Public Policy and Normative Economic Theory'. In *The Study of Policy Formation* R. A. Bauer and K. J. Gergen (eds.). New York: Free Press, 27–102.

Zehavi, Amos. 2008. 'The Faith-Based Initiative in Comparative Perspective: Making Use of Religious Providers in Britain and the United States'. *Comparative Politics* 40, no. 3: 331–51.

Zerbe, Richard O. and Howard E. McCurdy. 1999. 'The Failure of Market Failure'. *Journal of Policy Analysis and Management* 18, no. 4: 558–78.

Zielonka, Jan. 2007. 'Plurilateral Governance in the Enlarged European Union'. *Journal of Common Market Studies* 45, no. 1: 187–209.

Ziller, Jacques. 2005. 'Public Law: A Tool for Modern Management, Not an Impediment to Reform'. *International Review of Administrative Sciences* 71, no. 2: 267–77.

Zito, Anthony, Andrew Jordan, Wurzel Rudiger and Lars Brueckner. 2003. 'Instrument Innovation in an Environmental Lead State: "New" Environmental Policy Instruments in the Netherlands'. *Environmental Politics* 12, no. 1: 157–78.

Index

Page numbers in **bold** refer to figures, page numbers in *italic* refer to tables

'Michael Howlett's book is an important integration of various strands of the public policy literature. By focusing on the design of public policies he provides an innovative discussion of the policy process and also means of analyzing policies.'

B. Guy Peters, *University of Pittsburgh, USA.*

'Some policy books are indeed coherent though they funnel the reader into a narrower scope; some inspire a widening of views, but lack perspective. This excellent volume *Designing Public Policies* however combines both a wide and a coherent treatment of relevant literature.'

Hans Th.A Bressers, *University of Twente, Netherlands.*

'Using the lens of policy design, Michael Howlett has done a brilliant job in bringing together such a wide literature in public policy and implementation. Students and public policy scholars alike will learn a vast amount from reading this excellent book.'

Peter John, *University of Manchester, UK.*